GLASGOW 1919

• THE RISE OF RED CLYDESIDE •

KENNY MacASKILL

Biteback Publishing

First published in Great Britain in 2019 by
Biteback Publishing Ltd
Westminster Tower
3 Albert Embankment
London SE1 7SP
Copyright © Kenny MacAskill 2019

ISBN 978-1-78590-454-7

10 9 8 7 6 5 4 3 2 1

A CIP catalogue record for this book is available from the British Library.

Set in Adobe Garamond Pro

Printed and bound in Great Britain by
CPI Group (UK) Ltd, Croydon CR0 4YY

GLASGOW 1919

For Peigi – my constant companion when writing this.
Tragically taken and sorely missed.

*Crowds gather as the funeral cortège of John Maclean prepares
to depart his Glasgow home in 1923.*

CONTENTS

INTRODUCTION

Friday 31 January 1919 saw a cold winter's day dawn in Glasgow, the second city of a British Empire then so vast it was claimed that the sun could never set on it. But there would be little sunshine that morning, with daylight hours few and industrial pollution dimming natural light; it was an inauspicious start for what was to be a momentous day. Tensions were rising in the city as a strike for a forty-hour week was ongoing, and the fears and concerns of the authorities were mounting as the anger of protestors was rising.

Glasgow was then a teeming metropolis numbering well over a million people, which had expanded initially with the trade of tobacco, cotton and slavery and then with shipbuilding and engineering. It had also become the major city in the empire for munitions and military supplies and a vital part of the martial efforts for the Great War that had just ended.

Despite its growth, Glasgow was at that time a city where deprivation was rampant and where society was far from equal. Many lived in abject poverty whilst huge wealth had been accumulated by a few. Inequality abounded and was exacerbated, rather than reduced, when the First World War broke out. Whilst a few got rich profiting on the military contracts, many more continued to live in desperate circumstances. Hunger was common and infant mortality endemic, rickets blighted lives, and tuberculosis claimed them.

Huge sacrifices had been made by the city with thousands of lives lost waging war in the trenches and elsewhere. Meanwhile, on the home front, other battles had been fought by workers and women against exploitation, poor housing conditions and even by some against the war itself. Although the city (as with the entire country) had caught war fever in 1914, it retained a significant minority who publicly opposed it, probably greater than anywhere else, for whom there was still some respect and sympathy, even if not universal support.

For them the enemy wasn't the Germans, but industrialists, landlords and even the British government. Anti-war agitation had continued, and factory disputes and rent strikes had marked the war years at home, as shell craters had potted the battlefields in Flanders. It was also a city with a long radical tradition, which had seen a cadre of socialist and even revolutionary activists forged in its factories and communities, long before the Great War even broke out. Agitation for radical change had been strengthened, not subdued, by the conflict, and revolution in Russia and rebellion in Ireland had been celebrated by many and seen as the template to follow by some.

Industrial disputes during the war caused such concern that government ministers, including Labour members of the wartime coalition government, and trade union leaders had made appeals to support the war effort. But to little avail, as disturbances continued unabated and industrial peace was only restored through the arrest of leading activists and the deportation of shop stewards, using draconian wartime powers.

Now with peace declared the political agitators had been released, the militant shop stewards had returned, and were back in charge of the sites from which they had been forcibly removed. The Clyde Workers' Committee (CWC) that the shop stewards had established to coordinate activities had been resurrected, and the mood was militant. Battle lines were being drawn.

So concerned were the authorities about the threat and the potential effect upon the city that the War Cabinet in London had been closely monitoring events. The spectre of rebellion and revolution that had broken out elsewhere across Europe haunted them, and they were aware of the strength of support that existed for similar actions in the city. They were also concerned by the ability of the shop stewards to coordinate industrial action and to mobilise political support as had previously been shown when it had even threatened the war effort at one stage. As the situation escalated, consideration was even given to detaining strike leaders, and further legal advice was sought. In the interim, following briefings from senior military figures, the army was placed on standby.

The number of strikers was rising and the demands for action by both those who backed the dispute and those who opposed it were increasing. Factories and shipyards were shutting and large demonstrations had been taking place in support of the closures, with the red flag not only sung by protestors but also waved by marchers. Local political and industrial leaders were worried about the power supply, and demands had been made by the strike leaders to have the city trams stop running.

Crowds had been gathering daily in George Square and police from across the city were mobilised to confront them. Constables were deployed in front of the City Chambers that morning, with more including mounted officers in reserve. Confrontation was looming. Demonstrators were already standing in the central square and spilling into surrounding streets, as ever more were arriving by the minute. Nerves were on edge and the mood was tense. Fear was evident amongst the police, as was frustration for the strikers.

Then, through the growing tumult, a tramcar quietly turned into George Square. It was just one of many seeking to work its way through the milling crowds. But suddenly, a striker on board the trolley pulled the cord disconnecting the cable that powered it. Why he did so or even who he was is not known. It may have been frustration at the trams still running or just a desire to alight at that spot. But, stop it did, and that led to a fight in the tramcar between him and an off-duty soldier also seated there. The punch-up that followed between them quickly spilled out onto the street where others became embroiled. This was what sparked the riot and the events that became known as Bloody Friday, the Battle of George Square.

What had begun as a fight between a striker and an off-duty soldier quickly became a full-blown battle between protestors and police, and soon spread to other parts of the city. Baton-wielding officers and strikers charged and counter-charged. Heads were broken and officers were chased by angry demonstrators. Lorries were commandeered and used as barricades. Bottles and paving stones were flung, with windows broken and shops looted. Some were arrested and many taken to hospital from both sides. The Riot Act was read, or at least attempts were made to do so, but the unrest continued regardless, as police and civic leaders were overwhelmed by the situation. Trouble continued through the night, as gangs of men roamed the streets and incidents of looting took place.

The local powers in Glasgow sought support from the government in London, which was immediately provided (having already been prepared for), and the reaction was to be both swift and hard. That evening troops started arriving in Glasgow from barracks around Scotland, with tanks despatched from England arriving soon after. They were quickly deployed in George Square and at other key locations across the city, including the power stations. Pinkston Power Station, which supplied the electricity for the city tramways, was a particular concern, and was speedily guarded by armed soldiers.

In Glasgow itself, though, local troops had been confined to Maryhill Barracks for fear that they might mutiny. Similar orders saw soldiers from the west of Scotland left in barracks elsewhere around the country for fear they would refuse to act against families and friends. Without being told why, troops from the Greater Glasgow area were ordered to stand down, whilst comrades were mobilised for action.

At this point, the second city of the British Empire resembled a war zone rather than a vibrant industrial centre. Around 10,000 soldiers were garrisoned there, along with 100 lorries and six tanks. The City Chambers was surrounded by barbed wire, howitzers protruding from within, and machine guns were sited on the roofs of surrounding buildings, including upmarket hotels and the Post Office in George Square. Troops guarded power stations and were even positioned on street corners, and the cattle market was requisitioned for the stationing of tanks. This was a military response the likes of which the community had never seen, except on newsreel footage at the cinema and in cities far away. Glasgow was more akin to a city under occupation than one dealing with a strike, and the events were described by Robert Munro, the Secretary of State for Scotland, as a Scottish Bolshevik Revolution.

Much of what happened has entered into Scottish political mythology. For some on the left, including Willie Gallacher, who was later to become a Communist MP, and was downed by a baton in George Square that day as well as imprisoned for his troubles, there was regret that a revolutionary moment had been missed. He rued that strikers hadn't marched to Maryhill Barracks, the city's military garrison, to encourage local soldiers to come out and join them in their actions. But, was it really an attempt at a revolution, and could it have really succeeded?

For some nationalists it is a tale of English troops being billeted in a Scottish city to repress the rights of Scottish workers – yet another case of Scotland being defeated by the colonial might of its larger and more powerful neighbour, as happened many other times through the centuries. But although the tanks came from south of the border, and some English troops were involved, most of the soldiers were Scottish. So, what actually occurred?

Moreover, though the basis of the dispute for a forty-hour week was lost, political success would still be reaped in coming years as political power shifted in Glasgow to those that had been involved in the demonstration that day or otherwise represented the dispossessed. In 1922 the

Red Clydesiders swept into Parliament in the shape of the Independent Labour Party (ILP), winning ten out of fifteen Glasgow constituencies and being successful elsewhere, well beyond its boundaries.

David Kirkwood and Manny Shinwell, who had been pivotal in the strike and involved in the mêlée, would both be elected for the ILP. John Wheatley, who had been in the City Chambers seeking to negotiate for them when battle raged outside, would likewise be elected. Some, like Wheatley, would even become ministers in the first Labour government formed in 1924.

Those individuals and the events that occurred followed a long tradition in the city where strikes and insurrections had occurred over generations. As historians have argued, there was no direct correlation between previous revolts and strikes and the outcome of that election or indeed events during the war. But, the events didn't come about by chance and the individuals involved did not grow up in a political vacuum, rather they were nurtured and forged by events that occurred and by characters who inspired them. Accordingly, the story of the rise of Red Clydeside and its political success in 1922 cannot be told without reference to events that preceded it and were part of the journey the city made.

Finally, just as separate political paths were later to be taken, so some different views were held at the time by those involved. There were some who sought the revolutionary road and others who pursued radicalism through constitutional routes. Of course, there was always much more that united than divided them. But on specific issues, and more importantly on how to achieve the radical change they all sought, there could be digression and even deep political disagreements. Most had opposed the war and all sought peace, but some, like Kirkwood, were prepared to assist the war effort whilst others were conscientious objectors like James Maxton or vehemently denounced it like John Maclean. Whatever their personal views on the war, all participated in demonstrations and direct action in support of industrial disputes and rent strikes.

However, the majority sought social reform through democratic elections and the parliamentary route, whilst it was a minority who wanted revolution created through industrial and community actions and militancy. Unlike in Russia, which provided the backdrop to the events that were unfolding and inspired that minority, it was the social reformers, not the revolutionaries, who were ultimately to prevail. The ideological divides that existed within the socialist movement in those early yet turbulent years are also detailed. The disputes over theory as well as the practice that challenged the movement. And comrades made and friendships lost and how they developed and ultimately played out within the radical cause.

This, then, is the story of Bloody Friday in Glasgow, why and how it happened, who and what preceded and inspired the individuals involved and what became of them. It was an event that also heralded the political arrival of Red Clydeside, which was to leave an indelible mark on modern Scotland.

1

THE BACKDROP

January 1919 saw a world in turmoil. Although the Great War had ended, with the Armistice on 11 November the year before, an Allied army occupied the Rhineland and conflict still continued in some parts of the world. Moreover, humanity had been sorely bled, with eighteen million dead, including 148,000 Scots and almost 18,000 men from Glasgow alone. The number of men physically and psychologically wounded was even greater, with the consequences often lingering for a lifetime as medical science struggled to cope with injuries and amputations, and post-traumatic stress disorder remained largely undiagnosed and unrecognised.

It was certainly far from being the war to end all wars that many had hoped it would be, and it wasn't the prelude to social, economic and political harmony that others had sought. Instead, it was the precursor for demands for radical change and the clarion call for revolution and rebellion in many parts, which was often met by repression. Historic powers were breaking apart and new challengers were arising. Fighting continued not just between armies but, perhaps more worryingly for many, within countries.

Revolution had occurred in Russia just over a year before the war had concluded, and elsewhere centuries-old empires and their leaders were toppling. The February Revolution had seen the Romanov Dynasty overthrown, closely followed by the October Revolution, which saw the

Bolsheviks seize power under Lenin. Communism had been proclaimed and it was a dream shared by many around the world, including some in Glasgow.

Russian White armies opposed to the new regime, and supported by Allied forces, were trying to crush the nascent Bolshevik state. They were considered a threat that the established powers, victorious in the Great War, believed had to be nipped in the bud, lest revolution and Communism spread. Hence, British troops were fighting in Murmansk and Arkhangelsk, whilst soldiers from other countries were battling elsewhere across the vast Eurasian land.

Meanwhile, revolutionaries elsewhere also sought to seize their chance in the general turmoil to change the established order and challenge the capitalist system. A civil war had erupted in Finland between Reds and Whites in 1918, and the following year saw the Red Army under the command of Leon Trotsky, not only defending the gains of the revolution but supporting others seeking to replicate them. His forces advanced on other countries including Poland, Ukraine and Estonia, ostensibly to liberate them, but in reality, to back comrades seeking to emulate the Bolshevik Revolution and seize power. Revolution was in the air across the entire Continent.

In Germany, the Kaiser had abdicated following wartime defeat, bringing with it the fall of the House of Hohenzollern, but adding further turmoil to an already troubled land. The Kiel Mutiny that had helped bring about Germany's collapse had been closely followed by the Spartacist Rebellion, which broke out in the first days of 1919, and which had quickly and brutally been crushed. Karl Liebknecht and Rosa Luxemburg, two of the Communist leaders who had declared the Free Socialist Republic, had been brutally executed only a few days after. Fighting was also still ongoing in many parts, as others continued the struggle for the revolutionary dream.

The Habsburg dynasty, with links back to the Holy Roman Empire, had also fallen, and the great Austro-Hungarian Empire was about to splinter central Europe into a myriad of smaller states. Even countries that had not been involved in the war, like Spain, were afflicted by the global storm, with martial law soon to be imposed, as industrial disputes and social unrest escalated.

The maelstrom wasn't just in Europe, but crucially, struck at the heart of the British Empire. In Ireland, just across the sea from Glasgow, from where many had migrated during the Great Famine, Sinn Féin had been victorious in the general election. Held the month before, in December 1918, and in the wake of the brutal suppression of the failed Easter Rising of 1916, constitutional nationalism had been supplanted by radical Republicanism. Sinn Féin MPs had met in Dublin just days before, as the Dáil Éireann, to declare support for an Irish Republic, and shots had already rung out, killing two Royal Irish Constabulary officers and heralding the War of Independence.

Authorities and leaders faced challenges not only in military operations, but in civilian life as well. Governments everywhere were seeking to demobilise war-weary soldiers eager to get back to their homes and families. In Britain alone, two and a half million servicemen were due to be discharged, with 900,000 being retained for ongoing duties. Hundreds of thousands had already been demobbed and more were agitating to be discharged.

It couldn't come fast enough for some servicemen anxious to return to civilian life, and demonstrations had already taken place by troops angered by the conditions they were forced to remain in. 1919 was the opposite of 1914, when volunteers couldn't enlist quick enough to get to the front; now, many conscripts couldn't wait to be discharged to get home. Authorities knew that morale and discipline remained manageable, but the spectre of workers' and soldiers' councils on the Continent still caused unease. There was a desire to demobilise as speedily as possible before unrest in military ranks could grow, even if that simply passed the problem to the civil authorities.

For, whilst that eased tensions in camps where troops were billeted, it frightened many union leaders, because of the effect it would have on work and wages on their return. Unemployment had blighted industries and scarred communities before the war, and its spectre still haunted many where memories were still raw and painful. Eagerly anticipated reunions and the safe return of loved ones were tinged with worry about the future for all.

Compounding all these timebombs was Spanish flu. The pandemic was at its height and death was stalking towns and cities across the globe. Ironically, it was brought into Europe by American troops when that country entered the conflict. Wartime restrictions on news reporting meant coverage of the rampaging virus was repressed until news appeared in the Spanish press and the name was rather unjustly given. Over five hundred million were infected across the earth and more died than in the war itself, with estimates varying from twenty to one hundred million fatalities.

Glasgow was not be immune to those global pressures and a growing number of its inhabitants were agitating for change. The war had simply intensified the social troubles that already existed in the city and had also created networks for those advocating a different way, and even order of society. Many in Glasgow were inspired by what had already happened – whether in Russia or Ireland – and the possibilities these conflicts had opened up for their own city and country.

The February Revolution had been celebrated in Glasgow, as in many other cities, by left-wing supporters: demonstrations had taken place in support of it and the May Day celebrations in 1917 saw the red flag prominently displayed in the crowd of almost 100,000. That continued with further smaller demonstrations taking place in June as supporters mobilised and radical campaigners were energised (and backing for events in Russia was in tandem with demands for change at home). News of the Bolshevik Revolution in October of that year was more constrained. Wartime censorship also restricted information on what was happening, as the authorities were frightened by the revolutionary fervour. The peace treaty in March 1918 between the Bolsheviks and the Central Powers to take Russia out of the war was a bitter blow for Britain and its allies still fighting on the Western Front.

Again, though, some were inspired and anti-war sentiment and socialist fervour was further fuelled by revolutionary zeal. The mood in the city was also changing, as support for the war was replaced by stoicism and then supplanted by a desire for peace. The audience was becoming more restless, yet also more receptive. Most just wanted it to end soon through victory, although some were prepared to try to achieve that more quickly – and at any price.

Adding to that, revolutionary views now had a living example, significantly greater than the Paris Commune, which gave its name to Communism. The seizing of the moment, albeit by a minority, stirred many people's emotions, and the feeling in Britain was no different. In his memoirs, Lloyd George recalled that the

> Russian Revolution lit up the skies with a lurid flash of hope for all who were dissatisfied with the existing order of society … In Russia, they pointed out, the workmen formed a separate authority co-ordinate with the Government …Why not in Britain? That was the question asked in every workshop and at every street corner.

Glasgow, as the second city of the empire and with a significant radical base, could be no different and would be at the very centre of the clamour for radical change – and even revolution. There were many there who revered the Bolsheviks and sought to replicate those struggles in their own city. Lenin was even to describe it as the Petrograd of the West, and the revolutionary John Maclean was appointed Bolshevik consul. May Day 1918 saw 100,000 march through the city in socialist solidarity, despite the backdrop of ongoing war, and despite being held on the weekday that it fell, rather than the nearest Sunday. International Workers' Day wasn't a public holiday then, and absence from work meant forsaking a day's pay. Even if many who attended were shift workers and those losing pay were limited, it was still a significant event, and the massive turnout testified to the growing unrest in the city.

As well as revolution in Russia, rebellion in Ireland inspired many in the city. Red and green were interwoven and the Irish community was an important part of the city's life. It wasn't just through kinfolk that events across the Irish Sea were closely followed. The Irish community in the city was well organised and politically represented. The Irish nationalist cause had long been supported and had many activists associated with it. Michael Davitt had been a regular visitor who had worked closely with the local Irish community, which was not just well represented, but growing in influence.

Leaders of the insurrection in Dublin were also well known in left-wing circles in Glasgow, and contacts existed through socialist, as well as Irish nationalist circles. James Connolly, born in Edinburgh, had been active in several socialist organisations before moving to Ireland, where his parents were originally from. He had led his Irish Citizen Army in the (Easter) Rising and had been executed by the British days after it. His execution, along with many others, helped swing public opinion that had initially been hostile to the uprising towards their cause. This change in attitude was mirrored amongst the Irish community across the water in Scotland. As Ireland was stirring, so was Glasgow.

This then was the global maelstrom that Glasgow awoke to that Friday morning in January 1919. It was a city where left-wing activism had been growing before the war and had been steeled, not tempered, by it, and where there were campaigners in the community, as well as in the factories, with militants as well as moderates amongst those agitating for change. Radical reform was being demanded by many, and even revolution being advocated by some. It was a city with a long radical tradition, which had been inherited by many activists and inspired them as much as international events had enthused them.

2

THE RADICAL TRADITION

Glasgow has always had a strong radical tradition stretching back to the early days of the industrial age. In the latter decades of the eighteenth century, revolutions broke out around the world, as they did in the twentieth century. First in America and then France, as empires fragmented, monarchies toppled and a new strain of revolutionary political thought germinated; the old order being challenged, much to the concern of the establishment.

Calls for radical change from France were echoed as loudly then for some in Glasgow as they would be for others when revolution broke out in Russia more than a century later. Cooperation and coordination amongst groups of workers was growing; military presence was accordingly increased, not just to ward off attack from other armies, but to secure the state from revolution within. Barracks were constructed and militia recruited. Disturbances still occurred, though, around Scotland provoked by conscription and food shortages, but also with an undercurrent of demand for political reform. In some areas a tree of liberty was symbolically planted, coming from the French and American Revolutions, and it was as emblematic as the red flag would be more than a century later. It symbolised the demands being made for liberty, equality and universal suffrage, seen by many as being embodied in the French Revolution and articulated for them by Thomas Paine in his book *Rights of Man*.

In Glasgow the principal exponent of reform and its most able advocate was a lawyer, Thomas Muir of Huntershill. Born on the High Street in 1765 where his father was a successful merchant, he moved with the family to a house and lands at Huntershill in nearby Bishopbriggs. Graduating from Glasgow University in 1782, he forsook thoughts of entering the ministry and instead continued studying law. Becoming embroiled in the new developing political ideas, he fell out with the university authorities and left Glasgow to enrol at Edinburgh University. There he completed his studies and was admitted as an advocate in 1787.

Standing up for the poor and oppressed, and often working for little or no fee, his reputation quickly grew. Active in radical political circles, he was closely involved in bringing organisations together into the Scottish Association of the Friends of the People in July 1792, mirroring an English organisation set up a few months before – though more radical and with a wider social mix. Given the political ferment of the time, Muir and his colleagues also corresponded not just with the organisation in London, but with the United Irishmen in Belfast, who were revolutionary in nature. That latter organisation, already operating more covertly, would also move from simply advocating political reform to seeking to seize it by military means.

The establishment, though, was far from standing idly by: not only was military presence increased, but spies and agents abounded. Muir was quickly targeted as one of the principal ringleaders and the authorities soon pounced. Arrested on 2 January 1793 on a charge of sedition, he was released on bail and quickly headed south to London to advise colleagues of what had happened and seek support.

Meanwhile, however, revolutionary events in France were moving apace, as a republic was declared and increasingly radical elements took control. The King faced execution, which created panic amongst many reformers in London. Some were abandoning previous calls for change as horror at the revolutionary actions abroad mounted, and fear of repression grew at home.

Muir headed for France to try to persuade revolutionary leaders to spare the King's life and limit the collapse of support in London and beyond. Belated, if not doomed from the outset, he arrived in Paris just after the King had been convicted and shortly before he would be executed. Though his efforts had failed, he was still welcomed by the revolutionaries as a kindred spirit, meeting many leading proponents including Mirabeau, and Thomas Paine.

For the British establishment, revolution was bad enough, but regicide sent waves of fear and revulsion crashing through it. The French Ambassador was expelled and revolutionary France reacted by declaring war on Britain. Back in Scotland, meanwhile, the authorities were scheming to ensnare their own revolutionary. They accelerated Muir's trial date, knowing that he would be unable to return home from France in time to attend court. The most senior legal and establishment figures in the land eagerly conspired to convict and harshly punish him, as a warning to others.

When he understandably failed to appear, a warrant was taken for his arrest. Realising that he wouldn't be able to make the rescheduled date, Muir had decided to head home regardless, but with war raging, obtaining a passage wasn't easy. However, he eventually found an American ship heading to Ireland. In Belfast, he met with the United Irishmen and was enrolled as a member of the organisation before finally arriving home, landing at Portpatrick on 24 August, his twenty-eighth birthday. There, he was immediately detained and taken under military escort to Edinburgh for trial.

At the proceedings held on 30 and 31 August 1793, the full weight of state power was brought to bear against him, and charges including sedition and distributing inflammatory writings were levelled. Moreover, not only was the judge actively conniving to convict him, but the jury had been selected for their hostility to reform. In spite of this Muir remained unbowed, and rose to the challenge with his spirited speech from the dock becoming legend. There he stated:

This is now perhaps the last time that I shall address my country ...
of crimes, most foul and horrible, I have been accused. Of attempting to rear the standard of civil war, and to plunge this land in blood,
and to cover this land with desolation. At every step, as the evidence
of the Crown advanced, my innocency has brightened ... What then
has been my crime? ... having dared to be, according to the measure
of my feeble abilities, a strenuous and active advocate for an equal
representation of the people – in the House of the People ... It is a
good cause. It shall prevail. It shall finally triumph.[1]

His calm demeanour and his courageous oratory also brought public
sympathy behind him. That was reinforced when an unprecedented
sentence of fourteen years' transportation was handed down. Public
discontent not only continued, but escalated. As a result, the authorities moved him from Edinburgh to London where he was detained
under increased security.

The Friends of the People maintained their efforts with a further
convention bringing leaders together. Once again, state oppression was
unleashed, with other leaders of the organisation arrested and also sentenced to transportation to Botany Bay. Along with Muir, they became
known as the Scottish Political Martyrs.

Despite being sent to Australia, Muir's story was far from concluded
and, rather than settling down to penal life in Australia, he escaped. In
1796 he boarded an American ship departing the colony and crossed
the still largely uncharted Pacific Ocean before arriving off Vancouver
Island, in what is now Canada. Warned that a Royal Navy ship was in
the area, he transferred to a Spanish craft heading down the coast to
Monterey, California. Although upon landing there, he was detained
on spying charges and taken under escort to Mexico City, before being
put on a ship bound for Spain.

---

1   Murray Armstrong, *The Liberty Tree: The Stirring Story of Thomas Muir and Scotland's First Fight for Democracy* (Word Power Books, 2014), p. 187.

Nearing Cadiz harbour, the Spanish vessel and the ships it was sailing with were attacked by a British fleet, and during the fighting that followed Muir was badly wounded. The injury he sustained left him badly disfigured, which, ironically, resulted in him evading detection and certain execution after the British captured and boarded the ship. Unrecognised by his captors he landed in Spain where he convalesced in hospital, cared for by nuns. French authorities had by that point found out about his arrest and, angered by his treatment, sought his release. In September 1797 he returned to France, receiving a revolutionary hero's reception.

There, Muir sought to persuade the French revolutionary authorities to support a rebellion in Scotland. Lobbying leaders, he urged that soldiers be landed to support an uprising which he believed would garner popular support. He and some other exiled radicals were aided in their arguments by the imposition of the Militia Act in Britain, which allowed for conscription. It was the first time it had been imposed and was deeply unpopular amongst ordinary people who as ever, would face the brunt of it with the wealthy able to buy their way out of it.

Large protests against the act took place, which were in turn ruthlessly suppressed. Riots and disturbances took place across the country in numerous communities from the Borders north to Perthshire and from the east coast across to Ayrshire and Renfrewshire in the west. At Tranent, just outside Edinburgh, a confrontation took place between local colliers and English troops. A crowd chanting 'No Militia' were brutally cut down by soldiers, and others, including women and children, were pursued and slain by cavalry, killing between twelve and twenty. It became known as the Massacre of Tranent.

In Muir's absence and following the suppression of the Friends of the People a new organisation was formed. The United Scotsmen was modelled on its namesake, the United Irishmen, and was a revolutionary organisation advocating a Scottish Republic and universal suffrage. Similar to the Friends of the People, it was mainly based on working men with many weavers and other artisans, such as small shopkeepers, making up the bulk of the membership. Its operation, however, was much more clandestine, and was based on a cell structure taken from their Irish counterparts. Little is known about them for that reason, but it is clear that the authorities had reason to be concerned. Their strength in the weaving areas in the west of the country and in Fife and Tayside made infiltration by government spies difficult. Though they may never have been significant in numbers, plans for insurrection were being made with pikes and armaments under construction. It was for that reason repression was unleashed.

As well as the support of the French sought by Muir, overtures were made by the United Scotsmen to the Dutch for assistance. The Dutch Republic had been overrun after the French Revolution and become a client state of the Paris radicals. A landing of 15,000 Dutch troops in Scotland was even considered for 1797, with the intention of seizing the central belt and establishing a Scottish Republic before re-embarking to support a rising by the United Irishmen in Ulster. Many, including Wolfe Tone, the Irish organisation's leader, were sceptical and General Hoche, the French commander, died before authorisation could be given.

However, in any event, the Dutch fleets' defeat by the British Navy at the Battle of Camperdown off the Dutch coast put paid to any such landing. Ironically, the Royal Navy fleet was under the command of a Scot, Admiral Adam Duncan, 1st Viscount Duncan, from Dundee. As so often throughout Scottish history Scot was pitted against Scot. Divisions – whether over claims to the throne or religion – were dividing and scarring the land. Earlier that century the Jacobite rebellions had split the country, culminating in the Battle of Culloden in 1745. There, Cumberland's mainly English army were supported by some Scots as the Highlands were brutally suppressed.

The United Scotsmen were to be as ruthlessly crushed as the Friends of the People had been before them. The reaction of the authorities was once again swift and brutal. Fears of insurrection following the revolution in France and evident sympathy for the cause amongst many saw the start of the construction of barracks across the central belt. Edinburgh, Glasgow, Hamilton, Ayr and Perth were all constructed in the early to mid-1790s. This was all reminiscent in many ways of what had happened in the Highlands after Culloden. Britain militarised as the army grew from 40,000 in 1789 to 250,000 by 1814. Ostensibly, this was for war with France, but it was also was used to suppress the internal dissent that existed.

Leaders of the United Scotsmen were arrested, many imprisoned and some transported to Botany Bay with the organisation proscribed. George Mealmaker, a driving force behind the struggle (and ironically also from Dundee), died a lonely death, exiled in a foreign land.

Muir remained in touch with Scotland and was a minor conduit to the Directory, the five-member committee that was running revolutionary France. However, his efforts to gather further French aid for a Scottish insurrection were unsuccessful. With his influence waning, and doubtless tiring through ill health, he moved north out of Paris to the small village of Chantilly, dying on 26 January 1799 aged just thirty-three.

Although dead, his memory was not forgotten. Sympathy and admiration were widespread, even if they had often to be covert. It is suggested that 'Scots Wha Hae', penned by Robert Burns in 1793 as Muir's trial was commencing, was an allegory for the martyr's radicalism. Wary of possible accusations of republicanism, reference was instead made to the historic William Wallace, rather than to Muir, to avoid the poet himself facing charges of sedition and the often severe accompanying punishments.

Whilst Muir's revolutionary activities had ended and the final trial of a United Scotsman had taken place in 1802, the radical spirit hadn't been crushed. Widespread sympathies still lingered and others would pick up the mantle. In less than a generation, another attempt at revolutionary change was made, and Glasgow was again at the forefront of battle. For, 1820 saw a rising also known as the Radical War, which was yet another attempt at armed insurrection.

Following the Battle of Waterloo and the defeat of Napoleon, the economy faltered, with hunger and unemployment stalking the land. Moreover, demobilised soldiers home from the wars were adding to the ranks of the workless and increasing the destitution across the country. In 1816, 40,000 people demonstrated on Glasgow Green for political reform and against high food prices and the newly imposed Corn Laws.

Protests both north and south of the border increased, and in England bore witness to the Peterloo Massacre that took place in August 1819. There, fifteen were killed and hundreds more injured as some 60,000 to 80,000 peaceful protestors were attacked by the military in Manchester. This, in turn, provoked further demonstrations, and in Scotland a rally in Paisley the following month led to a week of rioting, and cavalry were required to be brought in to quell the disturbances. Protest meetings were held and there was fear in the establishment that revolution could occur. Further military recruitment and the garrisoning of troops followed. Still, though, the demands for reform continued. Once again, the authorities infiltrated spies and agents provocateurs into radical groups. Many were deceived with traps set for them, but for many, however, the fuse of revolution had been lit and it was too late to turn back.

In 1820 radicals met in Glasgow to elect a committee for organising a provisional government. It also arranged for military training under John Baird, a weaver from the village of Condorrat with army experience. By the beginning of April, proclamations had been printed and were being openly displayed in Glasgow calling for a rising and demanding equality of rights, as well as bearing revolutionary statements such as 'Liberty or Death'.

Meanwhile, industrial action in support of insurrection was also underway. Monday 3 April saw as many as 60,000 stopping work across west central Scotland, many of them weavers. This was a huge number, given the population was less than two million and the small industrial workforce in what was still a predominantly agricultural society. In many ways it was the equivalent of a general strike. Placards were placed in prominent sites across many communities, calling them to 'desist from their labour from and after this day, the 1st of April, and attend wholly to the recovery of their rights'.[2]

In many areas men assembled to drill in a military fashion, in other areas foundries and forges were raided for the manufacture and distribution of pikes to willing hands. In Glasgow, a few hundred radicals briefly clashed with cavalry billeted in the city, and in the following days further contingents of troops arrived as tension mounted. An attempt to march on Carron Company Ironworks, where military equipment could be acquired, was intercepted by soldiers. Skirmishes between radicals and troops began to occur on a frequent basis.

Tuesday 4 April saw government spies delude the would-be revolutionaries. A small band of men again marched off to Carron Ironworks for armaments, under the leadership of Andrew Hardie, and going by Condorrat to meet John Baird. They then proceeded to Bonnymuir, outside Falkirk, where they had been persuaded by the government agent that others would join them.

It was, unfortunately, a trap, and they were attacked by soldiers and cavalry. Though the small force resisted, they were soon overpowered. Nineteen men, including Baird and Hardie, were taken prisoner, but still the agitation continued. Another small force was similarly duped in Strathaven, Lanarkshire, and incited to march to Cathkin, south of Glasgow, ostensibly to meet with another force. Sensing something was amiss, many, including the leading radical James Wilson, turned back. Though it was too late; the marchers had been recognised and soon many were rounded up.

---

2   T. C. Smout, *A Century of the Scottish People 1830–1950* (Fontana, 1987), p. 233.

The protests continued in the weaving areas and well beyond. In many communities, both large- and small-scale drilling and the manufacture of pikes was still happening, and in Glasgow troops remained on alert as rebellion simmered. As captured radicals were taken to prisons around the country, further demonstrations took place. In Greenock, a riot occurred and shots were fired, killing eight civilian protestors. The angered mob continued their protest, breaking open the jail and forcing the release of some prisoners who then managed to escape.

The authorities responded by unleashing their full military and judicial power, and the radicals were once again soon brutally crushed. Special courts were established to deal with eighty-eight men charged with treason. There was, though, still great sympathy for those involved amongst the wider public. Juries acquitted several weavers, and even James Wilson was acquitted of three charges of treason and, on the fourth of 'levying war against the King in order to compel him to change his measures', they recommended mercy. But, clemency was not shown and he was hanged on 30 August. Likewise, the judge sentencing Hardie and Baird ensured that an example would be made of them and they were hanged and then beheaded, the last occasion such a punishment was invoked in the United Kingdom. Others who were captured were transported to New South Wales and Tasmania.

Steps were taken by government to ameliorate popular discontent across the land, recognising that force alone would be insufficient to maintain order. Measures to address unemployment and poverty through work schemes helped reduce the level of discontent. Additionally, a charm offensive was carried out with King George IV, who visited the country. Efforts were made by the likes of Sir Walter Scott to foster a new form of Scottish identity through the development of tartan and other fripperies, as a way of diluting discontent amongst the working people.

But still, demands for social and economic change remained undimmed. Insurrection was foresworn, but demands for political representation continued and the focus was shifted onto the franchise and

votes for working men. The first major Reform Act with separate legislation for Scotland was finally brought about in 1832. The electorate in
Scotland had always been lower than in England, some 0.2 per cent of
the population compared to 4 per cent. The changes were to increase
the electorate by well over tenfold. However, that still only resulted in
it rising from approximately '4,500 to 65,000',[3] roughly 13 per cent of
adult males. A further 400,000 men were still denied the vote, as were
all women.

It was an improvement, but still far short of what was wanted. Moreover, industrial unrest still remained. The west of Scotland was hit hard
by an economic depression, and in 1837 cotton spinners in Glasgow
struck against wage cuts. There were around a hundred cotton mills in
the city, and as one of the city's major employers, that meant hardship
in many households. During the dispute a blackleg worker was shot as
passions ran high. In another incident, a woman mistaken for a strike
breaker was killed, and the union appears to have helped those responsible flee to America.

The strike endured from July through to the end of August before
funds finally ran out and it collapsed. During the dispute the authorities arrested the leaders, who were brought to trial in Edinburgh on
charges relating to the strike, though the city collected £1,000 for their
defence, showing the support the accused had within the community.
Leaders were convicted and sentenced to seven years' transportation,
and though ultimately spared Botany Bay, they languished for three
years before being pardoned. Defeat in that strike was a bitter blow to
the wider trade union movement, which was compounded by a further
depression in the 1840s.

But, though down, radicalism certainly wasn't out. As the economy
recovered agitation returned. With the industrial revolution continuing
apace, a growing urban working class was evolving. Mines and larger

---

3   T. C. Smout, op. cit., p. 233.

factories began to supplant mills and smaller works, with the miners superseding the weavers as the leading industrial radicals. Demand for political reform continued, though it was primarily focused on the franchise.

In that struggle the Chartist movement was firmly to the fore, with its membership drawn primarily from the new working class that was evolving. Inheriting the radical mantle, they became the main outlet for the pursuit of political change. The name was taken from the People's Charter, which sought votes for all men over twenty-one, secret ballots and paid MPs amongst other demands – and which was garnering widespread support after its launch in 1838.

Chartism's electoral demands were aided in some ways by other social changes ongoing at the time. They varied from the growth in secessionist churches frustrated at landlord control and influence, to the temperance movement where alcohol was seen as the scourge of the working classes. All those issues helped colour its political convictions, but it was still primarily based on the quest for liberty and equality that had flowed from revolutions in America and France. In Scotland, it was based on the same principles as in England, though again with its own distinctive identity.

Clamour for further reform and votes for working men intensified. With the launch of the Chartist movement, huge meetings had taken place, including one in Glasgow. The movement was, in the main, non-violent; it was based on morality and legitimate political arguments. Most people, and especially those in Scotland, took the position of the Glasgow Chartist Association which declared 'that the oppressors would never heed moral force unless there was physical force behind it, but went on to say that violence should be used only as a last resort and in response to violence first used against the working classes'.[4] Elections were contested under the Association's banner and industrial disputes were supported.

---

4   T. C. Smout, op. cit., p. 235.

In the years following its launch, depression hit again, and in 1842 wage cuts were imposed by employers and strikes broke out. The west of Scotland and Glasgow were once more to the fore and demands, as in England and Wales, weren't just for the restoration of wages, but for the implementation of the charter. Upwards of 20,000 unemployed men marched from Glasgow Green to the West End of the city and troops were used to suppress disorder. But the strikes ultimately failed, and people began drifting back to work, primarily forced by lack of funds.

By 1848 demonstrations sprang up as Europe was once again convulsed by revolution, with the slaying of aristocrats as shocking to the British ruling class as the execution of the French king had been over two generations before. Authorities again clamped down on movements viewed as seditious, and these actions were also aided by a general improvement in the economy, which brought about a reduction in agitation.

However, a revolutionary wing had evolved in Scotland from within the wider movement, which saw an opportunity to be seized due to the support that remained strong in areas where hardship and inequality still lingered. But, again the authorities struck early with the use of draconian legislation and the arrest of leaders. Earlier that year 'Bread Riots' broke out in the city, which lasted over two days. On 6 March 5,000 attended a rally at Glasgow Green; there were demands for support for the workless and calls that people should simply take what they need. Rioting in the east end of the city followed and spilled into the centre. Shops were looted and goods carried off, windows broken and guns taken from a gunsmith and, as the crowd moved through the city, shots were fired in the air.

Confronted by police and militia they retreated to the Saltmarket where barricades were erected. Troops and police were assisted by special constables, many of whom were wealthy merchants enrolled to deal with the situation. The Riot Act was read (or at least partially) and cavalry charges took place at Glasgow Cross with parts of the city becoming a battlefield. Protestors then retreated to Bridgeton.

The following day the disturbances continued and a contingent of police and military pensioners taking a prisoner to Calton Police Station were stoned by local people. Shots were fired by the militia into the crowd, killing one man and wounding several others. Whether as a result of this, or simply because there was no real leadership or plan, the disturbance soon ended and participants simply melted away.

However, authorities sought to detain those they thought to be the ringleaders, and hoped to recover items looted from shops and stores. George Smith and John Crossan were tried and convicted for their role in speaking at the rally with Crossan sentenced to eighteen years' transportation. Order was restored and political turmoil lessened.

Some, though, still sought to pursue the revolutionary goals and later that year John Grant, Harry Sherwood Ranken VC and Robert Hamilton were charged with sedition and with planning an insurrection. Statements had been made in the press and at a public meeting suggesting support for an insurrection. It was alleged they saw the aims of the charter as insufficient, and a revolution like the one in France, was required. Formation of an armed National Guard was mentioned, with a rising led by them being used to tie up English troops to support a rebellion that was to take place in Ireland. Young Scots were also advised to go to Ireland and support rebellion there.

The trial of the radicals was conducted in a far fairer way than for those accused of such crimes in past decades. A sign, perhaps, that the establishment realised that the threat was ebbing? All three men denied the charges and argued they subscribed to 'moral force chartism'. An able defence by their lawyer meant the jury only found Ranken and Hamilton guilty of minor charges, and the court sentenced them to just four months in prison.

The Chartist movement thereafter faded, but left a legacy of political activism that continued not just in the community, but in the workplace. In the 1860s reform returned to the political agenda with demands for an extension to the franchise. The establishment soon conceded the Second Reform Act of 1867, which extended the vote 'to ratepaying male householders and ten pound a year lodgers and to small owners and middling tenants in the countryside'.[5]

However, this was still inadequate to satisfy the increasing demands of what was a growing working class, but the House of Lords in particular was being obstructive and opposing any further extension of any of the demands made in the original charter. A demonstration took place in Glasgow in September 1884 that saw 70,000 march from Kelvingrove Park to Glasgow Green, with tens of thousands more there to greet and support them. Speeches were made backing the changes, though there was also a subtext of agitation for land reform, which was running as an issue both in Highland Scotland and in Ireland.

A third Reform Act was finally passed in 1884, which extended the franchise to include the likes of crofters, miners and farm labourers who had previously been excluded by the original criteria. Although this increased the total electorate across the UK to five and a half million, meaning that roughly two out of three men in England and Wales had the vote, in Scotland it was more like three in five. Despite this, as many as 40 per cent of adult males were still denied the vote, due to being servants, sons staying at home, soldiers in barracks, or because they were destitute and either hadn't paid their rates or were on poor relief. Moreover, all women still remained disenfranchised.

But radical political parties were developing and trade unionism was growing as society changed. Demands for reform continued unabated, but rather than armed insurrection power would come through organising in the mines, factories and shipyards, as well as campaigning in the cities and communities. It would still face opposition, though, from the establishment, but the struggle continued as new battlefields were found. A Scottish Labour movement was being born.

---

5   T. C. Smout, op. cit., p. 245.

3

GROWING POLITICISATION

As industrialisation increased rapidly in the second half of the eighteenth century, thoughts of armed insurrection were supplanted instead by growing politicisation and increased union activity. The expansion of democratic franchise, even if still limited, offered a nonviolent political route for those seeking radical reform.

In spite of this, these were far from good times for working people in the urban communities springing up across the country and especially in west central Scotland. Life was hard, with work insecure and often dangerous. Hence why political activism in the community and the workplace increased with political parties and trade unions coming to the fore – protecting working people and championing their rights.

Politically, the initial beneficiaries of the demise of Chartism and the extension of the franchise were the Liberal Party. In some ways they supplanted Chartism and became the parliamentary vehicle for effecting change. They dominated both across Scotland and in Glasgow specifically for seventy years after 1850. Working with or through them became the political route. The Liberals won every election in Scotland from then until 1922 other than in 1900 in what became known as the 'khaki election' when the Boer war saw the Tories triumph. Glasgow was similar, with only one Conservative MP ever returned in the city between 1832 and 1886.

The historic support for the Liberals was based on many factors, but antipathy towards landlordism was a crucial part not just for Highland Scotland but in Glasgow as well. Poor housing conditions within the city provoked antagonism towards landlords, many of whom were rightly perceived as being Tories. High rents and poor accommodation left a bitter taste for many, and resulted in a rejection of those viewed as responsible for them and the misery they inflicted.

Moreover, the migration into the city of Scots from the Highlands and Islands and Irish from across the sea added to the unease, both bringing their historic loathing of landlords. Whether cleared from estates or simply departing for greater opportunities, many from the north brought with them a resentment towards the laird and landowner. That was matched by the arrival of the Irish community, commencing with the famine and which, at one stage, saw almost 1,000 a week streaming into the city bringing a legacy of bitterness and raw anger at landlords.

The liberal perspective and Liberal rule resulted in the growth of municipalisation, in which Glasgow would be at the forefront of development, both in Britain and beyond. From the water supply taken from Loch Katrine to address public health concerns through to the subway and tramcars, public facilities were established or taken over and operated municipally. It wasn't done through an ideological drive for public ownership, but from a paternalistic perspective of providing facilities for the public good. There was no desire for state control of the means of production, instead it was simply a recognition of the need for infrastructure to grow the economy and the requirement to take other actions to protect the common good. It not only mirrored the contributions elsewhere in the UK of wealthy individuals providing public facilities but institutionalised it within the council. It was an ethos of public-spiritedness rather than a desire for public ownership. This would be challenged as the decades at the end of the century approached and the extent of public ownership began to be opposed by a growing Tory presence, objecting to what they saw as profligacy and a threat to their own private ventures. It resulted in a slowing down of municipalisation and a more strident voice for the free market.

The Liberals themselves were an amalgam made up of three main groupings. Old-fashioned patrician Whigs, middle-class radicals and a growing body of what were described as Liberal/Labour all came together, though from vastly different roots. Moreover, initially, as trade unionism sought to get political representation it was done through the Liberal Party. Operating within and under the Liberal banner allowed for some working-class representation to be elected. It was only a small number and they were thereafter under the constraints of the wider Liberal Party group. However, it seemed the only feasible way to see working-class representation come about and was therefore the route pursued by many, with some limited success.

It wasn't just political philosophy that motivated many of the agitators. Religion also played a significant part in the early thoughts of many socialist and radical activists as the twentieth century approached. Even before the Disruption that affected the Church of Scotland in 1843 when, with the secession of the Free Church, there had been a splintering of many working-class adherents. That schism was over patronage in the selection of local ministers and relations between the Church and state. Trouble had been brewing for some time, but finally erupted. But, concerned at both the nature and structure of the Church, a growth in secessionist churches had begun with many Chartists particularly active in them. Thereafter involvement was maintained by many in often the United Presbyterian or other non-established churches. It affected their perspective of social change and helped forge the basis of their ideology. As was written, 'The labour leaders of early twentieth century Scotland very often saw their fight in terms of a struggle between good and evil.'[6] Similar no doubt to colleagues south of the border where Methodism

---

6   T. C. Smout, op. cit., p. 207.

and other non-established churches would be the genesis for many radicals.

That was also often allied to the support for temperance. Alcohol was seen as a huge problem that afflicted and blighted the working class. Fuelled by poverty and deprivation it was seen as a scourge that both harmed and held back the poor. Tackling it was therefore viewed by some as essential for both physical and spiritual well-being. It provided a moral basis for many in the city's labour movement, often in conjunction with the religious dimension.

Trade unionism was also growing and developing as factories expanded and the industrial revolution took hold. The nature of the membership also broadened as the new century advanced. It was much more than simply the miners replacing the weavers in radical leadership; the miners were now to the fore as leaders of the wider trade union movement, and would remain so for several generations to come. It wasn't just the scale of the industry and the numbers, where well over 100,000 were employed, but the level of organisation that they had established that made it so.

But other areas and new types of members were sought. In Glasgow, and especially in nearby textile towns, as elsewhere in the country, the National Federation of Women Workers (NFWW) was active in recruitment, thus increasing the size of the membership and deepening roots within the community.

Union membership in Scotland was lower than in England and heavily concentrated in the west of Scotland. Glasgow was also a city based primarily on skilled labour, enabling more workers to be persuaded of the benefit, if not the necessity, of being in an organisation to protect their trade. It was reckoned that over 70 per cent of the workforce could be classified as skilled at the start of the twentieth century.

However, the large industrial unions were also less dominant in Glasgow than they were in comparable cities south of the border, doubtless because of the skill base. Unions therefore evolved on a more federated basis, meaning control and influence was much closer to the grass roots than the union's leadership. Accordingly, it could be described thus: 'Scottish trade unionism was highly federated, more geographically concentrated and more activist led than was the case in England.'[7]

Trades councils in many ways became the basis for political campaigning where workers and political activists came together. Ironically, what had come about in some ways because of weakness with the need to work across factories and beyond the trade unions, became the base for a more radical political outlook and for wider collaboration than elsewhere. That growing trade unionism also sought to increase its political voice, and by the mid-1880s Glasgow Trades Council was calling for more working-class political candidates.

As the decade progressed, the grip of the Liberals began to lessen and the socialist movement began to evolve. Home Rule for Ireland had divided the Liberal Party and though both Scotland and Glasgow were less affected than other areas, seats were taken by both Conservatives and Liberal Unionists in the election of 1886. Those two parties would merge in the following century, but the result was the beginning of the end of Liberal dominance, though it would remain a major party for decades to come.

The difficulties experienced by the Liberals, however, proved to be opportunities for others – and not just on the left and in industrial areas. In Highland Scotland, a Crofters' Party emerged to challenge them on land rights. In Glasgow the focus though would be on the Irish community. The failure to deliver on Home Rule and the internal divide it caused resulted in them beginning to seek alternative outlets for their political representation, and crucially, in support of Irish nationalism. Moreover, facing religious and racial prejudice and blighted by poverty, they sought to ensure that their rights would be protected in their new home. So they began to mobilise for political representation.

---

7   Robert Duncan and Arthur McIvor (eds), *Militant Workers: Labour and Class Conflict on the Clyde, 1900–1950* (John Donald, 1992), p. 101.

More importantly still, in 1888, Keir Hardie, who had spent many of his childhood years in Govan, formed the Scottish Labour Party, which merged in 1894 with the Independent Labour Party (ILP). He had despaired of the representation through the Liberals and sought for the working class and the wider labour movement to have its own party. Working for the Miners' Federation in Ayrshire, he began to pursue political activism, seeing that as essential. Though he was never elected in Scotland, he retained his home in Cumnock, Ayrshire throughout his life and would remain the grand old man of Scottish socialism until his death in 1915. He also embodied that commitment to a socialism based on morality formed by his Christianity and support for temperance. The party he was pivotal in bringing into being became the dominant left-wing vehicle in Glasgow, even in his absence. Like him, its socialism was more pragmatic than doctrinaire.

The first president of the Scottish Labour Party was Robert Bontine Cunninghame Graham, who had been elected as a Liberal in Lanarkshire in 1886 and became the first socialist MP (an early sign of the drift of members and influence from the Liberal Party to the fledgling ILP). Cunninghame Graham had also helped establish the Scottish Home Rule Association the same year that he had been elected to Parliament, showing the intertwining for many of socialism and self-government for Scotland.

Initially, political representation for the working class in the city began to move from the patrician Liberals to what were known as the Labour stalwarts. They were elected to the council in 1898. Not all were socialist and many were linked with Irish nationalism. Most lost their seats in the elections in 1901, and had been viewed with some disdain by many when they seemed to focus on attaining office rather than delivering for working people. But it was the start of separate representation for the working class and this would only increase as the new century arrived and new political ideologies began to take hold.

It wasn't just the ILP that arrived on the scene, though it was to be the largest and most influential. Other parties such as the Social Democratic Federation, the Socialist Labour Party and the British Socialist Party would all appear on the scene in coming decades as the new century dawned. Socialism was blooming and its offshoots were flourishing. Radical thinking developed not just with Marx, but in Britain with William Morris, the Fabians and many others.

A few espoused revolutionary demands and took doctrinaire positions. Some would adhere to a more scientific form of socialism being espoused by Karl Marx and other theoreticians. They would begin to be heard more frequently as socialism in all its facets evolved and would have an influence on both the wider movement and the city. Allied to that milieu was the Irish community who began to slowly shift their longstanding political allegiance from the Liberals to the ILP.

The socialist movement was therefore growing in numbers and expanding in depth. Everything from Socialist Sunday Schools to a vibrant socialist press was now in existence. The newspaper *Forward* was founded in 1906 by Tom Johnston and supported both socialism and temperance. Johnston would become a stalwart of the ILP, yet it also provided an outlet for others, including the revolutionary John Maclean. It became the principal news outlet for the ILP, though several other papers and magazines would also be published across the socialist spectrum.

However, though growing, the socialist movement still remained politically weak in comparison to the established parties of the Liberals and the Conservatives. The ILP in 1896 had seventeen Glasgow branches but that number wouldn't be increased until 1910. An MP was returned in 1906, as one of only two across Scotland when George Barnes won the Blackfriars & Hutchesontown division, the other victory being in Dundee. Camlachie saw the ILP candidate poll 30 per cent of the vote, but that was insufficient to win.

That increasing representation came about as unemployment, poverty and poor housing increased. As the first decade of the new century progressed another depression had brought about another unemployment crisis. In Glasgow '7,000 people were dependent on a special relief fund by Christmas 1907, and *The Times* reported nine months later that 16,000 in Govan were on the verge of starvation'.[8] In July 1908, with up to 20 per cent of the workforce unemployed and relief funds proving inadequate, thousands marched for the Right to Work.

It was a breakthrough, but a modest one. Although it has to be taken in the context that despite the increase in the number of people afforded the franchise, working-class voters still faced significant limitations. There were considerable differences in voting patterns between working-class and more affluent areas. Some of the differentials could be stark indeed: 'In the poorer areas of the city such as Calton and Cowcaddens less than 40 per cent of adult males were on the electoral register, whilst in the middle-class suburban areas of Langside, Pollokshields and Kelvinside the level of enfranchisement was around 85 per cent.'[9] Accordingly, Barnes remained the only Glasgow Labour MP elected when war broke out, having retained his seat in the elections in January and December 1914. The other seats saw five Liberals and two Tories returned in both elections.

Moreover, the number of councillors – initially through the stalwarts and subsequently through the ILP – remained low. Cooperation took place between the left and Irish nationalists to try to increase representation, but success was still limited. In elections in 1911 they gained four seats, increasing their numbers to ten. However, in spite of losing three the following year, numbers actually increased to twelve as Govan, Partick and Shettleston came into the council area, when neighbouring communities were incorporated into the city boundaries. A further six gains were made in 1913, though there were again two losses. Victory in two by-elections and another gain in elections held in

8   T. C. Smout, op. cit., p. 261.
9   Alan McKinlay and R. J. Morris (eds), *The ILP on Clydeside, 1893–1932: From Foundation to Disintegration* (Manchester University Press, 1992), p. 45.

1914 meant that the Labour Group on the council numbered nineteen when war broke out. However, voting was even more skewed in municipal elections than in general elections; multiple voting for businesses and the disenfranchisement of the poor even more heavily weighed the scales against working-class representatives.

Meanwhile, militancy was also increasing in the factories; organisation into trade unions was increasing and expanding. The likes of Keir Hardie and many others were toiling away seeking to encourage membership. This continued not just through the good years, but into the hard times when work was absent for many and hardship befell them. Meanwhile, wages and working conditions were threatened for those who still remained in work.

Industrialisation proceeded relentlessly and by 1913 Glasgow and its wider conurbation made 'one-fifth of the steel, one-third of the shipping tonnage, one-half of the marine-engine horsepower, one-third of the railway locomotives and rolling stock and most of the sewing machines in the United Kingdom'.[10] But that growth came at a social cost, bringing poor housing and endemic poverty. The changes made by the Liberals, alongside the municipalisation of facilities in the city and the country, had ameliorated some of the conditions, but not radically altered them for many. Overcrowding was reckoned to be five or ten times as great as in comparable English cities, and the levels of mortality and infant mortality, in particular, were appalling. A national survey in 1902 had found Glasgow to be the most overcrowded city in the country and the situation had worsened over the first decade of the twentieth century. As late as 1898 infant mortality in the Gorbals was 200 per 1,000 births and the situation, though improved, still remained shocking in its extent. The poverty affected the living as well as those whose lives it claimed. A survey in 1906 found that a fourteen-year-old boy from a poor area in the city would be four inches shorter than one

---

10   T. C. Smout, op. cit., p. 267.

from a wealthy part. Poverty and poor housing were endemic in many communities across Glasgow.

Moreover, new manufacturing procedures were being brought in as capitalism and industrialism evolved. Many came in from America, increasing productivity for the employer at the cost of the employees' rights. It increased pressures on the workforce and threatened already poor standards of living. Militancy therefore increased, and demands for radical change grew as not just men, but women, too, were increasingly drawn into the industrial conflict.

As the second decade of the new century dawned, it was to be the start of a period of industrial militancy in Glasgow and surrounding communities, or as the revolutionary John Maclean described them, 'The times we are living in are so stirring and full of change that it is not impossible to believe that we are in the rapids of revolution.'[11]

---

[11]   Nan Milton, *John Maclean* (John Maclean Society, 2002), p. 61.

4

IN THE RAPIDS OF REVOLUTION

In Glasgow it wasn't just the outbreak of war or events elsewhere that made the second decade of the twentieth century a tumultuous time, and John Maclean could be forgiven for believing it was indeed the rapids of revolution. For the early years of the decade saw Red Clydeside being forged in the factories across the west of Scotland. As Labour historians have written, there were no direct links from those preceding years to the Red Clydeside that emerged from it. However, Red Clydeside didn't emerge from nowhere. The events that followed were fired – and the key participants moulded – not just in preceding centuries, but most especially in those preceding years. Ideas began to percolate, organisations were formed and radical action taken by workers. It was early days, but muscles were being flexed and preparations being made by some for more revolutionary steps.

That militant period from 1910 until 1914 saw strikes escalate and organised labour began to flex its muscle. It is reckoned that about forty million working days were lost in Britain in 1912 alone during both major and more minor industrial disputes. The impact on key industries in many urban areas, and especially on Clydeside, was huge. Moreover, when it tailed off elsewhere in the UK, it still remained militant in the west of Scotland. With many disputes spontaneous and led by the workforce, it added to a perception that something serious was happening. In establishment circles it was seen as politically motivated, and part of a wider attack on society, especially when many strikes were unofficial.

In April 1911 the *Glasgow Herald* fulminated that

> Glasgow has felt the surge of a movement that has swept the great centres of population throughout the country. To us the most deplorable feature of the troubles into which the country has plunged is the utter indiscipline of the forces which agitation has set in motion ... most of the restraints imposed by the older and more respectable type of trade unionism are flouted by workers who have come under the spell of incendiary advisers like those who have made the Confederation of Labour a menace to the structure of French society ... the present situation is the gravest that has been known for a century.[12]

Political activism and industrial militancy were increasing, but there was nothing beyond that in terms of concerted action. Information was shared and lessons learned, encouragement given and support offered, but it wasn't an organised series of disputes or part of a wider revolution. Other than coordination in the national dialogue that was taking place, this was mainly locally organised, and often carried out as an immediate reaction to specific local events.

However, increased militancy did see a growth in political activism which motivated many to join a union. Membership of those affiliated to the STUC (Scottish Trades Union Congress) increased from 129,000 to 230,000 between 1909 and 1914. The Glasgow Trades Council became the most powerful in the whole of the United Kingdom where 'over 400 delegates met weekly, from all trades in the Clyde area, to discuss local and national affairs'.[13] It became in many ways the political voice

---

12   William Kenefick and Arthur McIvor (eds) *Roots of Red Clydeside: 1910–1914? Labour Unrest and Industrial Relations in West Scotland* (John Donald Publishers Ltd., 1996), p. 2.

13   William Kenefick and Arthur McIvor, op. cit., p. 21.

of trade unionism on the Clyde. Female membership of unions also increased and all these changes were mirrored in towns both large and small across the Clydeside area.

Militancy increased, but for reasons not just to do with the poverty and deprivation, which were rampant. It was of course in part due to high rents and the overcrowding that created conditions of squalor and chronic ill health. However, it was also compounded by two additional other factors.

Firstly, new methods of working were being brought in, primarily from the United States, that were designed to increase productivity and enhance profits. Ranging from what might be viewed as the start of the modern production line through to the outcomes of time and motion studies, they resulted in speeded-up procedures. However, they did so at the expense of the employee, who faced working faster, with reduced rest and often for no more or even less pay.

Secondly, although Glasgow was a liberal city, many of its employers were far from benign. Some, obviously, objected to the liberality and municipalisation and were committed Tories. Others, perhaps, mirrored the likes of their fellow Scot Andrew Carnegie, and whilst capable of great acts of public philanthropy, remained ruthless towards their own workforce. Often autocratic and anti-union, blacklisting and victimisation of workers was common practice amongst industrialists of the time.

Employers' federations had been established and were numerous on the Clyde, spanning all sectors. They were used to protect industrialists' interests before, during and after any dispute. Collective bargaining was growing as a concept across the country, but it was far less prevalent on the Clyde. In Glasgow and the wider conurbation employers often refused to recognise unions, and sought to weed out employees they thought undesirable. In some sectors such as shipbuilding, where foremen often did the hiring, it resulted in sectarian employment practices, as well as seeking to avoid those who might be militant. By the same token, often those seeking to organise a union within a factory or site would be pressurised or dismissed from employment.

When industrial confrontation occurred, employers could be ruthless. Blackleg labour was frequently used to try to break a strike (a practice which occurred much more frequently in Scotland than south of the border). So-called 'free labour agents' were specialists who operated in hiring workers specifically for that purpose. Labour exchanges that had opened – ironically – to help the unemployed find work were also frequently used to try to provide the manpower for strike-breaking.

Employers were also supported by the state and other clandestine ways. Police provided protection for those being used to keep work going and undermine the stoppage. Likewise, the judiciary would come down hard on those arrested and charged with offences related to the dispute. Organised thuggery could also be unleashed, and Orange Order disruption of left-wing and union meetings occurred.

These problems also extended into housing, and where a tenancy was provided through employment, the threat of eviction would be used. Many larger companies had started to provide not just recreational facilities for their staff, but housing for workers. Whilst it provided many with better quality accommodation and often at a more reasonable rent, in an industrial dispute it also became a threat that not only would employment be lost, but so would the roof over their head be removed.

Despite all those challenges militancy increased alongside unionisation. National strikes took place with railways, seamen and dockers, which affected almost the entire country. The miners' strike in 1912 was that industry's first ever national dispute, with a million people taking part. Most strikes were local, though, and these were many and varied. Some of the larger ones were part of the forging of Red Clydeside; they laid a pattern of industrial militancy that would grow and develop and which was to be the training ground for many who would have a prominent role in future political and industrial events.

The dispute that is seen as signalling the start of 'Red Clydeside' occurred in 1911 at Singer's in Clydebank. It was to be the largest that took place at any single company, but also had other aspects that made it representative of the time. The strike was brought about by changes to the production system causing an increase in work and yet a reduction in wages. Moreover, it saw huge local support, as well as being given outside political backing. Individuals involved would also go on to play their part in future events on the Clyde.

The Singer's factory in Clydebank opened in 1885 and work moved out from the original site in Glasgow. At its peak in 1913 it employed 14,000 workers (most of whom were women); it produced over 1.3 million sewing machines and accounted for 80 per cent of the company's worldwide production. In 1911 it employed 11,000 people directly and was so vast that it extended over a huge site, which even had its own railway station.

The strike started on 21 March when twelve female cabinet polishers were faced with an increased workload, yet a reduction in wages. It triggered events which meant that within two days almost the entire factory was out on strike and the community rallied behind them. It was primarily led by the local strike committee, though they also had extensive political backing in the form of the Industrial Workers of Great Britain (IWGB) and the Socialist Labour Party (SLP). The former was the UK offshoot of the American Industrial Workers of the World (IWW), known affectionately as the 'Wobblies', who were pivotal in the leadership of the dispute. They were closely allied to the SLP, with both believing in industrial unions and political progress through workplace agitation. They were supported by other political parties within the wider socialist movement including the local ILP, who were also heavily involved in the factory and community and quickly put their resources behind it.

The company reacted venomously, closing the factory and threatening to relocate the work around the world. When that failed to break the strike, efforts were ramped up, culminating in the management issuing a ballot directly to employees. It went over the heads of the workforce leadership and was designed to undermine morale and divide the workforce, which it ultimately did. The ballot was sent to every employee's home and asked them to commit to a return to work if over half the workforce agreed. Steps were taken to agitate for a return to work and suggestions were put about that most were going to do so. As it was, 6,527 voted in favour with still 4,025 holding out against a return. Despite being independently adjudicated, there were still allegations of vote tampering, although it is more likely it was simply the sheer weight of pressure being brought to bear by the company that resulted in so many voting in favour.

As a consequence, the strike collapsed and its leaders resigned themselves to defeat. The workforce returned to the factory on 10 April with no additional terms having been achieved. The management's response, however, was not to show any magnanimity in victory. Instead, a purge of the workforce commenced, with strike leaders being dismissed along with others viewed as political agitators. All the strike committee and known members of the IWGB were fired, which totalled around 400. Other political activists were also identified by foremen and dismissed.

The purge had devastating effects not just on the individuals discriminated against, but on the left in Clydebank in general. They had rallied round the strike and would suffer with them in defeat: 'By 13 May 1911, sackings included sixty ILP members, a number of SDF [Social Democratic Federation] members and over twenty members of the Socialist Labour Party.'[14] Both the SLP and SDF virtually ceased to exist in the town, as former workers moved away in search of employment.

However, whilst it may have ended the dispute, it didn't diminish the fighting spirit in the community or even amongst those who had been sacked, and parties, in particular the ILP, regrouped. Arthur

---

14   William Kenefick and Arthur McIvor, op. cit., p. 205.

MacManus, who had been in the IWW and was dismissed having been a strike leader, would go on to be involved in the 1919 strike, as well as becoming the first chairman of the Communist Party of Great Britain when it was formed.

Disputes also took place across a wide range of sectors, and textiles continued to prove a major battlefield; 1911 also saw a strike at the United Turkey Red factory in the Vale of Leven around twenty miles north-west of Glasgow, in a community that would later be dubbed 'Little Moscow' because of its dominant Communist views. It was relatively high profile at the time and is now also seen as a microcosm of disputes at the time as it had all the hallmarks of the ongoing struggle between capital and labour. Unions sought to be recognised by employers and achieve better conditions for the workers, employers resisted that or demanded increased productivity – often without any increase in pay.

The town was a hotbed of radicalism and the dyeing and cloth factory had come about through a rationalisation of company sites, as closures and competition reduced profits, and the business contracted in size. Though there had been a modest wage rise, the workload had also been increased, causing union membership to grow – as did political agitation within the community. With the threat of punishment or dismissal hanging in the air, much of the organisation was done behind the scenes by the union.

At the beginning of December, the union advised the management that they were seeking a wage rise on behalf of the workforce. The company's response was to indicate that they would only deal with their employees and not with the union. That was rejected by the strike committee and a strike was called (though apparently it had been acceptable to union officials, indicative perhaps that though the union were leading the negotiations, much was driven by workforce representatives).

The dispute lasted for over a fortnight. A large meeting took place in Renton Town Hall to generate support and public demonstrations took place. Police were drafted in to patrol the town and monitor the situation, but all remained mostly calm, though there were reports of flour and other objects being flung at clerks going into the site by women picketing. Unions were ultimately recognised and a modest pay increase obtained, although the equality of pay between men and women that had been sought by the NFWW wasn't achieved. However, it showed that much of the leadership came from the local activists as well as public support, not the full-time union officials.

Women were to the fore in many other disputes, including some that preceded it. Mills in Paisley and Neilston had seen strikes by the mainly female workforce at the end of the first decade of the twentieth century. Then, in 1910, a strike at mills in Kilwinning in Ayrshire saw them withdraw their labour with not just the full support of local people, but solidarity pledged by local miners. That show of community support for the women was replicated in 1913 in Kilbirnie, Ayrshire where workers in a net-making mill went on strike. They were out for twenty-two weeks, which was then the longest female strike at that period. However, what was also commented on in the press was the backing that they received both from within the local community and from other workers including miners and steel workers.

And still the strikes continued across sectors. In 1911 just as the Singer's strike was ending, a major dispute arose in Glasgow where municipal workers (and in particular those working on the tramcars) went on strike. Brewing for quite a while, it finally blew up in the August and it was once again led in many ways by the rank and file, leaving a legacy of radicalism and bitterness in its wake.

The Municipal Employees Association had been established in London, but soon extended out to other large conurbations including Glasgow. There it quickly recruited heavily amongst growing numbers of tramway staff. Its Scottish secretary, Alexander Turner, was an ILP man active on Glasgow Trades Council. Though municipal workers tended to have better conditions than those in the private sector, the city council was still far from a benign employer, with the management style paternalistic and authoritarian.

New technology and changes in working practices were once again affecting workers as with private sector industries. Electrification made the vehicles faster and the distances they covered greater. The pressure on drivers and conductors increased accordingly, and the workers' demand was for increased leave and shorter hours – a 51-hour week and seven days' holiday per annum. However, these were rejected by management, despite the significant profit the service made for the city.

A strike ballot was held of the workforce, which was overwhelmingly supported by a margin of 1,667 to 171. The rank and file were angry: conditions were worsening and the strictures imposed by management increasing. Despite the hesitancy of the union leadership the strike commenced on 12 August 1911. Pickets appeared at every tram depot and police were placed on standby. Not just strikers but family, friends and supporters attended to jeer at strike breakers. Reports in some papers even suggested that the women at some places were worse than the men in their behaviour towards those still seeking to go to work.

Management tactics were similar to those in the private sector, and strike-breakers were hired to try to keep the tramcars operating and the city moving. That wasn't without its difficulties; there are reports of one inexperienced driver crashing and killing five passengers and injuring many more. Vandalism of vehicles also took place by strikers and protestors, with cables cut, and windows smashed and stones placed on tracks to derail cars. Approximately 150 vehicles were damaged and fights took place between demonstrators and police with many arrests. Tensions were rising and the situation was fraught.

Conversely, the vandalism was hugely counter-productive and resulted in public anger at the visible damage done. There was significant press hostility and the papers used the vandalism as an additional reason to attack the strike and demonise the workers. With management proving intransigent and public support diminishing the strike soon ended.

When it collapsed many who had been on strike were treated as having broken their contract and were refused re-employment. As at Singer's, the leaders were targeted by management.

However, though the dispute was lost, there was still a political fall-out which would benefit the wider socialist movement and the ILP in particular. In particular, the councils' handling of the dispute left a bitter taste for many, doubtless far too redolent of the excesses of the private sector. Those who had, it appeared, acquiesced, by allowing the council's management to act in that manner, paid a price. It changed the perspective that many ordinary citizens had about the council and their political representatives. As a result, as was identified by historians Kenefick and McIvor, 'numerous professedly progressive Liberal councillors on the corporation were deemed to have revealed their true colours by sanctioning anti-union exploits'.[15] The Liberals' loss would be the ILP's gain. They began to be seen as a credible force as their organisation improved and actions on the industrial front and on housing raised their profile. Meanwhile, others who had once obtained working-class votes and masqueraded as the friends of the unions were being exposed.

That dispute was quickly followed at the start of 1912 by a dock strike, which also garnered support from local seamen. A new union, the Scottish Union of Dock Labourers (SUDL), had quickly supplanted the former UK-wide union the National Union of Dock Labourers (NUDL), which had folded, partly due to dissatisfaction with the leadership in Liverpool. The new body had risen from the remnants and had been actively supported by the trades council.

Nearly 7,000 dockers were joined by 600 seamen when the strike came about in early 1912. Only the Singer's dispute and the later transport strike were bigger. It started on 29 January and the employers responded with a lockout. A settlement was reached between

---

15   William Kenefick and Arthur McIvor, op. cit. p. 236.

management and union officials, but was rejected by the workers. Over 6,000 came out again on 12 February, though it was quickly resolved thereafter. The union was recognised for the first time in the sector, although other gains were limited. Actively involved for the seamen was Manny Shinwell, who would go on to play a leading role in 1919 and would later be elected to Parliament in 1922.

Though strikes had been tailing off, elsewhere in the country militancy remained, and in Clydeside strike action continued to be taken, often locally led and occurring suddenly and on a variety of issues. In May 1913 shipyards in Govan and Partick struck over pay rates. Support for industrial struggles wasn't just offered to those in Glasgow, but to others elsewhere. The politicisation that had taken place saw links forged with others near and far. Backing was given to disputes around the country and beyond when they broke out. When the great Dublin lockout took place that year huge support was given from Glasgow. There were close political links between the two cities in both Irish nationalist and socialist circles. James Connolly wrote a regular column for *Forward* and the paper was very supportive of Jim Larkin the strike leader, as well as of the dispute itself. Both those individuals were well known in Glasgow and leading socialist activists in the city frequently went across to visit comrades in Ireland.

However, the support extended well beyond this, as funds gathered from Glasgow in support of the 'Great Lockout' were greater than from any city other than Dublin itself. They were obtained not just from political parties and trade unions at factory gates and meetings, but through street and community collections, in which the ILP and the trades councils in Glasgow and Govan were firmly to the fore. These collections even took place outside Ibrox Stadium, home of Rangers FC. Known then as now as a Protestant club, it is obvious that solidarity with fellow workers was then far more important for many than sectarian division.

Likewise, as with the factories, agitation on housing and other social issues was increasing. The ILP was growing in size and influence and other left-wing political groupings were also gaining numbers. Housing, in particular, was being pushed by the ILP, with demands for the building of cottage-type accommodation at affordable rents paid for through profits from the municipal services. This was one such demand that resonated with many, given the appalling housing conditions that afflicted so much of the city.

Basic social provisions such as pensions were beginning to be provided through the Liberal government, but they were nowhere near adequate enough, nor were they set at a level to satisfy demands. The push was for much greater social provision, and that required more radical social change. Growing militancy reflected a mood of working people being unwilling to meekly accept the conditions imposed or endured at work or in the community.

Red Clydeside's reputation was accordingly being forged, a cadre of leaders being moulded and a wider community becoming politicised. Not just in Glasgow, but across the country and beyond there was a growing belief within the socialist movement that change was coming, and that victory – if not immediate – was almost a historic inevitability. Progress had been made with the Labour Party growing in Britain, and across Europe social democratic parties were increasing in size and influence. A Labour Premier had even been elected in Australia, ironically an emigrant Scot, Andrew Fisher from Ayrshire, who had known Keir Hardie.

Although the membership of political parties was still not large, other organisations were growing and developing, including not just trade unions, but cooperative societies. They too were creating a spirit of solidarity, experience of self-help and a mood of optimism. So, hope sprang eternal for the socialist movement across Europe.

As summer 1914 arrived, storm clouds were threatening and war was looming. Many believed that socialist solidarity would see worker refuse to fight worker in a capitalist war. But, as nationalism and patriotism broke out, solidarity collapsed and the socialist movement was rent asunder, as was the world. Divides would also open up in Glasgow and in Britain over support or opposition to the war, both within the wider community and on the left.

However, the war also offered an opportunity, as established powers weakened and unrest grew. The legacy from the activities before the war would see confrontations on the home front as well as in the battlefield. War would arrive at the Clyde and its people would become combatants: many thousands in the trenches, but others in the factories and communities of the city.

5

WAR ON THE CLYDE
– THE COMBATANTS

When Britain declared war on Germany on 4 August 1914 it divided the growing socialist movement in Glasgow, as it did across Europe. Calls for the workers of the world to unite in refusing to take up arms against each other were ignored by most. War saw workers more often enthusiastically enlisting than declining to fight, and the Labour Party in Britain, as with the Social Democratic Party in Germany, was divided by the conflict.

Labour had opposed the war as storm clouds had gathered, viewing it, like other socialist parties, as being driven by capitalism. They also believed that the solidarity of the working class should transcend national borders and that war would only enrich a few, whilst resulting in the deaths of vast numbers of ordinary soldiers. Even just the day before war was declared the party leader Ramsay MacDonald had spoken out passionately against it in Parliament, describing the Germans as friends, not enemies.

However, the declaration of war changed all that, and just two days later the Labour Party came out in support of it. The invasion of Belgium was used as the excuse for the volte-face; it was likewise used by the British government. MacDonald was left high and dry, as well as isolated within the parliamentary group, where support for the war was overwhelming. Forty MPs had been returned in the 1910 general election and only a few amongst them continued to oppose the war. As a consequence, and abandoned by his colleagues, MacDonald resigned as leader.

Arthur Henderson replaced him. Born in Glasgow, he had moved to Tyneside at an early age after his father had died. Henderson would go on to join the government in 1915 as Asquith formed a coalition when his administration came under attack following Gallipoli and other setbacks. Becoming president of the Board of Education, Henderson would also advise Asquith on union affairs, having been an official for the Iron Founders as well as a Labour activist.

When Asquith's government fell in 1916, replaced by a coalition administration under the premiership of Lloyd George but with a majority of Tories, Henderson remained in Cabinet and was joined by two colleagues. One was George Barnes, who had been elected for the Glasgow Blackfriars & Hutchesontown constituency in 1906 as Labour remained committed to the war throughout. The other was John Hodge, who represented Manchester Gorton but who had been born in Ayrshire and gone to school in Glasgow.

Some did continue to speak out against it though, and not just MacDonald. Former leader Keir Hardie passionately denounced it and was supported by other senior figures including Philip Snowden and George Lansbury. Few of the leading left-wingers supported the war, and that opposition was replicated in the affiliated organisations such as the ILP and the British Socialist Party (BSP). But, a clear majority in the parliamentary and wider party rallied to the flag and voted to support combat. Trade unions in particular were much more pro-war, explaining the change in attitude within the British Labour Party. There were a number of reasons for that, from working-class patriotism and less commitment to international solidarity, to seeing opportunities for better wages and conditions to be obtained for members. They put a brake on left-wing ideas within the party, but equally were critical in changing the stance on the war.

Along with other anti-war proponents, MacDonald and Hardie faced vitriol in the press and even some hostility in communities where pro-war sentiment ran deep. Even mining communities with a strong support for the socialist movement faced splits over the conflict. Hardie experienced this in south Wales, where he was the MP for Merthyr Tydfil & Aberdare, and though there was strong backing for him personally from many of his constituents, there was equally significant resentment towards him from others. Meetings would often be disrupted and heckling took place as he travelled around the country.

Despite the growing feeling in support of the war, the Independent Labour Party (ILP) remained opposed to the conflict. It had met in Bradford for its twenty-first anniversary congress on 11 April, just a week after war had been declared, and remained resolutely opposed on moral grounds. It had a membership of around 30,000 by then and both at leadership and grassroots level the commitment to pacifism ran deep. Scotland was a significant part of the membership and one of the areas where the party was strongest; the ILP was the predominant political movement within the wider Labour Party in Scotland.

However, that position did see several leading figures leave the party, including George Barnes, the Glasgow MP, to join the wartime coalition government. He and some others left soon after the Bradford congress. Objecting to the failure to support the war, many joined the Labour Party directly rather than remain in the affiliated ILP with their pacifist stance.

In Glasgow, however, the ILP remained fairly solidly against the war though they, like other socialist groupings, had some members who supported it. Barnes wasn't alone as '16 out of 18 ILP councillors' supported it.[16] However, leading figures such as Tom Johnston, John Wheatley and Patrick Dollan remained passionately opposed to the war and that was the official line that would be reflected in both their

---

16   T. C. Smout, op. cit., p. 263.

journals and their actions. They were amongst the most influential figures and reflected the views of the overwhelming majority of activists.

As the war continued over coming years, the tack changed from opposing it to seeking peace, and disputes were more often about whether it should be a negotiated peace or simply an armistice called without any agreed terms. However, throughout the fighting, considerable sympathy was still shown by many in the wider public to those who continued to oppose the war on principle and who faced punishment and even jail for their conscientious objections. Coverage of this was extensive in the left-wing papers and journals, and respect was shown to them even by those activists and members of the community who either supported the war or believed in a negotiated peace.

Key leaders and activists began to emerge both across the factories and in the communities, and on the industrial and political fronts. Tom Johnston was born in Kirkintilloch in 1881, where his father was a grocer. Early on he became involved in socialist politics and, after working in a few jobs, persuaded some wealthier supporters to back him in the launch of a left-wing paper. *Forward* first appeared in 1906 and was avowedly socialist. It became the news outlet for the ILP and he was its first editor. Reflecting the moral streak of many in the party he refused to print alcohol advertisements and forswore gambling stories. He also found time to attend Glasgow University as a mature student, though didn't graduate, and wrote a book, *Our Noble Scots Families*, which was an excoriating denunciation of the landed gentry. It was through the paper that he came to prominence and he was to possess the greatest influence in the rise of Red Clydeside.

John Wheatley was born in Bonmahon, County Waterford, in Ireland in 1869, but came to Scotland with his parents a few years after when they arrived in search of work. Following his father down the pits in Lanarkshire at young age, he became a publican and then a printer, where his business specialised in left-wing works. He joined the ILP in 1907, where he became a leading activist and councillor. Devoutly Catholic, he founded and became chairman of the Catholic Socialist

Society, which was pivotal in moving the Irish vote over to the party. *Forward* started running a regular column on 'Catholic Socialist Notes', showing both the growing links being forged and the increasing importance of the Irish vote to the wider movement.

Patrick Dollan was also from an Irish background, having grown up in Baillieston, Lanarkshire, where he too followed his father down the pits, before becoming a journalist with *Forward* in 1911. Before joining the ILP he was active in local community and council politics, then, elected to the council just before war commenced along with Wheatley, he became a dominant force in politics; he and his wife Agnes, who was a Protestant, were leading opponents of the war.

When war broke out Tom Johnston fulminated against it, writing in *Forward* that it was 'a cause in which we have no interest, in which we were never consulted, and from which by no conceivable result can we derive any advantage – only starvation, hungry children, crying in the streets, bones lying in the battlefields, widows, orphans, tears'.[17] A clear reflection, not just of his own opinion, but that of the wider leadership.

There still remained some in the party, though, who felt that once war was declared support had to be given for the national interest. David Kirkwood, who had joined the party in the early stages of the war and would go on to play a leading role in the industrial disputes as well as becoming an MP, encapsulated the view of some in the party – and no doubt the feeling of many ordinary people. Deeply eager for peace, he believed it could not be at any price, and certainly not as a result of a military defeat. Writing in his autobiography, he said that he hated war:

I believed that the peoples of the world hated war … Yet I was working in an arsenal, making guns and shells for one purpose – to kill men in order to keep them from killing men. What a confusion. What was I to do? I resolved that my skill as an engineer must be

---

17   Russell Galbraith, *Without Quarter: A Biography of Tom Johnston* (Birlinn, 2018), p. 37.

devoted to my country. I was too proud of the battles of the past to stand aside and see Scotland conquered.[18]

That overt support for the war effort would lead to caustic criticism from those who were bitterly opposed to the war, and in particular, from John Maclean.

Born in the east end of Glasgow in 1872, Kirkwood became an engineer and then shop stewards' convenor at Beardmore's Parkhead Forge works, near where he'd grown up. Spread over twenty-five acres and employing more than 20,000, it was vital for war work. A key player in the Clyde Workers' Committee (CWC) that was soon formed, he was seen as the leader of the engineers. He had been a member of the Socialist Labour Party but left in September 1914 to join the ILP, persuaded by John Wheatley that 'if socialism was to have any power, all socialists must go into the Labour Party'.[19]

As there was a divide over war then commencing, there was also disagreement over how peace was to be achieved. When it became clear that the conflict was not ending quickly, this became an issue that required to be straddled. There were some who wanted peace negotiations and others who simply demanded that the war be ceased.

The biggest challenge that faced the ILP and all the others on the left who opposed the conflict was the pro-war fever that afflicted the city, as it did the land in general. Many members had family or friends who had either enlisted or would be later conscripted. Concern and understanding for them, as well as the wider political consideration of public attitudes, was required.

That divide was reflected across other smaller socialist parties. The British Socialist Party had seen regional conferences take place where Glasgow and London opposed the war but other areas didn't. Almost all the socialist groupings had seen some rift over the war and though

---

18   David Kirkwood, *My Life of Revolt* (George G. Harrap, 1935), p. 82.
19   David Kirkwood, op. cit., p. 87.

the likes of James Maxton and John Maclean held out resolutely, they were a minority within the city as a whole. For, in the city as elsewhere, ordinary citizens caught a war fever, which political parties were unable to contain – and sometimes even found contagious.

James Maxton (or Jimmy Maxton, as he was known) wasn't just a trenchant opponent of the war, but he even refused to serve in it. Born in Pollokshaws in the south of the city in 1885, he was the son of teachers. Moving at an early age to Barrhead just outside the city, he attended the local school which his father was in charge of before winning a scholarship to Hutchesons' Grammar School, Glasgow. From there he went onto Glasgow University and also became a teacher.

But, teaching aside, it was politics that inspired him. Both his family and his own early views had been more conservative, but he converted to socialism and in 1904 joined the Barrhead branch of the ILP. His experiences teaching in the city's deprived areas deeply scarred him and were pivotal in forging a commitment that drove his activities. As did his close relationship to John Maclean, with whom he collaborated on many anti-war activities. Maxton refused to be conscripted and as a consequence was sentenced to work on barges. His opposition continued undaunted, though, and along with other Red Clydeside stalwarts he was later convicted of sedition and imprisoned.

Maxton's friend and socialist firebrand John Maclean was another who zealously campaigned against the war. He was born in Pollokshaws in 1879 to parents who had moved to the city from the Highlands, with his father a potter hailing from Mull and his mother from Corpach. His father died when he was just eight years old (it is thought from silicosis, which was rife in the pottery industry), leaving his mother to bring up four children in very straitened circumstances. Training as a teacher through the Free Church and attending Glasgow University part time, Maclean graduated with a Master of Arts. His socialism was inspired, as well as driven, by the poverty he saw all around him. Joining the Social Democratic Federation (SDF), which later became the British

Socialist Party (BSP), he became a leading light through giving radical speeches and Marxist educational classes for working men. Embracing a revolutionary approach, he and others who followed him began to veer away from the more mainstream ILP.

Maclean was to become the most prominent anti-war activist, and most certainly the one the authorities targeted most. His opposition to the conflict increased his profile, as well as cementing his revolutionary views. He became the unofficial leader of what might be termed 'the revolutionary faction' in the city and Scotland as a whole. He and Maxton spoke regularly at peace meetings and he continued his promotion of workers' education and Marxist economics. As a result, he was sacked from his teaching post in 1915 and by the following year was in prison for his anti-war activities.

Supporting him was Willie Gallacher, who would soon come to fame as the chairman of the CWC. Gallacher was born in Paisley in 1881. His father was an alcoholic, and this was something that would scar him throughout his days and saw Willie initially drawn into the temperance movement. However, he subsequently joined the ILP before leaving to join the Social Democratic Federation, where he worked closely with Maclean. Leaving school at twelve, he had been a delivery boy and a steward on a transatlantic liner, before becoming an engineer at the Albion Motor Works in Scotstoun, which specialised in the manufacture of commercial vehicles. In 1913 he left to visit sisters in America with a brief stint working in Belfast before returning to the Albion Works and becoming works convenor just as war was breaking out.

Anti-war campaigning was carried out by the likes of Maxton, Maclean and Gallacher, alongside many others, and there were perhaps more anti-war activists in Glasgow than in most other cities, with perhaps also a greater tolerance for their activities shown. However, disruption and hostility could still be faced, despite garnering sympathy when imprisonment and clampdowns were imposed. Although they were given an opportunity to state their case and there was consideration for their suffering, it was certainly the case that they had far from widescale support across the city.

As there was a divide amongst the combatants over the war, so too would there be some divergence between those who were social reformers or radicals pursuing a parliamentary road and those who were of a revolutionary bent and wished to take direct action. In some ways the divide had always been there, as the socialist movement developed in the late nineteenth and early twentieth centuries. The ILP favoured the parliamentary route, as opposed to the Socialist Labour Party (SLP), who adhered to a syndicalist doctrine of change through action in the industrial field. The BSP was also more militant. The ILP and those supporting reform tended to pursue more social issues, especially housing in the community, whilst those seeking a revolutionary road sought militant change through industrial actions in the factories and yards.

However, the situation was fluid and both individuals and sometimes even entire parties could take differing positions on a variety of issues. Some who espoused a more revolutionary route could still stand for parliamentary or council election like John Maclean and the SLP, even if energies were concentrated elsewhere, whilst many others who pursued the parliamentary and democratic road were still heavily involved in industrial strikes and direct community actions. The ILP, for instance, would come to the fore in what, in reality, were actions of civil disobedience in the community, their radical convictions leading them to campaign actively and support extra-parliamentary acts. Likewise, individuals such as David Kirkwood were crucial in industrial actions, even if he sometimes rejected the demands of Gallacher and Maclean and others for more revolutionary steps.

But, despite this, there was always much more that united them than divided them. Whilst there could be deep disagreements and bitter words exchanged, there was also a mutual respect for the wider socialism that they agreed upon and a bonding from shared experiences as they fought their social and industrial battles. Although they may have had different ideological views on socialist theory, they stood united in efforts against the war and would work together for social and industrial change during and immediately after it.

As the ILP and the Communist Party evolved, however, the divide became clearer, the differences starker and, in many ways, the hostility much more evident. Accordingly, some of the memoirs and histories later written seem to reflect the antipathy and political sectarianism that developed, rather than the cooperation and even camaraderie that existed at the time. So, although there were profound disagreements between individuals it would be wrong to overplay them.

The initial challenge on the left, though, concerned the announcement of war and how to react to it. On 9 August 5,000 gathered in the city to demonstrate against the conflict just days after its outbreak. But that number was soon dwarfed by those flocking to enlist. The fervour to sign up and support the war was feverish. Young men flocked to join, fearful lest the war be over before they could see action. Belief in a short and glorious victory was all too prevalent, and the desire to be part of it overwhelming for many. 'Home by Christmas' was the presumption and missing active service would be a travesty – or so it seemed for some. Newspapers and the city establishment actively encouraged enlisting, and many ordinary people simply expected to do so themselves; it was both a patriotic duty as well as the opportunity for adventure. Churches and many other organisations were equally complicit in it. Sermons from the pulpit heralded the righteousness of the war and voluntary organisations extolled its virtues. Such was the atmosphere created that almost entire football teams and work- and schoolmates signed up together. Much of civic society rallied to the flag.

More, proportionally, would sign up from Scotland than any other part of the United Kingdom. Glasgow was no different and when, in September 1914, the City Corporation, as the council was then known, 'decided to raise and equip two battalions from the tramway employees:

within 24 hours, one in six – over 1,000 men – had volunteered, and by the end of the year recruitment had reached 1,756'.[20] Many of those recruits from the council would be killed on the Somme, but still they kept coming as the frenzy continued unabated for quite a while.

War had a huge effect upon the city and its legacy would be long-lasting – not just in terms of lives lost, but in its impact upon the wider socialist movement in Glasgow. For the war also increased the number seeing the need for radical change. It not only ignited a spark but offered many people an opportunity to try to light that fire in the city. As thousands of young men flocked to the front, Glasgow was well placed to benefit from the requirements of war. The city's engineering and shipyard base that had made it world renowned meant that it had the largest concentration of munitions suppliers anywhere in the country. Factories and shipyards boomed, and military orders flowed in, whilst people streamed into the city in search of work that was readily available.

The battle to stop people going to war had failed, but battles were about to be fought on both the housing front and the industrial front in particular. Skilled and craft workers were to the fore in the engineering factories, and protecting those skills from being diluted by less well-trained workers would become a prominent issue, as was ensuring that people were properly recompensed for their work.

Albion Works, Barr and Stroud's, Beardmore's, and Weirs were all hugely important for the production of war materiel, and the shipyards were also booming with the demands of war. However, other than a minor dispute at Fairfield's in 1915, the shipyards remained mostly peaceful and it was in the engineering works that battles would primarily be fought.

Each of those works would also have radical leadership changes from within, and that too would be pivotal. Many of those involved had been steeped in disputes or struggles before the war where their

---

20   T. C. Smout, op. cit., p. 264.

militancy had been forged – and some had even been in opposition to the war itself. Gallacher was at the Albion Works with his background having been in the SDF and with close links to John Maclean.

Barr and Stroud's in Anniesland specialised in rangefinders for artillery and other sophisticated military engineering products. There John Muir, born in 1879, and who had been a member of the Socialist Labour Party and joint editor of its paper (though he left it as he supported the war), was the shop stewards' leader. At Beardmore's at Parkhead Forge where they specialised in armaments and armour plating for warships it was David Kirkwood who was in charge. Though he had anguished over his support for the war, he was to have no qualms in being bullish in making his demands for the workforce.

At Weirs in Cathcart on Glasgow's Southside it was pumps, compressors and other sophisticated equipment for the navy that was particularly prized by the government. And there it was Arthur MacManus, a leading figure in the strike at Singer's in 1911, who was the senior shop steward. Sacked at the end of the dispute, he'd moved back to work in Glasgow. Born in Belfast in 1889, he had moved to the east of Glasgow with his parents at an early age. He was a friend of James Connolly's and was equally politicised by the endemic poverty he saw all around him. A member of the Socialist Labour Party, he had also been joint editor of its paper along with John Muir.

As workers organised many others came on board in various ways and through different organisations. Not just John Maclean and Jimmy Maxton, but Manny Shinwell, Neil Maclean, Harry Hopkins, Harry McShane and George Ebury would come to the fore along with countless others. Shinwell was born in the East End of London in 1884 to Jewish parents from eastern Europe and the family moved to Glasgow when he was young. Leaving school early, he became involved in the trade union movement and was on the trades council. Later, he was active in the seamen's strike, and became the local secretary of the British Seafarers Union and was a member of the ILP.

Neil Maclean was close to Shinwell, and was something of a mentor to him. Born in 1875, he had been in the Socialist Labour Party before joining the ILP. An organiser for the Scottish Cooperative and Wholesale Society, he would also be a conscientious objector during the war. Harry Hopkins was another engineer and district secretary of the Engineers Union, who was also in the ILP and was chair of Govan Trades Council.

Others were in more revolutionary organisations. McShane was born in Glasgow in 1891 to an Irish catholic father and a Scots Protestant mother. He became an engineer and a political activist who had initially enlisted, though he subsequently deserted. Like John Maclean he was a member of the British Socialist Party at that time, and was closely allied to him. George Ebury was another leading light in the British Socialist Party. Originally a Londoner, he was their national organiser, spending most of his time in the industrial communities, and accordingly soon gravitated to Glasgow, where he became closely involved in events.

It wasn't just in the engineering factories that a battle front formed, but also in the wider community. Alongside those mentioned, countless others also took part in the fight on the home front. Most were women and they were at the forefront of housing campaigns soon to be launched. Many of these had joined the ILP due to its support for votes for women and Keir Hardie's personal commitment to it. Their membership raised the housing issue within the party, as well as involving them further in political campaigning. Many were also opposed to the war and the drive for peace had likewise motivated them. Whilst many of the middle-class women in the suffragette movement quickly became very pro-war, the ILP ladies were very different, being predominantly working class and remaining resolutely committed to peace.

Mary Barbour was born in Kilbarchan in 1875 where her father was a weaver. Marrying an engineer, she moved to Govan. There she became involved in the cooperative guild, as well as being active locally in the housing association. She also joined the Women's Peace Crusade, which was established to oppose the war.

Helen Crawfurd was one of the founders of the Women's Peace Crusade and became its first secretary. Born in the Gorbals in 1877 she moved to England with her father, returning to Glasgow in her teenage years and marrying a Church of Scotland minister. Becoming politicised as a suffragette, she was imprisoned for breaking windows in London before joining the ILP.

Another woman who had helped found the Women's Peace Crusade was Agnes Dollan. She was married to Patrick Dollan, but was an active campaigner in her own right. Born in Springburn in 1887 where her father had been employed at the locomotive works, she'd left school at eleven to start work. She had been a suffragette as well as becoming a leading activist on several issues. Those women, along with countless others, opened a new front in the community campaigning for peace, socialism and, in particular, on housing issues.

But all those individuals and many more would be involved on the political, industrial and housing fronts, as the war on the Clyde was soon to see the first salvoes fired.

6

EARLY SALVOES ON THE INDUSTRIAL FRONT

By early 1915 it was clear that there was going to be no quick victory in the war. Initial bravura faded as the death toll mounted. On the Clyde, though, the opening attacks were about to begin on the industrial front, where trouble had been brewing since the final few months of 1914.

One of the main points of contention was the tuppence rise in wages, which was being sought across the engineering sector by trade unions, with employers holding out for considerably less. As negotiations were conducted employers referred to the need for patriotism and support for the war effort. However, this was quickly countered by the workers, who pointed out that several major employers had refused war work without an increase in payment from the government. That still didn't stop vitriol being heaped on the workers, with accusations almost amounting to treason being made in the press.

A leader in the *Glasgow Herald* on 17 February set the tone with a piece entitled 'The Responsibilities of Labour', which thundered at workers considering industrial action. It stated that the industrial effort was as important as that on the military front, and lambasted labour leaders who they accused of seeking to take advantage of the situation. It even called for government to lay down the law to them.

The dispute was the first major confrontation on the home front.

Employers had offered ¾d and negotiations were ongoing nationally with union leaders, but no agreement had as yet been reached. However, these events were quickly overtaken as action was taken in factories. The spark for the strike came at Weirs in Cathcart, where they were facing a shortage of labour for the war work that was flowing in and had recruited additional workers from the United States. However, not only were they having their passages paid, but they were on higher rates than their Scottish colleagues, with even bonuses paid at the end of the contract. In mid-February the workers at Weirs came out on strike. They were quickly joined by other works, including both the Albion and Yarrow's, and soon 10,000 were out on strike across the city.

Mass meetings were held in areas near the main factories and yards that were on strike, and a representative from each was sent to the central meeting. A central strike committee was formed from amongst those who attended. It was called the Labour Withholding Committee (LWC) and in due course it would become the Clyde Workers' Committee (CWC), which would be prominent in coming years. Between 250 and 300 delegates were elected directly from factories and yards and the committee met on a weekly basis.

The strike was led by shop stewards, as the national union leadership had been threatened and prevailed on to oppose the action. By the time the principal leaders of the unions arrived to meet with shop steward delegates and even attend mass meetings, it was evident they had lost control to the local representatives. Endeavours by full-time officials to have the men return to work were not just ignored, but even jeered at by the rank and file. It was the first sign of a sea change in control, and power would not return to the national unions for many years to come.

Press and even public opprobrium followed, especially for the likes of Gallacher and supporters like Maclean, who were denigrated and portrayed almost as war criminals. Such was the level of hostility that even *Forward* was muted in its comments and the support for the strike was led more by the growing revolutionary faction than the ILP.

Despite these conditions, there was still considerable unity and morale was high.

However, the leaders realised that they couldn't hold out for long despite that. Strike pay wasn't forthcoming, given that it was unofficial, and public hostility was marked. Engineers soon voted to accept the offer of one penny. To avoid the strike fragmenting the shop steward leaders through the LWC called for a return to work, which took place though some works, including Gallacher's, remained on strike slightly longer. However, the mood of militancy lingered on in the factories. As Gallacher recalled in his memoirs, 'It ended not on a note of defeat, but with a feeling of something achieved.'[21]

That sentiment was even endorsed in the press when, on 20 March 1915, the *Glasgow Herald* commented on the strike, writing that

> the Labour Withholding Committee can congratulate itself on having fought well. It can be sure that in the near future its efforts will again have to be exerted. Despite insults and threats, despite official pressure, the Clyde men have kept the flag of revolutionary trade unionism flying and that itself is something.

Although others, like Kirkwood, had a more sombre reflection on the strike in which they had been a key participant. His view was that though the public resented American workers being paid more than their Scottish colleagues, there was no sympathy for the strike with its potential effects upon the war effort. He even stated in his memoirs that they had got 'public opinion wrong',[22] evidencing the hatred amongst the general public towards the Germans, with even trade union officials describing them as disloyal.

Though the strike hadn't succeeded in winning any more concessions from the employers, it did mark a change in many other ways. Workers

---

21   William Gallacher, *Revolt on the Clyde*, 4th ed. (Lawrence & Wishart, 1978), p. 49.
22   Kirkwood, op. cit., p. 87.

were beginning to flex their industrial muscle both in their own defence and for political demands. However, the dispute also alarmed the government, who were conscious of the critical role of the Clyde to the war effort and the growing danger of union militancy. During the strike Lloyd George made it clear how important the munitions sector was:

> This is an engineer's war. And it will be won or lost owing to the efforts or shortcomings of engineers. I have something to say about that, for it involves sacrifices for all of us. Unless we are able to equip our armies, our predominance in men will avail us nothing. We need men, but we need arms more than men, and delay in producing them is full of peril for this country.

Then the Prime Minister went on to warn that the government wouldn't tolerate disruption and gave a hint of the stern action that they were proposing to take:

> While employers and workmen on the Clyde have been spending time in disputing over a fraction, and when a week-end, ten days and a fortnight of work which is absolutely necessary for the defences of the country has been set aside, I say here solemnly that it is intolerable that the life of Britain should be imperilled for the matter of a farthing an hour. Who is to blame? That is not the question, but how it is to be stopped?[23]

Though work had resumed on the Clyde and major industrial action had ended, the mood of militancy remained. In October 1915 the Labour Withholding Committee (LWC) transformed into the Clyde Workers' Committee (CWC), though it was still constituted in the same way. Willie Gallacher was chairman, David Kirkwood treasurer,

---

23   Prime Minister H. H. Asquith, *Glasgow Herald* (1 March 1915), p. 10.

but as well as the factory delegate representatives, political activists also attended along with them. Hence why not just shop stewards like Mac-Manus and Hopkins were there, but also political activists like Maxton, Maclean and McShane. The battlefront speedily moved from a strike over pay to workers' rights. For, as Lloyd George had stated, the government were taking powers to enforce measures against workers and protect military supplies. The CWC would become the major player in the confrontation with employers and authorities alike; the nature of its make-up meant it had representatives from all shades and parties, but it would be fair to say that it was heavily militant and would be dominated by the more revolutionary wing of socialist opinion. For, though Kirkwood was a member of the ILP, many more were aligned or sympathetic to the SLP, BSP or other such factions. The ILP, as such, remained in the community and in the background.

The government was not just concerned about the actions of workers and trade unionists, but by those of manufacturers and suppliers. Concerns were mounting about blockages in the industrial process and delays in the provision of munitions. The reality was that private business was not responding adequately to the urgent need of the military machine now engaged in a global conflict. This contributed to fears over the disruption threatened by the militant representatives of those working within the sectors. State intervention in the private sector was accordingly required and the rights of the state were going to supersede those of both employers and workers. Government was going to restrict what they viewed as any impediment to the war effort, whether by industrialists or from the workforce. The Cabinet instructed Arthur Balfour, a Scottish Unionist, and Lynden Macassey, an Irish jurist, to consider the situation on the Clyde, and their work was to form part of the basis to the Munitions Act soon to come into operation.

That legislation was rushed through Parliament and passed in July 1915. Its purpose, as historian J. A. R. Marriott recorded, was to ensure no private interest was to be permitted to obstruct the service or imperil the safety of the State. Trade Union regulations must be suspended; employers' profits must be limited, skilled men must fight, if not in the trenches, in the factories; man-power must be economised by the dilution of labour and the employment of women. Private factories must pass under the control of the state and new national factories set up. Results justified the new policy; the output was prodigious; the goods were at last delivered.[24]

Lloyd George was eager to be able to both direct the required work and ensure that there was no disruption to it. The government felt the powers the legislation provided were essential for the war effort and they also gave Lloyd George an opportunity to boost his own profile as a result of it. Union leaders gave it their tacit support despite the enormous effect on their members. Hugely extensive in its powers, workers' rights, wages, hours and terms and conditions were all affected, along with the restrictive trade union practices it suspended. It even made it a criminal offence for a worker to leave his job without the consent of his employer, if it was at what was designated a 'controlled establishment'. Not just engineering works, but even textile factories and docks were given that classification, and consent to leave was rarely granted. A munitions court was also established to deal with prosecutions under the act.

Trade unions may have acquiesced, but the CWC mobilised, and an early leaflet denounced union leaders for their treachery. And it wasn't just the union leadership, but the government itself that the CWC were prepared to confront, and there were some early skirmishes as workers were imprisoned. An incident at Fairfield's shipyard later in the summer saw three workers convicted at a munitions court of refusing work and being fined, in what had started as a strike by the workforce

---

24   J. A. R. Marriott, *Modern England 1885–1945: A History of My Own Times*, 4th edn (Methuen, 1948), p. 376.

against what they saw as the unfair dismissal of two of their colleagues. Action had been taken by the authorities under the new legislation and seventeen men had been convicted. Fourteen of them had paid the fine of £10 that had been imposed, but three refused to pay the penalty and were sentenced to the alternative of thirty days' imprisonment.

Both their union and the CWC became involved with strike action being threatened at Fairfield's and indeed elsewhere on the Clyde. The CWC were mobilising for action even though the union was reluctant to call an official strike. Agitation was growing on the ground and concern was mounting in boardrooms; steps had to be taken or there would be action. So, eight days before their scheduled release, the men were freed as their fines were paid for them. No acknowledgement of who had done so was given, but it angered many, including John Maclean, who felt it undermined the sacrifice being made and the opportunities that it might offer for mobilisation. An article appeared in *Forward* on 1 November 1915 written by Patrick Dollan, headlined 'Who "Paid" The Fines'. It surmised, probably correctly, that they had been paid by the government or someone acting on their behalf. In fact, it appears to have been an amalgam of both with the unions having done so, at the request of Lloyd George.

The incident left a bad taste in the mouths of the likes of Gallacher and others on the CWC, and this represented a further wedge that was being driven between shop stewards and the union leaders. It increased their doubts about the willingness of union officials to properly represent them and reminded them of the need to act themselves. The committee was transforming from an ad hoc grouping established for one strike to the organisational apparatus for concerted action – and not just in the workplaces, but across the community.

For, under the Munitions Act, not only were existing workers bound to their employment, but new workers were to be recruited. As more and more men went off to war, and as the military machine hugely expanded, the need for workers increased even with the restrictions on existing ones leaving. Even recruitment from abroad, as at Weirs, was inadequate and the solution was to bring in less well-qualified workers, and especially women. This was to cause friction as those coming in had neither undergone the same training nor possessed the same experience as the skilled workers. It was known as dilution and viewed as a threat by the engineering sector in particular, where skills had always been highly prized and stoutly defended. The craft sector so dominant on the Clyde was amongst those most affected by it, and accordingly reacted most strongly. It was something that even workers who weren't militant by inclination were concerned by, and it allowed the CWC to be more forthright in their objections.

Dilution also would see a further divide between Gallacher and Kirkwood, perhaps reflecting a strategic division. Gallacher and many of the more militant shop stewards were opposed to the bringing in of unskilled labour, not just on principle (as it affected deeply cherished craft skills), but also because of the opportunity it offered for pursuing industrial confrontation, as part of wider fight between capital and labour. Maclean had lamented the loss of the chance afforded by the earlier strike to take on employers in an industrial battle, but dilution more generally provided some prospects for Gallacher and others to continue that struggle.

Meanwhile, Kirkwood and the mainstream ILP were more sanguine about dilution and less keen on outright opposition to it. Kirkwood's objection was not to dilution as such, which he could accept, but the effect it had in the yards and works, where it could affect protected skills and rates of pay. He also accepted that he was more radical than his members, which was something he felt needed to be taken into account – though he still vehemently opposed the Munitions Act on principle, which he saw as undermining fundamental trade union rights.

At Parkhead Kirkwood had been engaging directly with Sir William Beardmore, who seemed to recognise the pivotal role the shop stewards' leader played, and no doubt developed a grudging respect for him. As a result, a closed shop seems to have been conceded in all but name, with Kirkwood claiming that all bar two of the new employees joined the union. His willingness to be more pragmatic would, however, have later repercussions for the CWC.

When the legislation had first been mooted industrialists had expressed concerns as to the unions' reactions. But the government was firm in stating to them that they wouldn't just deal with it, but would meet it head on. There was no room for dubiety about what was intended, either in the laws or their enforcement; actions would match the powers being taken. Speaking to Clyde shipbuilders and seeking their support, Lynden Macassey, one of the architects of the powers, made it clear that

> the provisions of the Munitions Act would be fully enforced. All customs – demarcation or trade traditions – opposed to the introduction of unskilled and female labour ... would be abrogated ... nothing would be left undone to increase production.[25]

The point was also made that once invoked, the legislation would be fully enforced using all and every power available. To show he meant business and no doubt to reassure the industrialists, Lloyd George decided to go out evangelising for the war effort and in support of his new legislation. That would mean meeting not only with the employers operating it, but with employees who would be working under it to persuade them of its necessity. He therefore went forth to meet both, and decided to include a series of meetings in Glasgow in late December. At an earlier meeting in Newcastle with some invited trade union leaders he was warned to avoid the CWC. The meeting was indicative of the clear rift between those leaders and the shop stewards. Heeding that advice, a press statement about the proposed visit stated that he wouldn't meet with 'unofficial'

---

25   Joseph Melling, *Rent Strikes: People's Struggle for Housing in West Scotland, 1890–1916* (Polygon, 1983), p. 106.

representatives. His intention was to ignore them and meet directly with selected workers at factories or in other set piece events.

That only angered and provoked the CWC, who refused to cooperate without official recognition and sought to avoid providing supine audiences for the minister. Accordingly, when the minister arrived in Glasgow he stayed away from Fairfield's, where the three workers had been imprisoned, and instead headed to Weirs, where presumably it was hoped he'd receive a friendlier reception. Instead, the workforce declined to meet him, preferring, as *Forward* reported on 1 January 1916, 'to get on with the making of munitions'.

At Parkhead Forge there was a rough reception from the workforce and the meeting with the shop stewards took place in the company offices, where *Forward* also reported that there were a hundred police officers guarding the entrance. Lloyd George had telegrammed Kirkwood, seeking to meet him, but had angered many by the police entourage that descended on the yard along with him. Tensions were also heightened by keeping the stewards waiting before being invited in to meet him. Some smaller and more pliant factories were visited, but he was floundering in his attempts to engage directly with large crowds of workers, where he no doubt thought his charms could be best utilised.

Arrangements were therefore made by the minister's office for a rally on 25 December at the St Andrew's Halls, where there was no doubt he could strut the stage and woo the audience. Though he may have been noted for his eloquence, a compliant audience was still preferred. Accordingly, tickets were given to more trusted union officials who were then to be responsible for their distribution. In addition, not insubstantial expenses of seven shillings and sixpence were being offered to all those who went, and it appeared that a receptive audience was being recruited.

However, the planned meeting came to the attention of Gallacher, who had gone along to an Engineering Union meeting where discussion of the event was taking place and even tickets for it were being distributed. Discovering this, he was outraged and vehemently spoke against any cooperation whatsoever. It was clearly a heated meeting with some either keen to accept the expenses or willing to simply comply, the union officials particularly so. The meeting and arguments went on late into the night before a vote was taken, which was comfortably won by Gallacher, and a decision to boycott the meeting was made. Members were advised not to go and tickets were taken from those who had obtained them for distribution.

A union official seeing the likely outcome had gone away to phone the ministerial delegation with the bad news. He returned to the discussion indicating that Arthur Henderson (Labour leader, and then Cabinet minister), who was accompanying Lloyd George on the tour, would like to meet with them urgently and had asked to be able to come and speak to them. Doubtless it was hoped that Henderson would be able to exert some influence over shop stewards and workers more generally, with his union background and Labour credentials. When contact was made it was already late, but the situation was urgent with the clock ticking for the scheduled event.

Gallacher recalled flippantly suggesting that they would hold back and meet Henderson, if taxis home thereafter were made available, given the lateness of the hour and with public transport soon to be stopping. It may have been said partly in jest, but was readily conceded by the ministerial delegation. Arrangements were quickly made for the stewards and Henderson hurried over to the Union Hall, seeking to rescue the event from looming disaster.

Despite the largesse of the taxi ride home coming at its conclusion, as well as the offer of expenses for those attending the meeting itself, the shop stewards still declined to participate. Entreaties by Henderson, who had rushed across the city centre, to give support to the Prime Minister and the war effort were dismissed. Moreover, not only did they stand their ground, but they subjected Henderson to a torrid time, treating him with considerable contempt for his role as an emissary for the government, as well as for other perceived sins of the administration. The impasse remained and the stewards simply enjoyed a luxurious ride home.

Lloyd George was both frustrated and outraged. The very people he had been warned not to meet and who he held in contempt were obviously more powerful than he had anticipated. He was, though, still eager to use his legendary charm and loquaciousness on the Clydeside workers, but was being thwarted by their local leaders. He no doubt still thought that if he could circumvent the leadership, he could engage successfully with the rank and file. Efforts to have that delivered therefore continued by his staff and aides.

A further private meeting with CWC representatives was therefore hurriedly arranged the following morning with Gallacher contacted at his work and asked to attend the Central Hotel, where the minister's delegation were staying. Arthur Henderson was again used as an intermediary, though others joined him and union officials were also present. Once again, though, it was to no avail and the shop stewards continued to deride him. Other trade union leaders and even some councillors were likewise brought in, but all were equally scorned in their attempts to have the planned meeting agreed to.

By this point it had also become clear to the government delegation during the meeting that tickets had got into the hands of the CWC, and that there was now no guarantee of having any control over the make-up of the audience. This came as a shock to them and they hurriedly departed from the room for a private discussion, returning a short time later with Lloyd George himself. The meeting was hastily brought to a conclusion with the minister simply acknowledging everyone's presence, before summarily dismissing them. As they departed, Lloyd George asked Gallacher to hang back, and then questioned whether he could organise a meeting with him and his committee that evening. Answering that he could, Gallacher agreed that he'd arrange for them to be at the hotel later.

That evening the CWC representatives returned to the minister's hotel with a delegation including Gallacher, Kirkwood, MacManus and Muir. Lloyd George headed up the government representatives that met them in a private room. There the minister's behaviour oscillated between charm and calls for patriotism whilst handing round expensive cigars to the shop stewards on their arrival, to a fierce oration on the importance of munitions to military success. Lloyd George then outlined the format of the meeting he desired, which would allow him to strut the stage and lecture the audience on the need to support the war effort. But, irrespective of his stance, the shop stewards remained implacable. If he wanted to meet with the workers then there would have to be conditions accepted, and that included workers' representatives having the right to speak. They were neither going to give him free rein, nor allow him to speak unchallenged, and that was far from the adoring crowd that he had anticipated (with the opportunity for further self-promotion in the press).

Eventually, after much toing and froing, and at a very late stage, it was agreed that he would address the assembled workers, but there would be both questions from the audience and, more importantly, speakers from the shop stewards' representatives. And so, on Christmas Day 1915, which was then not a public holiday in Scotland, a meeting took place in the St Andrew's Halls. The authorities, already concerned about the situation, had a phalanx of police stationed in the hall, which was already packed with stewards before the main attraction arrived. When the platform party entered the stage 'The Red Flag' was bellowed out from the audience, and it was clear they were in a festive spirit and were in no mood to be lectured to. The first speaker was Arthur Henderson, but he soon gave up, drowned out by singing and shouting.

It then fell to the minister to try use his noted Welsh articulacy to try to calm the proceedings, but still the barracking continued. The report of the proceedings in *Forward* on 1 January sets the scene. Headlined 'Wild Scenes', the article narrated:

On rising to speak Mr Lloyd George was received with loud and continued booing and hissing. There was some cheering, certainly, and about a score of hats were waved in the area, but the meeting was violently hostile. Two verses of 'The Red Flag' were sung before the Minister could utter a word. Owing to the incessant interruption, and the numerous altercations going on throughout the hall, it was quite impossible to catch every word of Mr Lloyd George's speech.

At one stage he appealed for calm, citing his friend Keir Hardie, which only resulted in 'The Red Flag' being bellowed out yet again. David Kirkwood, who was chairing, intervened to try to ensure some order for the minister to be heard. Lloyd George made further efforts to pacify the crowd, including referring to Ramsay MacDonald being yet another friend of his, but it was all to no avail and the clamour continued throughout. Finally, after marching up and down the stage for quite some time and tiring of trying to be heard above the ruckus, he eventually sat down, angered and exhausted.

That was then the cue for John Muir to stand up on his seat and seek to speak on behalf of the CWC, whereupon he delivered a denunciation of the plans. It got a rapturous response from some men around him in the hall who could hear what he was saying and others who no doubt had an inkling of the tenor of his speech. Many, though, would have been no more the wiser of his comments than those of the minister, such was the ongoing bedlam. That general disorder led to the meeting being brought to a premature end, with Henderson and Lloyd George walking off the platform enraged and frustrated.

It was a humiliating experience and ignominious departure for the future Prime Minister. However, reporting of it was restricted to avoid embarrassment for the Cabinet ministers. Instead, an official ministerial press release was issued, giving an entirely fictitious account, and portraying a sympathetic hearing being given when the truth was quite the opposite. The only paper to publish the actual events was *Forward* and, as a consequence, it would be shut down for several weeks.

The paper was closed down under the Defence of the Realm Act (DORA). For the Munitions Act was not the only wartime emergency legislation brought in as in the early days of the war, DORA had been rolled out and then further consolidated a few months later. It provided extensive powers for the authorities to suppress criticism of the war and detain individuals. It was used not just against those who were opposing the conflict, but also in the censorship of others who were simply seeking to report on the war or indeed events that related to it, such as the later outbreak of influenza.

Soon, those extensive restrictions would be used by the government against the workers, leaders and anti-war activists when the state decided to strike against them. But that was still to come. In the interim, authorities were facing battles not just in factories and yards, but on the housing front.

7

BATTLES ON THE HOUSING FRONT

Whilst opening salvoes had been fired on the industrial field, battle had also commenced on the housing front. For, as well as conflict on the factory floor, there was a struggle in the community and there it was rents, not wages, which were the issue.

Glasgow faced huge problems due to the lack of housing long before war broke out. A council report in 1912 indicated that the city required 65,000 new homes over three years and only 1,400 had been constructed when war broke out. This was then further compounded by wartime conditions and the burdens it brought. Additional workers streamed into the city for the work that was readily available, and housebuilding stopped as armaments became the priority. Rents rose accordingly, and pressure was greatest in areas with large engineering works; a problem that applied not just within the city itself, but across all Clydeside.

This in turn affected not just those already struggling to pay, but many others, meaning that some fell into arrears. As a result, notices of eviction began to be issued and evictions themselves would soon begin to follow. As early as Christmas 1914, councillors, community and trade union delegations were approaching the council concerned at what was happening, but the situation only worsened as the war continued and pressures increased.

Emergency powers that the government possessed under the Defence of the Realm Act and other regulations were, in theory, meant to protect soldiers' wives and other dependants. They allowed for a defence to an eviction application if the situation had arisen through wartime conditions. In reality, though, it didn't work out that way. Actions against war widows and those with dependants wounded in the war frequently occurred.

They weren't the only vulnerable group facing challenges from rising rents. Around 7,000 pensioners with fixed incomes faced increased payments for the roof over their head. Many found themselves facing eviction, and tales of the elderly being forcibly removed from their homes simply heightened the feeling of unfairness that existed across the country.

Then, in February 1915, landlords indicated an intention to increase rents across the city by 25 per cent. Enough was enough and, as in the workplace, so in the home, organising began. Trades councils also started to discuss action, but it was in the community that the real mustering began. As with the factories and yards, organisation around the housing issue sprang up from a local rather than national level and would be subsequently more militant in action.

Glasgow Women's Housing Association (GWHA) had been formed the year before, bringing together women from across the city. Though ostensibly a non-party political organisation, it was still driven by ILP activists including Mary Barbour, Agnes Dollan and Helen Crawfurd. Its first president was Mary Laird, another ILP member who, born in 1864 to Irish immigrant parents, had married a local shipping clerk. The ILP influence was strong both in its leadership and at grassroots level in the community. As well as the women, some men were also pivotal, including ILP councillor Andrew McBride and John Wheatley. McBride had been secretary of the Labour Housing Committee who, failing to make sufficient progress nationally, had turned to putting his efforts in locally.

Under their leadership a meeting was held in the Morris Hall, Shaw

Street to plan and prepare for action to be taken. Mary Burns Laird was in the chair and Patrick Dollan and Harry Hopkins were speakers, showing the links between the ILP in particular and the trade union movement more generally.

Posters for it declared it a 'Meeting of Women', with the aim 'to protest against the increase in rents'. It declared the basis of their actions: 'Whilst at this moment all sectors of the community especially women, are called upon to make sacrifices, the patriotic President of the Homeowners Association, at their Annual General Meeting, stated that '"That this was the time to raise Rents," and Rents are now being raised.'

Likewise, discussions were taking place in the community where tensions simmered, as they did in the factories. Govan was the first to organise, rent increases there being compounded by an existing grievance over rates for the area, which had only formally joined with Glasgow in 1912 when assurances had been of no rates increases for several years. Rent rises may technically have been different, but they still contributed to a feeling of injustice, compounding the financial problems many faced.

The Govan Women's Housing Association under the leadership of Mary Barbour began to mobilise. Meetings were held and support was canvassed amongst tenants in tenements and in the streets. The first rent strike was at Linthouse in Govan where accommodation was actually slightly better than in many other parts of the city as it housed skilled workers with a slightly better wage. But still, prices were rising and wages weren't keeping pace. Even those in good jobs were struggling to meet their existing commitments, reflected no doubt by the fact that 260 out of 264 households took part in an organised non-payment of rent.

By the beginning of summer 1915 the strike in Govan remained solid and was soon to spread far and wide across the city. The catalyst was the planned eviction of a Mrs McHugh in William Street, Shettleston.

Her husband had been wounded in the war and two sons were soldiers serving in France; there were also five other children living at home with her. She had fallen into arrears amounting to less than a pound. When a factor arrived with an eviction notice, word had got around the community and the people decided to make a stand against it. The official met not just the woman and her family, but hundreds of her neighbours, including John Wheatley, who was the local councillor. Blocking the factor from entering, they burned an effigy of him and pursued him all the way to his home, with Wheatley required to call for calm.

The case became high profile; it was reported widely in the press and embodied the clarion call for the mobilisation of tenants' groups all across the city. The groundwork laid was put into action, especially in Shettleston, Partick, Govan, Ibrox and Parkhead, where housing tenure and readily available war work made the cost of housing a particularly sensitive issue. A rent strike began and action was taken to oppose evictions that might follow. Political and public support was not just within the ILP and the left, for there was also widespread sympathy across liberal opinion.

By the autumn, tenants' groups almost invariably led by women were in action. At the forefront was Mary Barbour, though she was ably assisted by ladies from other parts of the city, including a Mrs Ferguson who was the secretary of the Partick rent strike committee, as well as Agnes Dollan and Helen Crawfurd, who were all also active in the Women's Peace Committee. They soon got to work, and street meetings were held across the city. Posters demanding no rent rises appeared in windows declaring 'Rent Strike against Increases. We are not Removing', and in some streets these were in almost every house.

Steps were taken to protect the protestors from landlords or their agent's actions. Prospective renters who came seeking tenancies that landlords had advised would soon be vacated were left in no doubt that it wasn't the case, and that they should try elsewhere. Landlords tried to dupe tenants into thinking that their neighbours had capitulated and paid their rent. Sometimes it worked, but more often it was shown up to be a ruse and the community remained united. Letters threatening eviction and dire consequences were nullified by the appreciation that there were thousands involved and it would be impossible to deal with all of them.

More intricate measures were also devised to deal with the specific threats of evictions that were still attempted by landlords and their factors. A system was invented where ladies sat in stairs with bells ready to be rung to notify neighbours of attempted evictions, allowing them to quickly mobilise crowds. Patrols were organised to ensure that homes where evictions had been threatened were protected. On occasions groups of women criss-crossed the city to thwart planned evictions, and Mrs Barbour's Army entered into folklore. Reports of her and a troop of her colleagues crossing from Govan to march on Partick, adding reinforcements to tenants facing eviction there, became legendary.

The women also began to receive support from the factories, as many involved in the rent strike were workers in the munitions sector. And it wasn't only women who had gone to work when their labour was required, but also the men who had been there throughout, who were active in the campaign. One planned eviction in Parkhead saw a demonstration of women, some with prams, who were joined by 5,000 men who had downed tools at Parkhead Forge to march and show support.

By October 1915 it was reckoned that at least 20,000 tenants, if not more, were on rent strike across the city, and it began to concern the government, already perturbed by disruption in the workplace. There were growing fears that the trouble in the community would spill over into the factories, and with good reason. Not only were many tenants working in the munitions sector, but the trades council and Clyde Workers' Committee were actively discussing it with the ILP and left groups active on the ground.

On 2 October David Kirkwood had chaired a CWC meeting at which the issue was discussed. Afterwards he had written to the city council indicating the serious concern that the shop stewards had over the issue and calling for action to be taken. Evictions, he wrote, would be viewed as 'an attack on the working class, which called for the most vigorous and extreme reply, and one which might have the most disastrous consequences ... If the nation is to have an adequate supply of the munitions for war, the workers must have adequate healthy housing accommodation.'[26]

That was quickly followed by a demonstration of over a thousand women to the City Chambers on 7 October, at which a delegation led by an ILP councillor, William Reid, attended and spoke. He made the mood of the workers clear, saying: 'The temper of the men was such that, in the event of wholesale evictions taking place ... they would not hesitate not only to prevent evictions but to influence Parliament by every other means in their power.'[27]

The political temperature in the city was rising and the government was monitoring the situation. As with the industrial front, so with the housing battlefield, there was concern about the effect upon the war effort. The Secretary of State came to the city to investigate the rents issue and action speedily followed with a Commission of Inquiry established under a judge and leading academic to consider it.

However, even though asked to report quickly, this still wasn't to be before the end of November, and frustration amongst landlords and factors was growing. Faced with that level of opposition in the community, they were at a loss to know what to do, as the usual threats weren't working. So, to circumvent that problem they decided to try a different method of attack. Rather than seeking to evict, they sought to raise actions in the small debt court. There they could successfully pursue a claim without ever approaching the tenancy. This then allowed them to deduct the arrears direct from workers' wages, all the while avoiding the necessity of carrying out an eviction.

That may have been the strategy, but it underestimated the strength

---

26   Joseph Melling, op. cit., p. 75.
27   Joseph Melling, op. cit., p. 75.

of feeling that existed in the community, never mind the level of support that there was in the factories (legal actions had started in mid-October). Rosslyn Mitchell was a lawyer and a leading ILP activist who appeared for the defendants and sought to have the cases adjourned until after the conclusion of the government-sponsored inquiry into housing in the city. Some cases were deferred, but in three cases decrees were granted, which only fuelled the political fires burning all across the city. Flames were further fanned by rent rises announced that month, and the fear many had of fresh increases thereafter.

All those fires finally combusted the following month. Mr Nicolson, a factor in Partick, raised payment actions against eighteen households, fifteen of whom were workers at Dalmuir. Women and workers mobilised for the first planned court action with a demonstration on 13 November. They prepared for the court battle as they had planned for evictions. As Gallacher said in his memoirs,

> All day long, in the streets, in the halls, in the houses, meetings were held. Kitchen meetings, street meetings, mass meetings, meetings of every kind. No halt, no rest for anyone, all in preparation for the sitting of the court when the test case came on. As in the streets, so in the factories. 'Will we allow the factors to attack our wages?' 'Never!' Every factory was keyed up and ready.[28]

The escalation was reported in *Forward* on 13 November under the aptly titled headline 'From the Tenants Trenches', written by Patrick Dollan. It detailed that

> the tenants strike is extending in Glasgow. Among the new areas affected are Whiteinch, Cowlairs and Springburn, while the old areas are as lively as ever, and the ranks of the strikers are being augmented

---

28   William Gallacher, op. cit., p. 54.

every day. By now there are at the very least over twenty thousand tenants on strike, each and every one determined not to pay any increase of rent during the war. These tenants have no fear of eviction and in Partick and Govan, the women have prevented any eviction taking place, although evictions have been attempted.

It went on to detail the actions being taken, describing 'the women fighters' as 'magnificent', and narrating that in Partick a number of them had picketed an empty house all night to stop a new tenant who had agreed to pay increased rent from moving in. They were proud to add that the house was still empty and also related how, in other Partick tenements, factors had been surrounded and forced to delete arrears marked by them in rent books.

What would have worried the authorities even more, though, was *Forward*'s report that the Partick strikers had been arranging committees in the 'shipyards and workshops for the purpose of organising the munition workers against the payment of increased rent'. Lunchtime meetings had been held and financial and other support had been pledged. Both the community and the factories were uniting and it was clear why, as the article concluded with the story of a wounded soldier back from France who found himself having to face the increase. It gave a further moral justification to the already strong social and economic arguments. The scene was set for a battle between landlords and not just tenants, but whole communities.

On 17 November when the cases were called in court, not just women but men marched on the Sheriff Court House. As Gallacher narrated,

From far away Dalmuir in the West, from Parkhead in the East, from Cathcart in the South and Hydepark in the North, the dungareed army of the proletariat invaded the centre of the city.

At the Albion we formed up at breakfast-time and were joined by Yarrow's and Meechan's. In the main road we awaited the arrival of the contingents from Dalmuir and Clydebank. Then on we went, leaving the factories empty and deserted, shouting and singing.[29]

As they marched the crowds passed soldiers embarking for France and were cheered by the troops as they headed towards their own fight. Moreover, marching from Govan, Mrs Barbour and her army had gone by the Lorne Street School, where John Maclean was still employed as a teacher, to recruit him to their ranks. He had just been advised that he was being dismissed from his job the following week. That had seen demonstrations at the school board meeting deciding upon his fate, whilst there were protests outside. No doubt both through sympathy for the cause and in the knowledge that he was being sacked anyway, Maclean simply left the school and joined the march to the court house.

It was estimated that anywhere between 10,000 and 20,000 demonstrators descended, though some newspapers suggested a lower figure. But, whatever the precise number, traffic ground to a halt in the city centre as the crowd headed past the City Chambers and on to where the hearings were to take place at the Sheriff Court House. Newspaper advertisement boards placed on the street were taken by marchers and used as improvised platforms outside the building for speakers. There, Maclean and others including Willie Gallacher and Helen Crawfurd addressed the assembled crowd.

The demonstration was peaceful but the crowd was still denied entry to the building, where a police cordon had formed. In due course the police removed the makeshift platforms, bringing the speeches to an end. Some of the crowd dispersed to march past the army recruiting offices on West Nile Street, but most just hung about outside the court house awaiting the outcome.

A few friends and representatives had been allowed into the building to support those involved and were crammed into the court room.

---

29   William Gallacher, op. cit., p. 55.

Inside, it had already been agreed between lawyers for both sides that one action only would be run as a test case. The one chosen was an action against James Reid, who was employed at Dalmuir but was also secretary of the local Tenants Defence Committee. He explained in court that his rent had gone up by two shillings from £1 18s before the war to £2. When he had indicated that he wouldn't pay he had been given two weeks' notice to quit. That period had passed, though no eviction had by then taken place, the factor no doubt thinking that the small claims court was an easier way of dealing with it.

The case caused considerable concern for the presiding sheriff, John Lee. He was becoming increasingly worried, not just by what was happening outside the court house where it would have been impossible not to have heard the chants and general hullabaloo, but also by the consequences of the actions proceeding. The report into the rent issue instructed by the Secretary of State had been published just the day before. Compiled by Lord Hunter and Dr Scott, who was Professor of Economics at Glasgow University, it had specified the issues but hadn't really provided solutions for either the wider problem or the specific issue before the sheriff.

The report was being lauded as a white paper and there was clear evidence that the government was planning legislation, but nothing was as yet in place. Sheriff Lee was obviously becoming more and more concerned, no doubt conscious that the law, as it stood, would favour the landlords and result in him having to pronounce court orders granting payment in favour of the landlords and with expenses going against the workers.

Highly unusually he then asked to speak to the factor's lawyer in private. There he sought to persuade them to drop the case on patriotic grounds, given that it involved munitions workers. Meanwhile, with the case failing to commence at ten o'clock as scheduled, by the time noon came many in the court gallery were becoming restless. An ILP councillor accompanying the tenants objected to the delay, resulting in cheering from frustrated supporters in the public area and bringing the sheriff out from his chambers to address the disorder.

Taking his seat on the bench the sheriff addressed the crowd crammed into the court room. Calling order, he accepted that these were exceptional times. Asked by the tenants and their supporters if he would meet with a delegation from them, he agreed, and four of them then went into his chambers to speak to him. There they explained that they were involved in war work and provided the background to their difficulties.

Entering back into open court the sheriff again sought to broker a settlement. In discussion with the factor's lawyer he was then advised that Lloyd George had been in touch with his client just the day before, seeking to have him either abandon or postpone the cases with a view to allowing for legislation to be enacted. With the Commission of Inquiry being reported in the papers that morning it must have increased the sheriff's unease about taking any preceptive decision – especially on an issue of such importance and where the government was involved.

This insight from the lawyer seemed to resolve matters for the sheriff, who had been reluctant all along for the case to proceed. He persuaded – or rather seemingly browbeat – the factor and his lawyer into a settlement. Initially it was to be a continuation for three weeks, but subsequently it was agreed that the cases would simply be dropped. Having forced the settlement from the factor and his lawyer the sheriff then turned his attention to the tenants. Addressing Mr Reid, he said that the case was being dropped on patriotic grounds and urged him to use his influence to ensure that there were no demonstrations against Mr Nicolson. The tenants agreed to that; however, despite the sheriff's remarks when the outcome was relayed to demonstrators outside they loudly celebrated.

There have been suggestions that given the workers demonstrating outside along with the women, the sheriff telephoned Whitehall and was put through to Lloyd George. This is certainly referred to in both

Gallacher's and McShane's biographies, but is not, however, referred to in other works or the news reports from the time. Given the publication of the inquiry report the day before and its reporting in the papers, it appears more credible that it was the contact made by the minister the day before with the factor's lawyers. This theory is also supported by the report the following day in the *Glasgow Herald* that was headlined 'Ministerial Intervention' and was followed by 'Pacific Sheriff'. It detailed the meetings in chamber both with the factor's lawyer and with the tenants' delegation, as well as the reference made to the communication received from the Minister of Munitions.

In any event, government action was quickly forthcoming. On 25 November, the government introduced the Rent Restrictions Bill where it was rushed through Parliament. It froze rents at pre-war levels and rent rises were restricted until a period of six months after the war. Both the women and the workers had won a significant victory, which had benefited not just Glaswegians, but tenants all across the country.

However, amidst all the agitation and organisation there had also been a grievous loss when on 26 September 1915 Keir Hardie tragically died. Suffering a mild stroke in January 1915, he had made his final contribution in the House of Commons the following month, but had continued writing articles thereafter. Though still MP for Merthyr Tydfil, he had returned home to Scotland, but never fully recovered, dying of pneumonia with his family by his side. Only fifty-nine years old, his constant political struggles had prematurely aged him and the war had been a bitter psychological blow.

There was, though, neither acknowledgement of it nor condolences paid to him in the House of Commons, despite it being standard practice for a member who had died. It appeared that the dislike for his socialist views (to say nothing of his opposition to the war) ran deep within the corridors of power. The mainstream press was likewise muted or damning with faint praise, other than the eulogies written in *Forward*. There, an obituary written by Jim Larkin was published as the major article. It eloquently expressed the sorrow at the grand old man's passing, but also the pride and gratitude that many people felt for what he'd done for working people.

His passing was at least properly honoured in his homeland. His funeral took place at Maryhill Crematorium, with thousands lining the Glasgow streets to pay their respects as the cortège passed. A memorial service was also held by the ILP on 3 October in the St Andrew's Halls, where over 5,000 attended to hear speeches from Ramsay MacDonald, the miners' leader Bob Smillie and trade union activist Mary McArthur. A hero had passed, but the struggle continued.

A leading light of the left may have departed, but the government still remained concerned about the factories. Emergency powers taken under DORA and other regulations were about to be unleashed as the government planned their counter-attack.

8

THE GOVERNMENT COUNTER-ATTACKS

Far from standing idly by, the government had been stockpiling firepower through the Defence of the Realm Act and other emergency legislation. The powers were extensive, could be deployed rapidly and would soon be unleashed across several fronts against anti-war protestors and shop stewards alike.

The war was not going well, and there were no signs of an early or easy victory. An impasse was faced, but it didn't deter the military leadership – who were still schooled in tactics from bygone wars – from seeking to break it in the time-honoured fashion. Men on all sides and from all countries died in their tens of thousands charging across barren terrain only to be thwarted by barbed wire and mowed down by machine guns. Conditions in the trenches worsened, with supplies of both men and munitions growing short.

The bravura of troops marching to war also transformed. Lightheartedness once displayed for a brief stint of soldiering in the confidence of returning home had long passed. Communities became all too aware of the death and destruction, as families were advised of casualties and notices of the fallen appeared in papers. The flood of eager young men rushing to the recruiting office dried up just as the generals needed waves more of men to send over the top.

This meant conscription was required to be brought in, and in

January 1916 the Military Service Act was enacted, which applied to single men between eighteen and forty with exemptions for the unfit, the clergy and other reserved occupations. Even that, though, was insufficient for the numbers required in the field and by the early summer it had been extended to married men as well.

The mood in Glasgow, as in the rest of the country, was one of resignation. War may have lost its allure, but that did not transmit into growing anti-war sentiment. Those opposed were vindicated in many ways by the unfolding slaughter, no doubt giving added impetus to further campaigning against it and continued calls for peace. But whilst conscription further fuelled their fight, having given another angle for them to pursue, it didn't see any growing public support for them or demands that government enter into immediate talks to end the conflict. As across the land, there was simply stoicism tinged with widespread sorrow, and the desire for a speedy victory.

There was still concern in government circles, both at the disruption to the war effort and about the effect of anti-war campaigning upon the wider community. Powers had been invoked through genuine fears about agitation against war. With Lord Kitchener's patriotic call that 'Your country needs you' diminishing in effect and widespread grumblings about conscription growing, anxiety only increased. Newspapers began to run articles condemning the likes of Maclean and MacManus for treachery that almost went as far as to accuse them of conspiracy. It was a sign of the nervousness of the establishment, as well as a hint of their intentions. For, the counter-attack on the home front was about to be launched.

First to feel the force was the newspaper *Forward*, which was closed down for five weeks after publishing a full and accurate account of Lloyd George's meeting. In Russell Galbraith's biography of Tom Johnston, it was claimed that when the 1 January edition of the paper reached London and was seen by the minister he completely lost his sense of proportion and ordered a complete raid of all copies of the *Forward* in every newsagent's shop in Scotland. A party of plainclothes policemen arrived at the offices of the Civic Press in Howard Street and took command of the building. They were acting, the House of Commons later learned, under the Defence of the Realm Regulations at the insistence of the Minister of Munitions.[30]

However, though he may well have been black affronted by the publication, it appears that action against the paper had been considered for some time. At a meeting at the Ministry of Munitions on 31 December attended by Lloyd George and including other ministers and officials, it was 'decided provisionally to suppress' the paper.[31] A later meeting in Edinburgh that included not just the Lord Advocate, but the head of the military in Scotland, confirmed the decision and arranged for the action to be taken.

Lloyd George denied that it was due to the personal slight, arguing that it was because of articles the paper had published over consecutive weeks that were 'designed to stir up friction among workers in the most important munitions district in the country'.[32] However, given the moderate stance that *Forward* had taken, few believed this and instead saw it as the revenge of a humiliated man. As the paper itself explained, it had never had any objection to the principle of dilution, but rather its concerns were that it should not be used by employers to attack wages.

The paper remained banned for five weeks until Johnston and his lawyer Rosslyn Mitchell signed undertakings 'not to issue or publish any matter calculated to prejudice the military interest or safety of the country in the present crisis'.[33] They were also required to give undertakings that the paper wouldn't impede or interfere 'with the production

---

30 Russell Galbraith, op. cit., p. 40.
31 Iain McLean, *The Legend of Red Clydeside* (John Donald, 2000), p. 54.
32 Iain McLean, op. cit., p. 54.
33 Russell Galbraith, op. cit., p. 40.

or supply of munitions of war or cause disaffection with the Munitions of War Acts or with the policy of the dilution of labour'.[34]

When *Forward* reappeared on 5 February 1916 it detailed what had happened under an article headlined 'The Raid on the Forward', explaining how on Monday 3 January their offices had been raided by military and police. It narrated how they had been informed in a House of Commons debate that it apparently wasn't because it had published an accurate account of Mr Lloyd George's speech. Instead, they explained, they had been 'suppressed' for the 'the supreme interests of the state'. No doubt the humiliation of the minister was critical, but it was also clear that the state was launching an offensive against those they believed to be a threat, whether newspapers or individuals.

In January 1916 a Russian émigré, Peter Petroff, a BSP member and an anti-war activist, was arrested and interned under powers held by the state over 'aliens'. A start was clearly being made with those most vociferous in their anti-war activities, as well as partly, no doubt, through anti-foreigner and spy hysteria. He would later be exchanged for British diplomats held by the Bolsheviks after the Russian Revolution. A divisive character, many on the left were suspicious of him, though he remained close to Maclean. On its own the incident was insignificant, but it was to be the prelude for far wider actions that were soon to follow.

Newly acquired powers were next turned on those campaigning against the war and disrupting military supplies essential to the war effort. John Maclean was arrested under DORA in October 1915, eventually being dismissed from his teaching post. Rather than reducing his activities his sacking simply increased them, as he became a full-time agitator and anti-war activist. Liberated from school work, he flung himself into anti-war activities, addressing street meetings and speaking at factory gates before doing lectures and talks at night.

---

34   Iain McLean, op. cit., p. 54.

The authorities arrested him again on Sunday 6 February 1916 after a meeting in Glasgow had ended, taking him to the central police station and then through to Edinburgh Castle. Charged with sedition, he was remanded in custody, and though demonstrations followed and strikes in support of him took place, they were limited in size and duration and were designed more to show solidarity than achieve his release. *The Vanguard*, the BSP newspaper and outlet for Maclean's views, was also shut down, but the political grouping (small as it was) rallied round to support Maclean and his family. Whilst he remained in custody pending trial, others soon joined him.

It was becoming clear that the state was viewing the CWC as both the source of revolutionary threat as well as a danger to good order in the munitions sector. On 9 February Lynden Macassey sent a note to the ministry including comments on the organisation, stating,

> It is ostensibly a Socialist Organisation if indeed it is not something worse ... I have been convinced for some days that the only effective way of handling the situation is to strike a sharp line of cleavage between the loyal workmen, who undoubtedly comprise the great majority of Munition Workers, and the disloyal Socialist minority who are pawns of the Clyde Workers [sic] Committee, and those, whoever they may be, behind the Committee.

He was not alone in his suspicions about the activities and intentions of the CWC, which appeared to be widespread across the Cabinet, and not simply angst by the minister at his treatment when in Glasgow. They were gearing up to take action against the organisation more widely, not simply against individuals who had offended him.

Next to feel the full force of the state was the CWC paper, *The Worker*. When *Forward* had been shut down another outlet was opened up. Ironically, it was partly funded by expenses paid to many attendees at the event that so concerned Lloyd George. Many donated them to the CWC, which used the money to the launch the paper. However, whilst *Forward* had merely been an irritancy, the new paper was seen as a considerable threat. Lloyd George commented when meeting with Tom Johnston: 'I thought your paper was bad, but it's nothing to this. This can't be tolerated.'[35]

The new paper's first edition covered a resolution that had been passed by the CWC, which opposed conscription, and read:

> This delegate meeting of the Clyde Workers' Committee, recognising that the purport of the conscription is not a fuller supply of soldiers but the cheapening of soldiers and the military control of industry and consequently the abolition of the function of our trade unions, resolves to take such action as is necessary to prevent conscription.[36]

Coming out on 29 January, with John Muir as its editor, *The Worker* was sold not just in factories, but on the streets, where workers and activists eagerly bought it.

Four editions had been published, but as the fifth was going to press disaster struck, and the authorities closed it down. Not only was its printing terminated, but Muir, along with Willie Gallacher and Walter Bell, the manager of the SLP Press, were arrested on 7 February. That was the day after the arrest of Maclean, and they, too, were charged with sedition. It was claimed that they had

> attempted to cause mutiny, sedition or disaffection among the civilian population, and to impede, delay or restrict the production of war material by producing, printing, publishing and circulating amongst workers in and around Glasgow *The Worker*.[37]

---

35   William Gallacher, op. cit., p. 100.
36   William Gallacher, op. cit., p. 116.
37   William Gallacher, op. cit., p. 102.

The pretext was an article that had been carried headlined 'Should The Workers Arm?' Written by a member of the Catholic Socialist Society, though unattributed in the paper, its conclusion was, in fact, that they shouldn't. It wasn't given any particular prominence and was carried without any additional attention given to it. Muir as editor refused to declare the identity of the author, believing that as he was unmarried and without children it was better that he faced the punishment than the actual author.

But this incident was only one factor, and it seems that the authorities were driven to act by the totality of what was in the offending paper or being published. The headline alone probably sufficed for the authorities, but additional items in that edition, from castigating conscription ('What Conscription Really Means'), through criticising the Munitions Act ('Slavery from Military Necessity – But Not if the Clyde Says No!') to a report on strike at a factory in nearby Johnstone ('Suburban Munitions Workers Revolt'), probably sealed the paper's fate. Reference was also made at the subsequent trial to pamphlets that were also published denouncing the treachery of union leaders. An Irish paper that included an article written by Countess Markievicz, who would go on to support the Easter Rising, was also referenced as implicating rebellion.

The three detained over the paper were released on bail when they appeared in court the following day. After they had been arrested John Wheatley and Rosslyn Mitchell were speedily in contact, and Kirkwood was also supportive. John Muir was a close personal friend of Kirkwood's and the Parkhead works leader did his best to mitigate the situation for all three, as well as giving them his full support. An attack on one after all was an attack on all, as they were soon to discover.

Though arrests did nothing to either diminish campaigning or quell discontent in the factories. When news of their detention broke, a demonstration took place outside the court and tools were downed at several factories, with some 10,000 workers involved. But the stoppage ended and workers returned to their machines when the three were released after the £50 bail was posted.

Throughout this, the Munitions Act remained the main source of discontent, and although the CWC was united in its opposition, there was a division between Kirkwood and Gallacher in how to respond to it. This rift would go on to become the source of some considerable disagreement between them, and would ultimately undermine the solidarity that had existed across the factories represented by the CWC.

For an agreement was signed by Kirkwood with the government commissioners that accepted the reality of dilution for Parkhead and restricted the power of shop stewards. It was signed by Kirkwood whilst Gallacher was under arrest and prior to his release on bail, and without their being any discussion either at the CWC or with leading stewards from other major sites. It appears to have been written for him by Wheatley and was an attempt to defuse a situation that was obviously becoming increasingly tense.

Kirkwood's position on the war was of course vastly different to the views held by many of the others, and his bragging of shell production and war efforts brought open contempt from the likes of Maclean. As a result, Kirkwood had grown ever closer to Wheatley, who, already his mentor, had been pivotal in persuading him to join the ILP.

But the signing of the document had the effect of breaking the solidarity that had previously existed across the factories. When he heard about it, Gallacher was angry, and spoke to others including John Muir, who had been detained with him from Barr and Stroud's, and Mac-Manus, from Weirs. They had been equally unsighted on it and were likewise unhappy. In response, Gallacher negotiated a deal directly with management at the Albion factory that again recognised dilution but, in this instance, preserved the power and the status of the stewards, as well as excluding the government commissioners from the discussions; that was replicated by Muir at his factory. Although, as a result, the united front against dilution begun to fracture.

The document signed by Kirkwood would soon have another major effect – and one he hadn't anticipated. When he sought to continue his shop steward activities across the huge Parkhead factory site, issues arose with management about his free movement around the factory. The employers referred to the terms of the agreement signed by him with the government commissioners, the strict terms of which appeared to limit stewards, including him, to their own department and restricted them from accessing other areas. This was not Kirkwood's understanding of what he had signed, and it was certainly a strict interpretation of it.

However, when he remonstrated with management, they were adamant that the terms stipulated that he was confined to the one unit where he had worked. Discussions even took place with owner Sir William Beardmore, but to no avail. Whilst Kirkwood had seen his close relationship with the owner as a positive when preaching about his commitment to the war effort, it was to prove no benefit whatsoever when the state turned against him. Stewards were to be restricted to their own section or department, and Kirkwood was included amongst them. The ability to organise across the factory – never mind the city – was being fatally undermined, and Kirkwood reacted by resigning as senior steward.

A strike followed at Parkhead starting on 17 March, where the workforce stood behind their elected union leader. Despite their hostility to what had been signed at Parkhead, Gallacher and others sought to coordinate action in support, and a few other factories came out on strike a few days later, including North British Diesel Engine Works and Whiteinch as well as gun departments at Weirs and Dalmuir. Though numbers were limited, the effect upon the authorities was significant, with the action at the gun departments causing special concern as artillery and howitzers were required for a planned military offensive that spring.

The pressure being applied by the state was mounting, and it wasn't simply in the arrests being made. Press hostility was being unleashed against those seen as disrupting the war effort, and it was all set against a backdrop of carnage in the trenches. Whatever doubts ordinary people had about the war, they grieved for loved ones and reviled those viewed as besmirching the sacrifices being made. Kirkwood recalled that the strike was condemned by the wider public, on occasion he was spat at and his wife verbally abused whilst shopping.

Despite that change in the public mood, the authorities were still gravely concerned by the strike's effect on military production and, accordingly, the government struck again on 24 March. Restricted in what they could libel as criminal charges, and floundering to find the evidence that they might need to justify an arrest, another weapon in their armoury was used. For, as well as wide-ranging criminal law sanctions, the state also had widescale emergency powers over where people could live and work. So, the state chose simply to deport leading shop stewards from Glasgow under DORA, removing them from the factories and the area, thus taking the CWC leadership out of circulation.

That morning Kirkwood was woken up at 3 a.m. by a violent knocking at his door. When he answered, he was met by armed detectives announcing they had a warrant for him under DORA. Taking him to the central police station, he was told that he had to leave the Clyde Munitions Area. Escorted home to gather some clothes, he was one of three others from Parkhead who were also removed in what was the start of the deportation of stewards.

MacManus and James Messer from Weirs quickly joined them and within days three more Weirs stewards were apprehended and deported. Not all could immediately be located, but they were soon tracked down and detained. Irrespective of when they had been seized, though, the outcome was the same, they had to remove from the city and it mattered not if they had wives, families and jobs. The state's powers allowed for them simply to be removed forthwith – and removed they were.

They were, at least, allowed to choose where they went so long as it was furth of Glasgow and the west of Scotland, though in reality, that left few options for those being removed. Kirkwood opted for Edinburgh, almost on the spur of the moment, as it was close to where he came from and he knew it reasonably well. Besides, he also had some friends and colleagues there. Given a one-way ticket, he was also provided with ten shillings, but other than that he had little else. Moreover, he was ordered to report to the chief constable in Edinburgh upon his arrival and was warned that surveillance would continue thereafter. The others likewise followed, embarking on trains following detention. They too opted for Edinburgh where their comrade had already gone and like him were required to report to the police on arrival and thereafter on a daily basis.

Dr Christopher Addison, who became Munitions Minister when Lloyd George became Secretary for War, made a statement to Parliament on 28 March where he justified the action taken and indicated that it had been targeted against the CWC, stating:

> At different times strikes have been brought about, sometimes on the most trivial grounds, by a self-appointed body known as the Clyde Workers' Committee. This committee ... decided about a fortnight ago to embark on a policy of holding up the production of the most important munitions of war in the Clyde district, with the object, I am informed, of compelling the Government to repeal the Military Service Act and the Munitions of War Act, and to withdraw all limitations upon increases of wages and strikes, and all forms of Government control. The present series of strikes commenced on the 17th of March ... From that time the series of strikes appears to have proceeded upon a systematic and sinister plan.[38]

During that debate Sir Edward Carson, the Ulster Unionist, had the temerity to enquire whether the men were not, in fact, guilty of high

---

38   Iain McLean, op. cit., p. 81.

treason? Addison, answering him sympathetically, indicated that deportation had been chosen as it was quicker than a trial. In his biography Gallacher couldn't help noting the irony of the Ulster loyalist leader questioning the minister about having the men charged with treason. Not only had Carson established his own private army to oppose Irish Home Rule, but he'd actively encouraged British officers to mutiny. But, as was often the case, preservation of the empire was one thing, socialism and workers' rights were quite another.

When the War Cabinet discussed the events on 30 March, a report from the meeting highlighted the extent of concern had by the government about the activities of the CWC.

> It was shown that the principal danger of the situation depends not so much on the proceedings of the small (by comparison) number of workmen holding syndicalist views and revolutionary aims, as on the fear that the vastly larger body of patriotic and loyal trade unionists may be deluded by misrepresentation of the facts into expressing sympathy with the violent minority believing them to be unjustly treated.[39]

So, the organisation was targeted and its leaders deported. There appears to have been some perception within government that this was all part of a larger plot to destabilise the state. It was that fundamental threat to public order, never mind the effect upon the war effort, that seems to have decided their actions. But this is entirely without foundation, as was an equally spurious suggestion of some links with Germany. However, with German assistance being sought for the rising soon to take place in Ireland, nerves were clearly on edge.

The strike underway following Kirkwood's treatment had seen a few others join in, after the deportations widened the nature of the conflict. But it was neither large scale nor did it enjoy widespread unity,

---

39   Iain McLean, op. cit., p. 82.

as other than the artillery men, workers at Fairfield's, Barr and Stroud's and Weirs refused to join over Kirkwood's signing of the agreement. The administration's fears seemed perhaps overplayed, given what was actually happening on the ground.

However, although 200 Clyde stewards did travel through to Edinburgh and march down Princes Street to show their support, the cracks were already beginning to show in what had been a united front. There was antagonism towards Kirkwood and Parkhead and many men of other occupations felt this to be an engineer's strike, rather than part of the wider conflict. This was doubtless compounded by both the severity of the government crackdown and the general mood of hostility towards industrial action.

Many, though, were still out on strike and the remnants of the CWC stalwarts were seeking to keep it going. But, not only did they face disunity at the bottom, they were confronted with disloyalty from the top. The Amalgamated Society of Engineers (ASE) and other unions refused to become involved, taking their cue from Labour Cabinet minister Arthur Henderson, who had assured colleagues he would make further efforts to placate the Clyde. Nationally the unions had been cooperating with the government throughout, and almost appeared to collude in the deportations. The stewards were no doubt an irritancy to the unions as well as the state, and their removal meant a respite from troublesome agitators, much the same as the state saw them.

However, the CWC leaders that remained sought a political solution. Despite being on bail, it was agreed that Gallacher and Muir would go to London to lobby for support. Arrangements were made for the two of them to meet with Ramsay MacDonald and William Pringle, a radical Liberal MP for Lanarkshire North West. Through them a meeting was to be arranged with Addison, the Munitions Minister. They were presumably unaware of the involvement of Henderson or the active role of the Cabinet in the planning of it all. The day before they even departed for Westminster, Addison had already made his statement to the House of Commons as detailed above, and outlined how seriously the government considered the threat of their actions and the view they held of the CWC leaders.

A meeting was held between Gallacher and Muir and the minister and, when a further meeting was arranged for the following day, there was some hope of a reconsideration of the deportations. In the interim, though, Lloyd George returned from France and it appears that whilst Addison was willing to compromise, Lloyd George most certainly was not. The War Secretary insisted on sticking to the hard line and, according to Gallacher, directed the minister to cease the talks. It also appears that Ramsay MacDonald was either leant on or prevailed upon. When the issue was discussed in the House of Commons the following afternoon, the erstwhile Labour leader distanced himself from munitions strikes, cravenly declaring he had appealed to workers in his own constituency to support the war effort. Pringle was left alone to represent the CWC in the parliamentary fight.

Obeying his new orders Addison went on the attack, railing against both the CWC and their sole remaining political champion. He claimed of Pringle:

> He has chosen to make himself the spokesman in this House, of the Clyde Workers' Committee, a body which with a treacherous disregard of the highest national interest, has made itself responsible for promoting strife and putting obstacles in the way of the full and rapid equipment of our armies in the field.[40]

Lloyd George also waded in, accusing the CWC of being 'purely an organisation for sedition, not merely against the government but against the trade unions'.[41] There was to be neither compromise offered, nor a political agreement available.

---

40 William Gallacher, op. cit., p. 112.
41 William Gallacher, op. cit., p. 112.

Gallacher and Muir returned to Glasgow to find that Parkhead Forge was still on strike; but with only Dalmuir, Albion and another contractor's factory supporting them, even that effort would soon crumble. On 29 March thirty strikers were fined under the Munitions Act at Glasgow Sheriff Court; unlike the occasion the year before, all paid the punishment this time. Two days later a large demonstration took place at Glasgow Green, organised by the trades council and the CWC, but it was clear that the strike was fragmenting with men drifting back to work. By 5 April only thirty-three remained on strike and the commissioners delivered the *coup de grâce*: levying fines on those who had remained on strike until the 4th, threatening similar action against anyone who did not return to work and deporting Thomas Clark (who had replaced Kirkwood as treasurer of the CWC). The strike was over and the CWC defeated.

Kirkwood's signing of the agreement had certainly caused a rift between him and Gallacher, as well as lessening the unity once displayed across the many factories. However, the defeat of the strike was more likely down to the swift and ruthless nature of the state's assault, all at a time when the public mood was bitter, with scant sympathy for those opposing the war. Added to that was the perception, not entirely without reality, that it was an engineer's strike and not for the wider workforce. Moreover, with the arrest and deportations the leadership of the CWC had been removed, and the wider membership subdued. The CWC was dealt a critical blow and it wouldn't recover for quite some time.

But the state was still not finished with its crackdown on dissent and agitators. Next to feel the power of the establishment were James Maxton and Jimmy MacDougall, a close confidante of John Maclean. Maxton had, like Maclean, been dismissed from his employment as a teacher due to his absences for political activities, as well as the fact that his actions generally seemed to prove too much for the school board. The authorities detained him and MacDougall following speeches made at Glasgow Green, where they spoke against the deportations. They were joined by Jack Smith, a shop steward at Weirs, who had also spoken and was also charged with possessing revolutionary leaflets. As with Kirkwood, Maxton recalled the hostility faced from the public when he was arrested. The mood swing was against not just those impeding the war effort, but those speaking out against it.

It is suggested by Harry McShane in his biography that they were encouraged by John Maclean to be arrested on a political charge as that would be better than the punishment imposed for conscientious objectors, although this is not supported by either Maxton's biography or other comments made by or about his actions. The speeches may well have been in the knowledge that arrest would follow, but Maxton was still willing to face the punishment for being a conscientious objector after his release. So, whilst the arrest may well have been tactical, it most certainly wasn't from any unwillingness to face the penalties imposed, as subsequently on his release he maintained his refusal to be conscripted and was forced to work in the yards.

Those who had been arrested still faced trial and that came after the deportations. First to be dealt with was Maclean, and the witnesses against him were mainly police or other professional witnesses, testifying to him having criticised the war. Maclean conceded that, but defended the charges on the basis of the context in which he'd been saying it. Maxton, Helen Crawfurd and others were all called to give evidence on his behalf, but to no avail and he was convicted and sentenced to three years of hard labour.

Others were to follow in quick succession with Gallacher and Muir next, both receiving a sentence of one year's imprisonment and their co-accused Bell given three months. Then it was Maxton, MacDougall and Smith. They were also sentenced to a year, with Smith receiving an extra six months for the leaflets he had produced. So, before spring 1916 was over, both the leadership of the CWC and the main anti-war agitators had been either deported or imprisoned.

A dependants' fund was set up to support deportees and their families with John Wheatley as treasurer. Substantial sums were contributed by ordinary workers on the Clyde, showing that even though militancy had died with the deportations there was still a lingering sympathy for those who had been forcibly removed. Initially Kirkwood and several stayed with John Clarke, another SLP activist who had moved to the capital before finding accommodation. Others found lodgings or bedded down with comrades from the political and trade union movement.

Some moved on to work in Liverpool or Manchester where skilled jobs were more plentiful, but Kirkwood refused to go, arguing that he'd work at Beardmore's or nowhere. Despite offers of employment, the possibility of union activity in Sheffield and Coventry and even encouragement from some Labour leaders including George Lansbury, he refused to relocate or seek work elsewhere. But this still did not mean that either the pressure or watchful eye of the state reduced. Reporting to the police continued for him in Edinburgh and for those elsewhere. He was asked to sign a document which would have been tantamount to admitting having impeded the war effort, and was likewise threatened with jail – though neither happened. Other deportees were similarly harassed, but none agreed to either recant or sign.

Disruption in the factories greatly reduced and the political coordination of left-wing agitation across the city was severely hampered. Meanwhile war on the Western Front was about to enter a calamitous stage. The Battle of the Somme started on 1 July 1916 with almost 20,000 dying on that first day alone. More than 400,000 British and Commonwealth soldiers alone would die before it finally ended in November. Over a century on, the name of the battle still resonates with the slaughter that took place. It had an equally chilling effect on communities at that time, as trains were arriving at Glasgow carrying the wounded, many with appalling injuries, who were destined for Bellahouston Hospital. The sight of severely wounded men became commonplace as the toll of wounded mounted along with that of the dead. Newspapers carried not just lists of the dead and missing, but graphic photographs detailing the gruesome nature of the conflict. The public was now becoming conscious of the full horror of war.

It didn't result in increased anti-war sentiment, more a numbed acceptance of the carnage. Grief was evident and pain raw for many families who had lost sons, husbands and fathers. For some it must have been easier to cope with the pain through anger at the enemy, rather than questioning the basis of their loss. With others the sorrow was all consuming and the war too hurtful to even consider. Numbers attending anti-war rallies dropped considerably and the anti-conscription campaign by the ILP was replaced by calls for peace.

The ILP were in a different position to that of the CWC, where the leadership had been decapitated. Although they also opposed the war and had confronted the government, they had lost far fewer of their major figures and community campaigning had seen them grow in strength. They had lost Kirkwood and a few others, but many more key leaders still remained, such as Wheatley, Dollan and Johnston. On the ground, membership of the party increased considerably, rising by 116 per cent in Glasgow between April 1915 and April 1917.

Dilution was by and large accepted and though issues remained in the factories, with the leading stewards removed, the coordinated actions were reduced considerably. Conscription and dilution of labour were replaced by food and housing as the critical issues for workers and citizens. As the issues changed so did the organisation leading the campaigns, with the ILP supplanting the CWC as the major political organisation in the city. However, as with the war on the Western Front, there was a lull in activities. One side licked its wounds, whilst the other got its breath back. But the battle was most certainly not over, as the underlying issues remained and many of the leaders of the left would soon return to the front. Rebellion was about to break out.

9

REBELLION BREAKS OUT

hough disruption had been quelled in the empire's second city, peace
was fragmenting elsewhere. For, whilst the Clydesiders were being
dispersed or going to jail, the Easter Rising was taking place in Ireland.
Initially the response to the rising in Glasgow mirrored that of most of
Ireland, and many on the left were hostile to it. *Forward* was astonished
at their erstwhile columnist James Connolly's involvement, and was initially condemnatory, writing shortly after its occurrence that it was 'not
only a futile insurrection, but one in which the insurrectionists were
apparently being used as pawns and tools of the German government'.

But following the brutal British response the paper's sympathy, like
that in Ireland, began to change. For the ILP, the execution of Francis
Sheehy-Skeffington, an artist who hadn't been directly involved in the
insurrection and indeed had been seeking to quell looting, appears to
have been pivotal in their change of heart. However, the political direction was in support of Home Rule rather than for a republic (as sought
by Sinn Féin), and armed insurrection stood condemned. The official
line was perhaps best reflected by comments in the magazine *Socialist
Review* in September, when it was made clear that 'in no degree do
we approve of the Sinn Fein rebellion. We do not approve of armed
rebellion at all, any more than any other form of militarism or war.'[42]

---

42 Nan Milton, op. cit., p. 130.

The Irish community, though, was more supportive of those involved directly in the rebellion, viewing them as having died for Ireland. Writing in *Forward* in June 1916 weeks after the failed rising, John Wheatley commented that 'Connolly's death has removed a mountain of prejudice against Socialism. "He was a socialist and he died for Ireland." This is a common remark among the Irish population. They are now interested in Connolly and in Connolly's views.'[43] Comments like this helped to further ally the wider Irish community with the ILP, even if they weren't in support of it.

However, whilst the ILP condemned the armed insurrection, others were fully supportive of the actions taken. Lenin fully backed it, seeing it as an uprising against imperialism, which was something that must be supported whether there or anywhere else, be it Africa or Asia. A portent no doubt for events in Russia just over a year later, and why the likes of Maclean who supported the revolutionary path would come to fully support the Irish struggle along with other rebellions.

It was also a salutary reminder of the actions that the British state was prepared to take in defence of its interests. The shelling of the centre of Ireland's capital city and the execution of many involved put the arrest of anti-war campaigners and the deportation of shop stewards in context. Actions like this also must have left an impression upon many, whether they supported reform or revolution.

For the authorities, the war wasn't going as they had hoped and the Easter Rising was a worry, but peace at least seemed to have been restored on the Clyde. In the factories the disruptive shop stewards had been removed, and within the community the main anti-war agitators had been imprisoned. But, as the war and world events turned, so would the mood in Glasgow.

In the interim, though, it was a damp prison cell for some or a cold flat in a strange city for others. Prison conditions were grim indeed, and

---

43   Nan Milton, op. cit., p. 130.

would severely affect the health of many of the prisoners. Calton Jail stood in Edinburgh on the site where the Scottish government's principal office now stands on Regent Road, and in the shadow of Calton Hill cemetery, which contains a huge obelisk to Thomas Muir and the Scottish martyrs.

However, it held no fond memories for the likes of Maclean, Gallacher and many of the others imprisoned there. It is doubtful that they could have seen the monument from their cells, and with the harsh regime they endured probably couldn't have cared less. Visits were few and limited, though supporters came to cheer and rallies took place in support of them, with even a socialist choir convening outside on occasions to sing for them. Still, it must have been a cold and lonely existence, and one which must, in some way, explain the bitter memories that Gallacher and others had.

Peterhead, though, was even harsher, and not simply because it sat on the very edge of the North Sea. It had opened in the later decades of the nineteenth century after transportation to the colonies ended, built to take those previously bound for Botany Bay. It would hold Scotland's most high-risk prisoners throughout its existence, and that would include John Maclean. Initially sent to Calton Jail, he was quickly moved to Perth, before arriving at Peterhead. The regime there merited its notoriety and was even harsher than Calton and other local jails. Prisoners were taken under armed escort to a quarry to break rocks and their diet would be just as poor as in the other jails.

Prison took its toll on Maclean's physical and mental health. Harbouring suspicions that his food might be poisoned he refused to eat, resulting in the authorities seeking to classify him as insane and remove him to an institution. However, the Peterhead Prison doctor refused to concur in this assessment and the attempt failed. But Maclean's suspicions remained, and he went on hunger strikes and suffered force-feeding. This also led to rumours of mental ill health, and though he was clearly a very damaged man both physically and psychologically, mentally ill he most certainly wasn't.

The others remained in Calton Jail, which Gallacher described in his memoirs as 'cold, silent and repellent, the discipline was brutal and the diet atrocious. There was no "association" labour, most of the prisoners working in their cells at mat-making and similar occupations. The one hour's exercise in the morning was the only opportunity they had of seeing each other, when desperate attempts were made to exchange a whisper or two.'[44] Whilst not as damaged as Maclean, several of the others also suffered both physically and mentally during their incarceration, Maxton, McDougall and Muir in particular.

Maxton would be plagued by ill health, some of which was easily attributed to the incarceration, and MacDougall appears to have suffered mentally from the experience he underwent. Maxton, however, appears to have been very popular with both the prison staff and prisoners alike, and later health difficulties were simply as a result of the basic conditions of the jail, rather than any additional punishments imposed by warders. Muir suffered greatly and would die still relatively young, perhaps as a result. Gallacher also attributed his former colleague's subsequent joining of the ILP and growing estrangement from him as being down to the period of incarceration. Though it is more likely that it was simply a political decision influenced by a feeling of the futility of his incarceration.

Conditions for the deportees were less harsh, but they were still away far from their homes and families and dependent on handouts. Their situation was further complicated by the possibility of conscription for those of military service age unless they were employed in a reserved occupation. Accordingly, it was decided that they should go to northern English cities where work was available and conscription could be avoided. (Although this didn't apply to Kirkwood as he was older and exempt from service.)

So, MacManus and some others headed south where life was still

---

44   William Gallacher, op. cit., p. 122.

difficult as it took time to pick up work and some were required to pawn possessions, despite a modicum of support being available. Kirkwood remained in Edinburgh, where he was supported by the dependants' fund administered by John Wheatley. There he was able to maintain contact with colleagues in Glasgow and the political agitation continued. Gallacher perceived this as preferential treatment for Kirkwood, and an abandonment of the others, which seems quite an unfair judgement given the circumstances.

By January 1917 Kirkwood was growing increasingly frustrated at his enforced exile and set out to try to force the issue. After discussions with other leading members, he decided to attend the Labour Party conference being held in Manchester. Initially, he had planned to travel in disguise as his movements were still restricted, but a government informant notified the authorities of the plans. Kirkwood was then contacted by them and advised that they were aware of his intentions, but were willing to allow him to go anyway, though they would require him to return thereafter to Edinburgh.

In Manchester he met with Ramsay MacDonald as well as with Wheatley and Johnston and advised them that it was his intention to return to Glasgow, of which they all approved. Taking the opportunity to speak at the conference in a resolution on trade union rights, he passionately gave vent to his plight. He referred to the 'persecution' he and the others were enduring, going into detail about how they had been deported and could only return if they signed an undertaking to 'work loyally and faithfully and behave obediently to their trade unions'.[45] Receiving thunderous applause from the packed hall and a standing ovation from the delegates, he then made a heartfelt plea: 'No charge has been made against us; no trial has been afforded us. On my return I shall have no means of life but labour. I am no criminal … I will not go back to deportation. I go home to Glasgow or I go to prison.'[46]

---

45   William Gallacher, op. cit., p. 128.
46   David Kirkwood, op. cit., p. 140.

Though his plight was rapturously heard by delegates, it was much less appreciated by the party leadership. Arthur Henderson responded for them and, doubtless trying to placate matters, called for a Committee of Enquiry to be established, seeking to defuse the clamour within the hall. Bob Smillie, the miners' leader, sought to keep the focus on the issue of the deportations, which had taken place without charge or conviction, but the leadership were keen to downplay it and avoid confrontation with the authorities, and hence the wider consideration was driven through.

That the issue was side-lined by the leadership was further confirmed when Tom Johnston of the ILP failed to be elected to the committee established to report on the deportations. Though it has to be said that even the ILP itself seemed to disapprove of some of the actions that had been taken when, in *Forward* on 10 February 1917, they commented that 'the deportees have in effect won their battle. It is generally agreed that their attitude about shop management was misrepresented by Lloyd George, that, at the same time, they were disloyal to their Trade Union leaders, and were trying to force to the front a rival organisation.' An indication, perhaps, that it wasn't just the Labour Party but the ILP that were distancing themselves from some of the actions of the CWC.

Kirkwood returned to his home city the following day. His wife and family, who had moved to join him in Edinburgh, had earlier returned there. The next day two detectives called at his house asking him to sign a declaration not to interfere in the war effort. When he refused to do so they departed, but stated he should remain in the house whilst they obtained further instructions.

However, after a few days, and before the officers had returned with new orders, Kirkwood went to Crieff Hydro, a popular hotel in Perthshire, for a period of recuperation, with the costs met from the dependants' fund. There, though, he was met by police who once again arrested him and took him back to Edinburgh, where he was this time imprisoned in the Castle. A few days later he was liberated again, this time on an undertaking not to return to Glasgow without the consent of the military authorities. Arrangements were then made by Wheatley for him to go to Moffat Hydro, in Dumfriesshire, this time to rest, again paid for by the fund, whilst negotiations to have the order withdrawn continued.

By then it was February 1917, and those who had been imprisoned also began to be liberated as their sentences had been served. Maxton and MacDougall were freed and the following week it was the turn of Gallacher and Muir. As they had been in custody and not deported there were no restrictions on their returning to Glasgow, and indeed, the authorities had transferred them back to Duke Street Prison the night before their release for convenience. There, on their liberation the following morning, they were met by John Wheatley and a few others who had been made aware of their impending return.

Wheatley advised that he had made arrangements for them to all go to Moffat Hydro where Kirkwood already was. So Gallacher, Muir, Maxton and MacDougall, accompanied by wives and fiancées, travelled there by train. At Moffat Station they were met by Kirkwood, who was already resident at the hotel. It was a much-needed respite after the prison, as well as a chance to relax and reunite with loved ones. It must have been a strange atmosphere in the large and opulent hotel, which was almost devoid of guests due to the war (other than some off-duty soldiers). Apparently, one resident was a drunken army officer clearly suffering from 'shell shock', who berated the group regularly about the actions and dangers of trade unions and agitators, oblivious to who he was actually speaking to. That was tholed for a while, though it is suggested in Gallacher's memoirs that Kirkwood eventually became irritated by the soldier and had the hotel management intercede.

Gallacher also suggested in his recollections that the atmosphere became too much for him and he objected to the costs at a time when austerity was being imposed on ordinary people. He stated that Kirkwood sought to assure him that there were sufficient funds to cover them, but he wouldn't be placated and insisted on returning to Glasgow, suggesting that the others also should accompany him to leave Kirkwood alone. That isn't mentioned by Kirkwood in his biography or indeed in other accounts, and it may well be that Gallacher, the ascetic revolutionary, did find it uncomfortable and perhaps even objected to the use of funds at a time of poverty for many, but it does not appear to have been made either an issue at the time or recalled by any of the others. Maxton's account simply recalls five days' rest and recuperation before a return to the fray in Glasgow, where he shared a platform with Gallacher at a rally. It seems more likely that the divide that grew between Gallacher and Kirkwood by the 1930s when he wrote his autobiography jaundiced his recollection.

Negotiations continued with the authorities over the following weeks about the return of the deportees, but in the interim those who had been released from prison sought to return to work, or in the case of Maxton, to find it. Maxton still refused to be conscripted and that was accepted by the military panel before whom he appeared, but he was still obliged to find employment. Refusing to countenance work that supported the war effort, he eventually found a job in July 1917 in a civilian shipyard that wasn't dealing with naval contracts. Muir returned to his old job at Barr and Stroud's from whence he been removed.

But there was to be no such forgiveness for Gallacher. When he sought to return to his old job at the Albion, he was told that the Ministry of Munitions had barred him from all large factories, with only firms operating with a handful of staff to be open to him for employment. Gallacher subsequently recounted how Lloyd George's memoirs later provided the reasoning for the differentiation. Kirkwood was described thus: 'despite a theatrical frown he was fundamentally easy to get on with', whereas Gallacher was 'a Communist, whose manners were quite perfect, and whose tones were soft, but he left no doubt in my mind that his was the most sinister influence'.[47] Barred from the yards and

---

47   William Gallacher, op. cit., p. 139.

factories, he obtained work in a small shop in the city centre involved in ship telegraphs. However, this did not stop his union activity, which continued unabated as steps were taken to try to revive the CWC and reinstate the coordination that had previously existed.

The deportation orders were finally lifted at the end of May 1917. During the negotiation period Kirkwood's wife had remained in Glasgow along with the family, whilst he had gone to Edinburgh. She became ill in the middle of May and, seeking compassionate leave to visit her, he found himself taken to Waverley Station by police and put on the Glasgow train, where he was met by other officers who advised him that he could stay whilst she recuperated. Then, on 30 May, the deportation orders against him and the others were finally revoked, and he was allowed to stay and the others were able to return.

But obtaining employment proved difficult for Kirkwood, just as it had with Gallacher, despite the high regard in which he had been held by fellow workers and the close relationship he thought he possessed with Sir William Beardmore. Initially he was excluded from his Parkhead site, and other munitions works seemed equally closed to him. After several weeks, and supported by representatives of Glasgow Trades Council, he even approached Winston Churchill (who had, by that point, succeeded Addison as Munitions Minister), arguing it was discrimination. Churchill accepted his arguments, and within a fortnight Kirkwood had returned to a shell factory operated by Beardmore's where he again became foreman. The other deportees likewise drifted back into work.

Back in Glasgow Gallacher and the others soon got back into the swing of political agitation and, in particular, they sought the release of John Maclean, who remained incarcerated. As the acknowledged – if unelected – leader of the revolutionary section, there was considerable support from activists, as well as widespread sympathy from a wider public who viewed his punishment as overly harsh. Meetings were held to demand his release and street agitation was increased.

The authorities were aware of the tension his incarceration caused and seemed to hint that an early liberation might be possible. Whether as a gesture of good faith or otherwise, Maclean was transferred from Peterhead Prison to Perth Jail and though it, too, was a forbidding institution, it was neither as feared nor as infamous as the north-east citadel.

Whilst required to release the convicted prisoners at the end of their sentence, the decision by the authorities allowing the deportees to return indicated a mellowing of their attitude towards them, and a slight relaxation of their tight grip. The lull in the conflict that the state had managed to achieve couldn't hold for long, though, as news of events elsewhere reached the city. Coinciding with the return of many of the political and industrial leaders, the level of agitation and campaigning increased considerably, just as difficulties on both the war and home front increased. Revolution was in the air.

10

REVOLUTION IN THE AIR

Change was on the horizon for those who had been deported, as they were released and returning home. The February Revolution that had occurred in Russia had huge significance not just for the war in Europe, but for the political mood throughout the country. Whilst the overthrow of an autocracy resonated with the general mood of why the war was being waged, as well as enthusing more radical elements with its possibilities, it caused fear and alarm to military strategists and the government.

What started as a local demonstration in the then Russian capital, St Petersburg (or Petrograd, as it was known at the time), became a full-blown revolution that convulsed the entire country. Disturbances broke out and, as the weather worsened with heavy snows falling, anger over food rationing increased. Strikes spread, demonstrations grew and troops on leave joined in. Soon, riots were breaking out and soldiers began to mutiny.

Finally, after days of upheaval Tsar Nicholas II abdicated, and a provisional government was established containing liberal- and reform-minded socialist parties. At the same time, revolutionaries formed the Petrograd Soviet to represent workers and soldiers. A system of dual authority of the provisional government and the Petrograd Soviet now ruled the capital, whilst across other areas of Russia control varied, depending on the local situation and who was most powerful.

In Glasgow as elsewhere, people celebrated the revolution. It was a view shared by many, not just of the left, but liberals who had viewed the Romanovs with contempt, and few shed any tears for the end of the old order. Disputes were never about restoring the monarchy to power, but which faction was to be supported in the new democracy: reformist or revolutionary.

More importantly, the opinion of the British establishment was firmly rooted in protecting the interests of the empire and keeping Russia in the war. This was reflected in the *Glasgow Herald* editorial on 14 March, which narrated, 'Those who have been watching the development of the internal affairs of Russia closely will not be surprised to learn this morning that a revolution has taken place in Petrograd.' But which then went on to add:

> It is Russia's business to determine under what form of government and under what Emperor it shall work out its own salvation. Our sole interest is the Revolution in its relation to the war. The Revolution can only really be interpreted alright as a grim proof of Russia's discontent with the methods of the ruling caste and of the new desire to fight on with us for victory with a greater concentration of powers. We accept the fact and wish the new rulers Godspeed, for their business, like ours, is to achieve peace speedily – peace with honour and liberty.

This theme continued throughout the media over the following days, with the *Glasgow Herald* of 20 March even reporting that Lloyd George told the House of Commons that the revolution was 'the first great triumph for the principles for which we entered the war', and the headline on 21 March read 'Army and People Behind the Government'. A few days later on 23 March, they reported Parliament congratulating the Duma on its 're-establishment'. The coverage was factual, without regret at revolutionary events and simply concern about the impact on Russian involvement in the war. Dissatisfaction at the effectiveness of the Tsar's leadership saw hopes raised for a more vigorous prosecution of it on the Eastern Front. The emphasis was clearly on the military interests of Britain and its allies.

Others, though, were much more enthused. Ramsay MacDonald welcomed the revolution, putting great faith in Alexander Kerensky, then leading the provisional government. He recorded in his diary that 'a sort of springtide of joy had broken out all over Europe'.[48] The Labour Party was intrigued and, keen to learn what was happening, sent Arthur Henderson to Russia in the summer to meet with Kerensky. Their support for the moderate social revolutionaries rather than the Bolsheviks was clear; for them, as for many, it was progress with hope not just for democracy, but for social and economic change.

Though those of a more revolutionary disposition were even more inspired, with Gallacher recording in his memoirs that 'Free Russia was emblazoned on our banners and mighty demonstrations in support of the revolution were organized all over Scotland'.[49] It was acknowledged by him as 'one of the most potent factors in the revival' of the movement after the deportations and arrests. Those who had been locked up and the organisations that had been subdued were given a second wind by the revolution in Russia. John Maclean was still imprisoned and efforts to have him released intensified as the left was revitalised.

The May Day celebrations that year offered the ideal opportunity to show support for the revolution. They were scheduled to take place on the Sunday following the day itself. Plans to change them to the specific day had been impeded by the arrests and deportations, and preparations for the weekend event had already begun before Gallacher was liberated, so no late attempts were made to change the day.

But that did not hinder the enthusiasm of those participating. The *Glasgow Herald* on Monday 7 May conceded that 'the May Day demonstration in Glasgow was elaborately planned and the result was

---

48   Kenneth O. Morgan, *Labour People: Leaders and Lieutenants, Hardie to Kinnock* (Faber and Faber, 2011), p. 44.
49   William Gallacher, op. cit., p. 137.

a comprehensive representation of the variegated labour movement. Conventional trade unions, cooperatives, socialists and Anarchists assembled forces.' The report described the demonstration as 'numerically imposing' and that official estimates were that 70,000 took part, representing 224 affiliated organisations. However, they didn't add that tens of thousands more lined the streets of the procession.

They did, however, provide a report of the march stating that 'George Square was the rendezvous and the organisers forming into procession marched with banners flying and to the strains of revolutionary music to the Green, where oratory was supplied from the platform'. The views expressed varied from ILP through to Socialist Labour with a Labour MP from Sheffield also contributing. Despite minor factional differences, everyone attending deplored the capitalist system, and food and housing were the major issues for those speaking – indicative, perhaps, that it was on the home front that most socialist energies were being spent – rather than the war itself. Opposition to the war continued, and those opposing the fighting or conscription maintained strong support from the left. But the public mood was less supportive and that meant a change of tack by many, even if a minority continued campaigning against the war. The major efforts by the ILP in particular were to go into campaigning on living standards and housing conditions.

Gallacher's recollection of the event was understandably of an even more enthusiastic celebration still. He recalls in his memoirs that

> never had there been such a May Day demonstration as Glasgow witnessed that Sunday. It was estimated that between seventy and eighty thousand people marched in the procession itself, while about a quarter of a million lined the streets. Bands and banners, slogans and streamers, singing and cheering, all contributed towards a scene of mass enthusiasm.

He also recalled the solidarity expressed with the soviets of workers, peasants and soldiers. For some like him, it wasn't enough just to address conditions at home, it was also the opportunity to overthrow the capitalist system.

A major rally was also held the following week in support of the Russian Revolution at the St Andrew's Halls. The venue was packed to capacity and thousands more were unable to gain entry. Realising that the venue would be unable to cope with the crowds, the organisers made arrangements for all those who wanted to attend but who were unable to access the building. Both within and without the hall speakers including Ramsay MacDonald and Bob Smillie addressed the jubilant crowds. As Gallacher recalled, 'Revolutionary Russia was hailed while continued calls were made for Glasgow to follow the lead of Red Petrograd.'[50]

Both the May Day rally and the meeting that followed were clear evidence that the mood was generally buoyant and positively enthusiastic amongst many. The broader socialist movement had been inspired by revolution in Russia and the CWC was beginning to come back to life, which was opportune as further changes were being made to conscription criteria.

The reason being, as the *Glasgow Herald* reported on 1 May under a headline 'Industry and the Army', that selection criteria were to move from trades to occupations: 'In order to provide the men which are required for general service in the army, a large number will have to be released from munitions work, and the only question is how the men are to be selected.' It meant that exemption from military service would no longer apply simply because a man was a member of a certain trade union and instead would be based on the work he carried out. A schedule of protected occupations such as shipbuilding and marine engineering, where there was still a shortage of skilled labour, was drawn up and from where there would still be no conscription.

Termed the 'comb-out', it was brought in as the authorities needed

---

50   William Gallacher, op. cit., p. 147.

ever more men for the front as casualties mounted. The procedure had been agreed with the trade union leadership, but that was never likely to appease Gallacher or some other stewards on the Clyde. Nor indeed did it find favour in many areas in England, with strikes taking place in major cities like London, Manchester, Birmingham and Coventry.

Now recuperated, Gallacher scented the air of revolution, and was eager to see it replicated on the Clyde. However, there was less willingness for confrontation by this point from many others. Some of it was down to political ideology, with many in the leadership that had taken over at the CWC (in the absence of Gallacher and others) forswearing wider political action to concentrate on factory control. Moreover, there was doubtless some acceptance of the situation faced, with the state's power and the reluctance of the workforce to take any action or undermine critical war efforts.

In some ways Gallacher appeared aggrieved that other cities in England had supplanted Glasgow in the vanguard of the revolutionary movement, and he wanted to ensure that they took their rightful place within it, if not return once again to its forefront. It was agreed by the reconvened CWC that he would head south after the St Andrew's Halls rally to make contact with stewards there, find out what was happening then report back. In the interim, stewards in Glasgow factories would take soundings amongst the workforce on attitudes towards industrial action.

Heading first to London, he was disturbed by what he discovered, which was evidently little appetite for strike action. Then proceeding back north to Birmingham and Manchester, he found that mood of little resistance even more pronounced, noting that only in Coventry and Sheffield was there any 'spirit' at all. The strikes in England, though unofficial, were still significant in scale, but did seem to lack coordination and leadership. They soon ended with the arrest of several strike leaders and a settlement made by trade union officials resolving matters. The reasons for the lack of enthusiasm were no doubt similar to what Glasgow had experienced before, with assurances, if not inducements, to encourage settlement. That was no doubt compounded by other factors from considering action futile (given the power and determination of the government) through to concern either about harming the war effort or being seen as doing so. Besides, there was also the fact that for many skilled engineering workers, in England as in Glasgow, it was unlikely to affect them. The importance of so many factories to the war effort ensured that workers were still in 'protected occupations', and the comb-out would pass over them.

Returning to Glasgow, Gallacher found the situation was much the same there, as though many delegates reported some sympathy for industrial action, other, newer delegates were adamant that there was only apathy amongst the workforce. So it was clear that there was still no mood amongst the wider workforce for militant action on a wider political issue. Strike action in Glasgow against the comb-out wasn't to be.

However, despite that failure to galvanise industrial militancy, there was still a mood swing across the land, with both renewed optimism on the left politically, and a growing frustration amongst the population as a whole over the conduct and progress of the war. The authorities grew concerned as the conflict dragged on, increasing the pressures on ordinary people not just through conscription, but also through food shortages and rationing. As it turns out they were right to be concerned, as grumblings against the war were increasing and the issues for civilians were being highlighted by radical and revolutionary groups.

A gathering of the leading figures on the British left took place in Leeds in June, with delegates from the Clyde including not just Gallacher, but also Maxton and others for the ILP, as well as MacManus and colleagues from the SLP. Two thousand people turned out to listen to the leading lights of the Labour Party, including Ramsay MacDonald, Philip Snowden and George Lansbury. They sang the praises of what had occurred in Russia and rejoiced at the coming of parliamentary democracy, expressing hope that Germany would soon follow.

Although others, like Gallacher, took a different view. For him the revolution wasn't finished, but had to be continued by taking on the capitalists and industrialists. Moreover, he felt that it was the duty of the British left to seek revolution in their own land to support the cause elsewhere. The *Glasgow Herald* on 9 June 1917 reported him as saying:

> This conference seems to be agreed that the Russian revolution is definitely settled. But is it? No. The Russian workers and soldier's delegates have the biggest fight on, not against the capitalists of Russia, but against the capitalists of other countries who are determined that they have to be beaten back. Give your own capitalist class in this country so much to do that it won't have time to attend to it.

In Britain, as in Russia at that time, the revolutionary element was in the minority. Gallacher returned to Glasgow with the convention having agreed the Labour line, rather than endorsing his revolutionary demands. However, in both countries, the divide was growing more marked and the political debate was heating up. Tension was rising and in Glasgow confrontation was to come later that month, albeit on a significantly lesser scale than the revolution that would break out in Russia just a few months later. The direct action was planned and coordinated by the radical elements and, whilst it saw the state struggle to maintain order, it did enjoy not inconsiderable support amongst the wider community. It was a significant event, involving the British Prime Minister, and one that neither then nor after has received the coverage it merited.

Lloyd George had replaced Asquith as Prime Minister in December 1916. There were several reasons for this, but chiefly it was due to the limited progress in the war. That and a specific crisis over the production of shells that had rocked the administration had seen Asquith form a coalition government in 1915. By the end of the following year Lloyd George sought to have a war council established, which would have taken control of war affairs away from Asquith. When it was refused

Lloyd George, joined by Bonar Law the Tory leader, resigned. Asquith did likewise, fully expecting to be restored to office, but instead the King approached Lloyd George and asked him to form an administration. Lloyd George was supported by the Tory leader as well as the Labour leader in Parliament, and this, along with powerful support from press barons, seemed to persuade the monarch of the need for change. Lloyd George offered a new and invigorated leadership (although it split the Liberals and he was primarily backed by the Conservatives). There may have been a Liberal Prime Minister, but the reality was a Con-servative-dominated government. The Liberals continued as one party, but effectively operated as two separate entities in Parliament. Arthur Henderson remained in the Cabinet unofficially representing Labour. Glasgow councillors were therefore keen to venerate Lloyd George, and invited him to come to receive the freedom of the city on 29 June 1917.

This would be the new Prime Minister's first visit to Glasgow since his ignominious speech the year before. If he had hoped that great-er respect would be paid to him on this occasion, he would be badly mistaken. He may have been assured of a warm reception from most councillors, but it would be a much more hostile reception from many others. Demands were made for the freedom of the city to be given to John Maclean, as well as to Kirkwood and the other deportees. Threats of disruption and demonstrations abounded, and given the mood, in conjunction with what had occurred on his last visit, they were taken very seriously by the authorities.

Accordingly, to try to placate feelings in the city, the deportation orders against Kirkwood, MacManus and the others had been with-drawn at the end of May, allowing them to return to Glasgow. Doubtless it was hoped that the gesture would defuse some anger and placate the evident hostility. Gallacher recalled in his memoirs the irony that Lloyd George's first visit had led to the arrests and deportations and his second resulted in their revocation. Hints were also dropped that an early release from his lengthy prison sentence might be possible for John Maclean, presumably to dangle some inducement to behave respectfully and quietly for the Prime Minister's visit. However, if that was hoped to suffice it was to prove far from successful.

Before the Prime Minister had even arrived, the deportees had returned home and were given a huge reception themselves at an event at St Mungo Hall. There, old and new comrades gathered and were treated to rousing speeches from the returning heroes. Kirkwood thundered: 'Some workers you can find who are afraid of the Germans, but they forget one thing, they forget that the greatest Huns in Christendom are the capitalist class of Britain.' And as Gallacher recalled, 'MacManus spoke of the need for carrying the fight into the factories and for developing the political character of our work, and was followed by Messer, who appealed earnestly for a rebuilding of the organization.'[51] It was clear that they were back – invigorated and eager to get on with their campaigning and agitating.

When Lloyd George arrived a few days later the mood was still angry and the reception far from what the Prime Minister would have wished. Though there were no organised stoppages in the factories or yards, it appears many – if not thousands – still left work to join the protest that was gathering. It is suggested in Maclean's biography that the crowd that gathered on Glasgow Green as part of the protest numbered close to 100,000, and whilst that may be an exaggeration it was certainly substantial. Moreover, according to Gallacher there were some rumours circulating that there was a plan to kidnap the Prime Minister, which whilst doubtless absurd, still caused some concern with the authorities.

Accordingly, the police and even military presence was substantial. Police with batons and soldiers, many with bayonets fixed, surrounded the Prime Minister and his entourage, as well as encircling the hall where he was to speak. Demonstrators were unable to get anywhere near Lloyd George's reception due to the uniformed and even mounted

---

51   William Gallacher, op. cit., p. 153.

ranks that shielded them, nor could they access or many even see him as he moved from train station to venue and back because of the security presence.

But the security protection still couldn't insulate the Prime Minister from the sound of voluble jeering from the huge crowd gathered as they approached the hall where the reception was to take place. There an old woman, Mrs Reid, in a flat opposite the west entrance that was being used to try to smooth the access for him, was waving a huge red flag from her window and earning loud cheers from the crowd below. According to Gallacher, she was seen by Lloyd George and, ever the showman, he doffed his hat and bowed towards her. The crowd continued with their opposition as the leader of the empire was hurried into the hall.

After the formalities the Prime Minister was spirited away once again, requiring to be heavily shielded by a police and military escort. The mood remained tense, if not potentially ugly, as demonstrators sought to locate where the Prime Minister had been taken, intent on continuing to vent their opposition to him. It was rightly assumed he would be departing by train and groups gathered at the many stations the city then possessed. Police spread out across the city centre, seeking to block access by the crowd and thwart any attempts to reach him. It was quite an incredible situation for the Prime Minister in the second city of the empire, especially during wartime.

Anger and rage were visible and there must have been concerns about a potential riot. Workers who had gone to protest about Lloyd George's visit were also clamouring for the release of John Maclean. According to Gallacher, he and other leading stewards were therefore approached by senior police officers who advised them that John Maclean was to be released the following morning, presumably to defuse the anger that was swelling. Maclean's biography adds credence to this theory, which details that his wife received a telegram that evening notifying her he was to be released the following day. The authorities had, after all, previously been hinting at his possible early release and whether it had been pre-planned or brought about by concern that day, it saw him released the following day. It was also successful in defusing the tension as the crowd thereafter began to disperse. Thoughts moved from jeering the departure of the Prime Minister to welcoming the return of the revolutionary leader.

And so it was that Maclean was released on 30 June almost fifteen months into his three-year sentence. The following day the gates of Duke Street Prison opened and the revolutionary leader once again walked free. Maclean returned to his family, but there was no retiral from his commitment to campaigning for peace and revolutionary socialism. Whether the authorities had harboured any hopes that he would forsake his activities is unlikely given the strength of his convictions, steadfastly maintained, even under difficult penal conditions. But they must still have been aghast at his speedy return to the front line and the warmth of the reception he received.

Protests for peace continued with the Women's Peace Crusade (WPC) next to organise an event. They had been formed in Glasgow earlier that year and had then gone national, soon organising across 100 branches across the length and breadth of the country. Prior to Lloyd George's visit they had initiated street meetings in communities across the city, as well as in other areas of Scotland. Those protests culminated in a march just over a week after the Prime Minister's visit. Over 14,000 attended, many of them women whose husbands or sons had been killed in the war, and others pushing prams or with young children bearing placards pleading for their fathers. Workers and members of the public lined the streets, as others joined with the women and children solemnly processing to the venue.

Only a few days after the WPC rally on Glasgow Green, a meeting in John Maclean's honour was arranged. Thousands gathered to greet him and the premises hired were unable to cope with the numbers that arrived despite both the main hall and a smaller hall being pressed into use. Those unable to gain admittance simply hung around, happy to cheer him from afar. Despite the hardship that he had endured in prison Maclean did not shirk from carrying on from where he'd left off before his arrest. Now his convictions were given added fervour by the revolution in Russia and the political battles being waged there. Continuing with his denouncement of allied war aims, he gave his full support to the revolution in Russia, insisting that the fight in Britain likewise had to be not just against the war, but for the overthrow of the capitalist system. Maclean was clearly aligning himself with the Bolsheviks, even if Labour Party support more widely was for those pursuing the parliamentary route.

The divide in strategic direction may have been developing, but the unity of the left was still shown by Tom Johnston acting as chair and the reception containing more moderate socialists and revolutionaries alike, all gathered to welcome home a favourite son. Even those who disagreed with Maclean's revolutionary policies appreciated his courage and convictions.

Despite the public showing of solidarity, the revolutionary atmosphere was stimulating debate and heightening a divide not just between parties, but also within them. Maxton noted a political tension that had been growing within both Labour and the ILP, who had been moving further left in Scotland. Pressure had mounted within the former to oppose conscription and demands were made for the parliamentary party to leave the coalition. The latter's drift leftwards had also caused concern in London, and according to Maxton, 1917 saw the beginning of the divide within both the ILP and broader left: between 'parliamentary socialists' and 'syndicalists'.

That divide was reflected in continuing actions following the conference that had taken place in Leeds in June, where there had been discussions about the formation of workers' and soldiers' councils to mirror those in Petrograd. Later meetings saw steps taken to try to organise events to promote them around the country. This step certainly concerned the authorities, not simply with the backdrop of previous industrial action, but no doubt added to by the spectre of the rising that had taken place in Dublin, and so in early August, the Cabinet approved the Home Secretary's decision to ban those regional conferences. Approval was also given to the Secretary of State for Scotland's plans to do likewise in Scotland, where a meeting in Glasgow was also proposed.

It had been planned to hold the meeting, as with many such events, at the Scottish Co-operative Society's St Mungo Hall, who were normally sympathetic to hosting such meetings, but even they were unwilling to allow it to proceed following the ban and cancelled the let they had given to the organisers of the event. Denunciations of the planned rally were made by many and likewise threats made to its security. A similar event that was attempted in London was disrupted by Australian soldiers attacking it.

Undeterred, the organisers arranged for a rally outside the halls with a makeshift platform erected. Given the threats being made no chances were taken about attacks from counter-demonstrators. Shop stewards were lined several deep in the surrounding streets, providing a cordon guarding the entire area surrounding the hall. Ramsay MacDonald was brought in by taxi through the cordon to provide a keynote address and was supported by others including Wheatley and Shinwell.

The tenor of speeches from the Labour leadership both nationally through MacDonald and in Glasgow through Wheatley was to support democracy in Russia. Others though, such as Gallacher, were intent on using the opportunity to mobilise for more revolutionary action. However, as Kirkwood recalled in his memoirs, attempts made to establish 'Soldiers, Sailors and Workers Councils' on the Bolshevik model soon died a natural death as 'workers laughed and went on with their jobs'.[52] There may have been many who were seeking to copy the Bolsheviks,

---

52   David Kirkwood, op. cit., p. 171.

but the popular mood (whilst angry at the government) most certainly wasn't revolutionary.

However, though workers' and soldiers' councils faltered, the CWC was revived. Gallacher and others soon manoeuvred to take back control from those who had succeeded them during their absence and were intent on getting the organisation back agitating once more. The *Glasgow Herald* reported on 29 September that

> the Clyde Workers' Committee had been definitely established as the result of a workshop conference at the weekend, with Willie Gallacher as chairman, and J Messer as Secretary. Some delegates wanted to change the title, but the majority agreed to stick by the name which made the committee famous all over Britain in the early months of 1916. Immediate steps are to be taken to link up the workers in every industrial establishment, and before long the Clyde Workers' Committee will be a greater power than ever.

The CWC was back and mobilising, even if the reality was that it had never formally disbanded. Rather, it had simply grown moribund in the hands of a changed leadership who followed a different political bent. Those who had been arrested or deported were now back in charge, supplanting those who had presided over its pacification, or more accurately, its change in emphasis. Most had remained militant, but had seen the route as through their factories, not in wider political action.

That newly restored leadership soon set to work with a will, refreshed from their absence and eager to mobilise the factories once again. Though the workshops and yards had seen many strikes and disputes in their absence, the coordination and political direction had lapsed. That would now all change with the old leadership back in command and the war grinding on.

Despite the United States of America's entry into the war on the side of the Allies in April 1917, it was still not going well. Public enthusiasm for the war had long since worn off, but even stoic acceptance was now being challenged by the death toll of soldiers and the price being paid by the living. That was evidenced not just by the fall of Asquith and a new coalition government under Lloyd George, but more widely in society. People were disturbed by the mounting casualties and the additional conscription being required, as well as by the social and economic conditions the conflict was imposing with pay restraint and food shortages.

Hence efforts by the government to bolster morale and encourage the population for one final heave to achieve victory. Lloyd George's speech in Glasgow when he had received the freedom of the city was indicative of that as he spelled out a road map to bring the war to a speedy conclusion and deliver peace. Even he was conscious that the mood was changing and it required fresh tactics and a different tone. The war needed to be concluded or criticism would intensify; more soldiers and more munitions were vital to that even if such plans increased anxiety and caused anger at home.

Discontent increased amongst civilians and disputes in factories occurred, giving an opportunity not just for demands for peace to be amplified, but for the CWC to seek to flex its muscles once again. An early opportunity came along in September 1917 when a dispute arose in Scotland within the moulding craft. Given the nature of industry in Glasgow there were many involved and they were represented on the CWC, though it was a dispute that was also spread across all of Scotland. It was largely over wages, but the difference between what was being sought and what was offered remained considerable and a strike took place that lasted for over three weeks. Those leading the dispute appeared to have been closely tied in with the CWC and to have learned from their organisation, and so formed a committee from every branch. The outcome was a 12.5 per cent rise which, at the time, was substantial, and when brought in provoked understandable agitation by other crafts for similar rates. That wage rise brought about by the strike was soon granted across the wider engineering sector, doubtless to avoid disputes demanding parity following from the settlement.

This enthused the likes of Gallacher, who, though conscious that the workers were still not ready for revolution, was keen for them to still be mobilised to confront their employers and indeed the state on particular issues. Likewise, in the communities, agitation against the war by John Maclean and others increased. Those who had continually opposed the war were increasing their efforts, driven by the senseless slaughter they saw continuing, whilst others who had been more circumspect or felt a negotiated peace was necessary were undergoing some reflection. That was shown at the Scottish Advisory Council of the Labour Party that same September 1917 when an overwhelming majority of delegates supported a resolution demanding peace without annexation or indemnities. That was a clear shift from before and indicative of a swing by parties and public towards bringing an end to the war. The mood was changing and morale on the left had been reinvigorated. However, there was still no mood or appetite for revolution on the Clyde amongst the wider population.

Russia, though, was different. Troubles had been ongoing since the revolution in February as parties fought for control and power. The country continued in the war on the Eastern Front but was plagued with dissension and disputes within it. It was a situation that couldn't continue, and in October it exploded with the Bolshevik Revolution. That also enthused many around the world – not least on the Clyde where some echoed it with demands for their own Bolshevik Revolution.

11

THE BOLSHEVIK
REVOLUTION

The Bolshevik Revolution exploded in Russia and reverberated around the world with tremors felt even on Clydeside. Deep-rooted political disputes had neither been resolved by the February Revolution nor had they addressed the underlying economic problems that Russia faced. Instead the country stumbled along, still bleeding in a war on the Eastern Front and haemorrhaging combatants.

The economy was collapsing and food shortages were increasing, and across the land strikes were breaking out and peasant uprisings occurring. The military remained equally restless with mutinies frequently taking place. Lenin returned from exile and the Bolsheviks seized power. A civil war broke out that would continue for several years with armed intervention by Britain and others before the Soviet Union was finally established in 1922. But, the Bolsheviks were now in control and that was something that many on the Clyde welcomed but which equally also worried the British establishment.

Events unfolding in Russia were followed with great interest on Clydeside, though a thorough understanding of what was happening was difficult given the distance and the speed at which events occurred. The lurch towards the crisis was noted and reported on, and the difficulties besetting the country were mentioned in the *Glasgow Herald* on 8 October under the headline 'Russian Chaos'. By 20 October the paper was narrating that there was 'no precedent in modern history for the complete breakdown of a great and powerful nation in the middle of a war'. Concern was evidently growing for Russia's continued military involvement, as reports of the ongoing political chaos continued.

The 9 November report detailed that the Bolsheviks had deposed the provisional government and were offering a programme including 'an immediate democratic peace, the handing over of the large proprietorial land of the peasants and the convocation of a constituent assembly'. It was not, however, something that the paper or the British government supported. The editorial lambasted the new regime, declaring, 'Detention, espionage, jealously, hatred, suspicion – all the dark forces that ravaged France during the Reign of Terror have been unleashed in Russia.' It noted that there was going to be a power struggle and gave its unequivocal backing to the moderate elements around Kerensky and within the army. Blame, as far as they were concerned, still lay with the old regime of the Tsar, but it was clear that they opposed the new order in the Bolsheviks and were worried over Russia's potential withdrawal from the war.

As the revolution raged across Russia they maintained their condemnation and support continued to be given to those opposing them. But the real cause for concern was made clear a few days later, on 13 November, when they commented:

> We can only hope for the gradual reestablishment of order, the reorganisation of the Army and the introduction of a political regime which will hold the promise of permanence. It matters not to us whether Russia finds her ultimate salvation in one form of government or another, provided it maintains her in loyal adherence to the allies.

Maintaining Russia as a war ally was what mattered, and it was growing increasingly likely that the Bolsheviks weren't committed to that.

Reports through November and into December were therefore

supportive of actions to defeat the Bolsheviks, and expressed concern about discussions between them and the Germans that might lead to peace on the Eastern Front. What had begun as worries over Russia's military situation soon started to turn to rage. On 23 November the *Glasgow Herald* wrote, 'While the world is regarding with admiration the splendid achievements of British soldiers on the Western Front, it is being bitterly amused by the puerile tragic farce that is being enacted in Petrograd.'

Scathing condemnation of the Lenin regime continued as news filtered through that fighting had ceased on the Eastern Front. There was further concern about reports of discussions between the Bolsheviks and the Germans and fears that peace was being sought. As revolution raged, stories followed the successes and failures as the tide raced between the respective forces. Through December reports continued to indicate there was fighting in many areas of Russia where civil unrest was taking place, but also that peace had broken out on the Eastern Front with Germany and her allies.

Finally, news of the Treaty of Brest-Litovsk, which saw an armistice signed between Russia and Germany, was carried on 17 December. Though agreed a few days before, the ceasefire was to begin at noon that day. It was a bitter blow to the paper and the British government. The *Glasgow Herald* leader on 22 December vehemently castigated Russia and quoted Lloyd George as saying that the Allies would 'cut their losses' with them. Although later recognising that the majority of Russians were for peace, it didn't stop further articles condemning the Bolsheviks' actions.

As 1918 broke, the establishment's hostility towards the Bolsheviks only increased as events continued to unfold and the Soviets consolidated power by abolishing the Constituent Assembly.

However, that was not the view held by all within the country and certainly not of some on the Clyde. When news of the revolution first broke *Forward* was critical of mainstream press reporting and even alluded to the doctoring of news against revolutionary Russia. That continued into early December, where they argued that there was neither sufficient information about what was happening in Russia, nor was enough known about Lenin to rush to judgement.

This was equally reflective of mainstream Labour and ILP opinion where, though there was scepticism over the Bolsheviks, there were also some hopes harboured for peace because of them. Indeed, at the Labour conference in January 1918 delegates had broken into a rendition of 'The Red Flag' when it was mentioned. However, leadership opinion was much more muted, if not hostile. Ramsay MacDonald addressed a meeting in Rutherglen in early January where he argued that Lenin was seeking peace not just for Russia, but Europe as a whole. He seemed almost to deny the reality of the Treaty of Brest-Litovsk, which took Russia out of the war, but no doubt saw it as an opportunity to try to bring the entire conflict to an end, adding that war was always a political problem – not merely a military one. Beyond that there was little support for the Bolsheviks within the Labour leadership who, in any event, had always been more politically aligned with the social revolutionaries who they had removed.

Others, though, were immediately supportive of the Bolshevik revolution. As Willie Gallacher noted in his memoirs,

> While all the Labour leaders, including Lansbury, remained silent about this world-shaking event, the Clyde workers received the news with a wild shout of joy. For the first time in history, the workers, ordinary men and women, had thrown off their oppressors, had expropriated the parasites, and taken the land and industries into their own hands.[53]

John Maclean was even more fervent and his support was recognised by the Soviets. In January 1918 he was elected chair of the Congress of

---

53   William Gallacher, op. cit., p. 174.

Soviets as a mark of respect and 'English Avenue' in Petrograd was even renamed 'Maclean Street' in his honour. He was appointed Bolshevik consul in Scotland to represent the regime. A consulate was even opened by him in South Portland Street and a Russian assistant hired to help staff it. There was a significant Russian community in the city – which was itself quite diverse – including Lithuanians and a small Jewish populace that had previously fled pogroms. Others had simply sought better opportunities, with many having come to work in the mines over past decades. The consulate was very busy with visitors and enquiries, as many were concerned as to whether they would be conscripted into the Russian Army.

However, the consulate wasn't recognised by the British government, who remained implacably hostile to the Bolshevik regime. Funds being brought into Britain to support both the embassy in London and the consulate in Glasgow were confiscated. Not only were the banking arrangements fractious, but the UK was refusing to recognise the regime and normal diplomatic niceties did not apply. The Post Office even refused to deliver mail to the address, declining to recognise the title or building. However, Maclean struggled on, all the while continuing his political campaigning, as well as seeking to represent the needs of the Russian community.

As civil war raged in Russia the divide on the Clyde between revolutionaries and more moderate elements also increased. Maclean, Gallacher and others were strident in their support for the Bolsheviks. However, the ILP was far less so with some senior figures in Glasgow being openly opposed. During February and March *Forward* published articles both supporting and opposing the Bolsheviks. However, it was notable that it was John Wheatley who wrote the critical piece in the latter month, which was responded to by some far less notable Marxists. Though a few within the ILP were supporters of it, the major influencers were moving against, which was quite logical given support they had held for other Russian parties and their opposition to the revolutionary road.

So, as 1918 progressed, the left in Glasgow was working away with confidence growing once again. However, it was becoming much more obvious that two distinct paths were being followed. The ILP was campaigning in the community and following a route for social reform, albeit of a very radical nature. They were growing in numbers and in influence, as Wheatley and Dollan, in particular, began to grow in stature and influence. Others, such as Kirkwood (albeit on the industrial front), were also drawing ever closer to them, and John Muir was also doing so following his release from jail.

Meanwhile, there was a smaller section that had been enthused by the Bolsheviks and wished to replicate that revolutionary road in Scotland. There, Maclean and Gallacher would be to the fore and the CWC would be a vital part of the grouping. Whether in the community or in the factory and whether in opposing the war or seeking to mobilise industrial workers, they were anxious to take any opportunity and be ready to seize their moment. With the CWC now reconstituted and re-energised by the return of the former radical leadership, action would not be long in coming. The primary issue once again was conscription, as further combing out was required.

Despite the entry into the war of the USA additional troops were required even though almost six million men had already volunteered or been conscripted by then for the army and the navy. Russia's withdrawal from the conflict was argued as a factor along with the general necessity for more bodies and greater flexibility between the needs of the battle front and the industrial front. The military reality was that the British Army was hugely overstretched. By late autumn 1917 it was becoming obvious as the Western Front had lengthened, but troop numbers hadn't increased. Arras, Passchendaele and other campaigns had drained the front line, and resources were equally required in Mesopotamia and across other areas. American troops were still to arrive in sufficient numbers to make a difference and high command was pleading with the government for ever more men.

But it wasn't going to be welcomed on the Clyde, either by stewards in the factories and yards or by anti-war activists in the community, and it would become a recipe for conflict. Things came to a head as the Manpower Bill was introduced to Parliament in early 1918 by Sir Auckland Geddes, who had been appointed Director for National Service by Lloyd George. It varied from the Military Service Act of 1916, both in terms of age, by extending the age range to between seventeen and fifty, but also in further changes to those who were exempt. These amendments would affect those working in protected occupations and, in particular, engineering. However, this time there was also opposition from within the trade unions, whose officials had historically been more supportive of government. The ASE had expressed objections themselves, but in moving the bill the minister was clear that he couldn't give preference to any organisation.

However, if there was opposition within the union leadership, it was met with even more hostility by the CWC, and Gallacher even referred to it as the 'Man-Slaughter Bill'. His objection wasn't simply the effect it might have upon Clyde workers previously exempted, but to the war itself. With the heightened atmosphere caused by both the Bolshevik Revolution and the new conscription criteria the level of militancy was rising. A meeting of trade union officials on 14 January in Glasgow with only a few standing against the motion endorsed a resolution demanding a downing of tools if the bill wasn't withdrawn and it was unanimous in a call for an international peace conference. Conscious of the sensitivity of the legislation and in an attempt to try to defuse the growing clamour against it, Sir Auckland Geddes was despatched to Glasgow to engage with those trade union officials.

It seems a rather strange decision given the reception that Lloyd George himself had received, not just when being granted the freedom of the city some six months before, but more importantly when, just over two years before, he'd sought to gather support for previous legislation. Either undaunted by that or oblivious to it, Geddes headed north.

A meeting was organised for the City Halls on 28 January where the minister and trade union officials would address workers and stewards. However, the night before the meeting the CWC leadership met and planned to take charge of the event and move a resolution both against the war and for an immediate armistice.

When the meeting took place, the hall was packed with almost 3,000 present and, as with Lloyd George's ill-fated attempt in 1916, the crowd was boisterous with songs sung and slogans chanted all before the platform party even appeared. The appearance of the minister flanked by trade union officials was the cue for 'The Red Flag' to be once again belted out by all and sundry. Geddes sought to speak, but was unable to be heard over the din, and suggestions of inviting Willie Gallacher up to quieten the audience were initially refused.

However, with the pandemonium showing no sign of abating, the organisers eventually conceded and asked him to try calm the proceedings and restore order. That he did, and the crowd eventually fell silent as Gallacher quietened them. He proposed that they listen to Geddes, which would be followed by questions from the audience, and after which Arthur MacManus would move a motion. Once again, plans to sideline the CWC had been thwarted, and what had been planned as a set piece event for the government representative had been hijacked.

Geddes was given a hearing, but it was far from listened to intently or even politely. Some disturbances continued and much was delivered to obvious derision in the hall. Compounding that, the pressure of an obviously hostile crowd seemed to unnerve Geddes, who was fumbling and uncertain in what to say and how to deal with the situation. It was a relief for both speaker and listeners when his time was up, but his muted contribution was then followed by some hostile questions which he struggled to answer and was derided when he did.

The experience for the minister then went from bad to worse. Gallacher had prepared for the event and arranged for a young man aged eighteen and recently issued with call-up papers to be situated close to him in the hall. Like so many of his peers the apprentice from Dalmuir was undersized, thanks to the poverty they had been reared in, and was just over five feet tall. Called up on the stage by the CWC chairman, who now turned master of ceremonies for the occasion, the shy youngster was towered over by the well-fed and well-bred minister, who stood only a few inches short of six feet tall.

In an icy and almost menacing voice Gallacher then demanded to know from Geddes if he was intent on sending the pint-sized lad to the front. All of this took place before an audience already hostile to the war and far from satisfied by the stumbling director's performance. Shell-shocked by the events unfolding and over which he had lost control, the minister clarified the youngster's age and then said no, adding that no one under nineteen was being despatched. His response was met by hoots of derision from the seething crowd, which was then followed by Gallacher inflicting the *coup de grâce*, and boldly asking him to confirm that he therefore would been right to have ripped up the youngster's conscription papers.

Humiliation continued for the beleaguered minister as MacManus then took to the stage to move a resolution opposing the bill and demanding peace. His fiery contribution demanded an immediate end to the war, as well as loudly opposing conscription. The condemnation continued as Maxton came up onto the platform to second the motion and continue the ordeal. The motion was clear and unequivocal with opposition to the conscription plans, demands for an immediate armistice and a commitment to do nothing in support of the war. The resolution was adopted with only six dissents amongst the 3,000-strong crowd, and the meeting concluded as it had begun in a bedlam of noise and song.

The following day the press fulminated over what had happened. Reports of the meeting itself were circumspect, no doubt to save embarrassment for the minister, but there was caustic condemnation of the shop stewards with allusions of treachery. The general theme taken up by many was of battle-weary troops bravely fighting in difficult circumstances whilst being shamefully undermined at home by revolutionaries.

The *Glasgow Herald* editorial on 29 January 1918 bore the headline 'A British Soviet', and went on to state that what the 'public had thought was an industrial process [was] now revealed, [to be] a political movement directed against the government, the country and the Empire. Hostility to the government was a mere camouflage.' It also berated them for treachery, referring to Britain, the empire and the Allies still fighting, whilst Russia alone had deserted and betrayed them. Describing the position being taken by the stewards as rebellion, and stating that 'pacifism has become militant and threatens to put down a righteous war by means of an unrighteous strike', it concluded by threatening, 'If the down tools policy is undertaken, let there be no more timorous handling of the issues.'

Even *Forward*, when it was published later in the week, was limited in what it reported, referring to 'uproarious scenes' before concentrating on the anger of the establishment press and the *Herald* in particular. No doubt mindful of its closure two years previously, *Forward* restricted its coverage and tempered its comments, perhaps with a watchful eye to the authorities seeking retribution and again imposing restrictions on individuals and outlets. Tensions were running high and with a German spring offensive about to be launched the authorities were under considerable pressure both at home and abroad. Equally, as well as being alarmed at the possible consequences, the more moderate social reformers were perhaps also unhappy at the stridency, which wasn't reflective of wider public opinion.

But the stewards and activists were far from cowed by the press denunciations or the demurring by more moderate colleagues. Instead invigorated by what was happening in Russia, they pressed on with their campaigning and agitation. Next to endure their wrath was Sir Lynden Macassey, previously involved in the dilution committee, and now appointed to be in charge of the Shipyard Labour Department.

Sallying north to meet the Clyde stewards to discuss changes to working practices, he was equally rebuffed by both the stewards and local trade union officials. Faced with counter-proposals, he returned to London and sought further meetings with the stewards there.

Those opposing the war were becoming increasingly active and not just on the factory floor but within the community. Even before Sir Auckland Geddes had ventured north activity had been underway. Authorities in the city had been sufficiently concerned by the activity that in December 1917 they had proscribed the publication of leaflets and pamphlets without the consent of the Press Bureau, which was in effect the official censor. This soon resulted in a confrontation with the Women's Peace Crusade, which had marched poignantly in the summer to Glasgow Green and had been continuing ever since with street meetings and strenuous campaigning.

That prohibition not only outraged the women but incited them to take action, and they reacted by publishing more leaflets, then organising a march on the City Chambers. It was not a huge demonstration in numbers, but was still significant given the make-up of the protestors. Arriving in George Square, they were initially subjected to some booing and jeering from schoolchildren who were hanging about there. Partly, no doubt these were just hijinks, but may well also have reflected the mood of the wider populace and their parents, as most people were still supportive of the war effort and denigrated those opposed to it.

Later though, a counter-demonstration by the Scottish Patriotic Federation, a right-wing organisation often used to break up anti-war meetings, appeared on the scene. As the women continued their protest police sought to hold them back from entering the building, and in turn the women were forced to fend off verbal abuse and attempts by the Patriotic Federation to grab their banners. The women retaliated, striking out with their umbrellas to protect their banners, some of which were still pulled from them and ripped apart. Despite that, they gave as good as they got, landing numerous blows upon the heads of those attacking them, and the Patriotic Federation moved away to hold their own separate protest meeting.

Whilst all that was ongoing, two WPC activists got into the building. Agnes Dollan and Helen Crawfurd had been signed in by an ILP councillor and had peacefully entered to be allowed to watch proceedings from the public area. Once present, though, they interrupted the council meeting, shouting for the regulations to be recalled and demanding peace, all the while strewing leaflets about where the civic leaders were gathered for their deliberations. In the end, they had to be removed by police, and the ILP councillor was upbraided for his actions though he strenuously defended his visitors' actions. The women were taken away, but released – it appears – without charge.

According to Gallacher, when the stewards heard about it there was anger and meetings were held across the city, not just to protest, but to consider what action to take. However, the authorities seem to have appreciated the potential for further disorder, and calmed the situation by releasing the women and having the police keep a low profile. Moreover, the behaviour of the schoolchildren was also telling. For, whilst there might be real anger amongst militant sections of the community, there was far from widespread support for the anti-war activists. The ordinary people in the city were most certainly ready neither for revolt nor for rebellion over the arrest of peace activists.

Moreover, the war was still far from over – even if the desire for peace was growing. In March 1918 Germany, now able to move men from the Eastern Front, launched a major offensive aimed at putting France out of the war before American troops could land in ever greater numbers. Nerves were jangling as the army faced the offensive and prepared for a counter-offensive. Likewise, the state was prepared to endure some anti-war activities, but was about to launch its own counter-attack upon those they considered enemies or dangers at home.

12

OFFENSIVE AND
COUNTER-OFFENSIVE

Spring 1918 saw the German offensive start to cause alarm in military high command, whilst also having an effect on the government's actions at home. Although America had officially entered the war in April 1917, the arrival of troops on European soil would take far longer. In the interim, the British and French were required to face the German offensive alone. The Ludendorff Offensive, as it was called, started in the early hours of 21 March with attacks all across the Western Front. Allied forces reeled and, in many places, were forced to pull back. However, German supply lines became stretched, the Allies regrouped and by late April the danger had passed.

But the German offensive was still massive in its scale and intensity. Even before its launch, concern over troop numbers caused by the constant carnage had been increasing, hence the actions from tightened conscription criteria and combing out, as the generals pled for ever more recruits to replace the fallen. The offensive confirmed the dread the authorities had, and they increased their efforts to speed up enlistment, but also to reignite their own efforts to close down open dissent. As with the preceding year when the arrests and deportations had occurred, 1918 would bring an internal spring offensive against the leading opponents of the war and the principal target would again be John Maclean.

The Bolshevik consulate had been an irritancy that had obviously piqued the authorities as shown by their unwillingness to even recognise it as a postal address, despite its obvious existence. Still it had been tholed despite the impediments placed in its way, but all that was to change when the German offensive was launched and fear ran deep in both the civil and military establishment. For, the day after the Allied lines came under attack, the consulate was raided. The Russian assistant employed there (required as Maclean didn't speak the language) was arrested, compounding the refusal to either recognise or accord any diplomatic status to it. Detained in custody, he was soon to be deported as the authorities ramped up the pressure upon both consul and consulate.

As the offensive continued on the Continent, so did the suppression of those most vocal against the war. On 15 April Maclean was taken into custody once again and charged with sedition under DORA regulations. Detectives this time went to the consulate, where they arrested him and took him once again to the central police station, where he was charged and refused bail when he appeared in court. The following day the *Herald* carried a factual report of his arrest and narrated that it was on the basis of his advocating revolution, with specific reference to speeches he was alleged to have made seeking to 'raise the red flag as in Russia' and for workers to 'down tools'. It went on to narrate that further calls had been made to 'copy methods', including 'seizing' hostages and 'buildings', including the City Chambers, the Post Office, banks and newspaper offices.

Though, nothing had changed in his activities since he had been released the previous summer in an attempt to try to defuse tensions and with concern over his health. His activities, supported by others such as Maxton and Gallacher, had continued unabated, but hadn't been escalated and it seems that this was a reaction to what was happening militarily on the Continent, as well as to fears caused by the effects of the Bolshevik Revolution that were rippling across the land.

Refused bail, his trial was set for 9 May, but before then the 1918 annual May Day parade was to be held. The scale of the demonstration the previous year had obviously concerned the authorities and the events since, from the Bolshevik Revolution to the war in France, further added to their anxieties. It appears some consideration was even given to banning it, but that was viewed as a step too far, or perhaps just an incitement to civil disorder if steps were taken to hold it anyway. Practicalities doubtless mitigated against anything as repressive as an outright ban, but overt and covert steps were still taken to try to minimise attendance and involvement.

A variety of measures were invoked, from downplaying the event through to accusations of disloyalty as British troops engaged in a titanic struggle on the Western Front. Newspapers were used to question the actions of the organisers when a huge struggle for the preservation of the empire and the values they believed it enshrined was ongoing. Likewise, employers were encouraged to, and often did, threaten dismissal for attendance or encourage absence from it by offering to assist in avoiding conscription through the comb-out.

As it was, not only did the parade take place, but was the first to be held on the official day of 1 May and not the Sunday following (if it didn't fall on the actual day). Notwithstanding that, even the *Herald* reported that it was larger than usual despite the change of day, stating,

> in point of numbers the procession was larger than any that have yet been held but the composition did not suggest that there had been any widespread movement among the men on Clydeside to make the occasion a holiday. During the day work in the big industrial establishments of the district went on much as usual. Though there were instances of workers taking the day off.

It also noted that there were large numbers of women taking part.

The view of others on the left was vastly different, with the *Worker,* published by the BSP and now back in print, headlining it as 'Labour's Greatest May Day', providing a full report on the celebrations – and with good reason. For, despite all the efforts to restrict or diminish the march, it had proceeded and for the first time ever on a weekday. The attendance of in excess of 100,000 was significant, and though work continued as the paper reported, many did leave or rescheduled their shifts. In addition to the marchers and others just watching, bands, banners and streamers travelled in their wake, and eighty cooperative lorries also formed part of the procession – all bedecked with socialist propaganda. It was by far the biggest and brashest that there had been. Moreover, the numbers of women participating and the frequent references at the rally which followed it on Glasgow Green to housing, testified not just to anti-war sentiment, but to the growing anger at abhorrent conditions endured in the community.

At its conclusion, a large crowd also marched to Duke Street Prison in Glasgow's East End to cheer Maclean, who was being held pending his trial. Anticipating this and potentially fearing even an attempt to free him, the authorities arranged for forces to be deployed within the prison. As it was, no such attempt was made and the large crowd restricted itself to volubly giving him their support and registering their opposition to his imprisonment.

His trial, though, was not to be long in coming, as on 9 May he appeared at the High Court in Edinburgh, brought through the night before from the Glasgow jail and charged with sedition and incitement to mutiny. The trial was not held in Glasgow, which was no doubt considered as too dangerous or difficult given local support for him. Presiding was the Lord Justice General, Scotland's most senior judge, another factor confirming the seriousness with which the authorities viewed him. Not only that, but it was the High Court and not the Sheriff Court with its increased sentencing powers, that he was to appear in. Senior and junior counsel appeared for the Crown to conduct the prosecution, but Maclean chose to represent himself. Whilst he may have been without legal support he wasn't short of moral backing, as some supporters set out overnight from Glasgow to Edinburgh to show solidarity and crowded into the court room with others to watch.

Despite, or more likely due to, the absence of legal representation, Maclean gave a spirited defence of his actions and his oration from the dock has become famous in Scottish radical folklore. Refusing to plead when asked if he adhered to his plea of not guilty, he then compounded his display of contempt by indicating his rejection of the jury in its entirety when asked if there was anything to which he objected. Though selected in the normal fashion, the jury was still composed of people entirely unsympathetic to his stance – never mind unrepresentative of wider society. Maclean knew this, and it was clear he viewed the proceedings as political and was intent on treating them as such. Witnesses were led, all of whom were either police officers or other government officials, including shorthand writers, who narrated a litany of excerpts from speeches that he had made and which they had been despatched to attend.

A special constable told the court how he had attended a meeting Maclean had addressed with nearly 450 men of military age present where he had called for the 'downing of tools'. Other evidence was of a similar nature, lambasting the neglect of working people and the exploitation that they endured. The most damning evidence was perhaps that he had called for direct action, including urging workers to 'take control of the Post Office and the banks, compel the farmers to produce food and if they did not, burn the farms'.[54] He no doubt further infuriated the authorities still reeling from the Treaty of Brest-Litovsk by praising the Bolsheviks and denouncing the war.

Maclean didn't dispute most of what was narrated, his objection being that they were taken out of the overall context of his arguments against war and the capitalist system. Much attributed to him sounded

---

54   Nan Milton, op. cit., p. 167.

far harsher and made him appear much more culpable of seeking sedition or revolution, than had been either his intention or indeed the tenor of the overall speech. Questioning and sparring between him and police witnesses took place, as he sought to clarify or justify what had been said. His attempts in cross-examination to elucidate that, though, were simply ignored or batted aside. Those were the comments made and the context was neither here nor there as far as the court was concerned. Having heard those witnesses the Crown concluded its case.

Doubtless, that simply confirmed to Maclean that it was a political trial, justifying the stance that he was taking, and he advised the court that he was neither calling any witnesses in his own defence nor giving evidence himself. The King's counsel for the Crown then addressed the jury, denying that socialism, social revolution or the like was on trial, though caustically adding, no matter how inappropriate those views may be. Instead, he argued that there was nothing in the country's laws, and even those that had been required to be brought in to deal with the emergency they faced had precluded that. People were entitled to talk about politics and express their views, he said, and Maclean would have been entitled to try to persuade them of the soundness of his case. However, he argued, there came a point when Maclean's statements changed in character and simply became attempts to plant seeds of disunion, disloyalty, sedition and mutiny amongst the people. Arguing for rebellion and violence could not be afforded, argued the prosecution, at a time when the enemy was at the gates. The Crown submitted that the case was absolutely and completely proven.

Maclean was then given the opportunity to address the jury and his speech from the dock has gone down in Scottish socialist history. Lasting for approximately seventy-five minutes, it was both an oration of his socialist conviction and a denunciation of war and capitalism. His peroration set out his background and philosophy, and though he did use some notes, he also employed also the full weight of his rhetorical experience, harnessed from a lifetime of street corner meetings and lectures. The court listened without interruption, doubtless conscious that he had neither led nor given evidence, and aware of the almost inevitable decision of the jury still to come.

That was to be Maclean's opportunity not so much to state his case, but to give full vent to his denunciation of the system that was trying him and against the war he bitterly opposed. Getting into full flow, he declared:

> For the full period of my active life I have been a teacher of economics to the working classes, and my contention has always been that capitalism is rotten to its foundations and must give place to a new society. I had a lecture, the principal heading of which was 'Thou shalt not steal; thou shalt not kill', and I pointed out that as a consequence of the robbery that goes on in all civilised countries today, our respective countries have had to keep armies, and that inevitably our armies must clash together. On that and on other grounds, I consider capitalism the most infamous, bloody and evil system that mankind has ever witnessed. My language is regarded as extravagant language, but the events of the past four years have proved my contention.

He gave vent to his pain and anger at what he felt was enduring by stating:

> No human being on the face of the earth, no government, is going to take from me my right to speak, my right to protest against wrong, my right to do everything that is for the benefit of mankind. I am not here, then, as the accused; I am here as the accuser of capitalism dripping with blood from head to foot.

Continuing with a defence of the Bolsheviks and a condemnation of empire he predicted:

All the property destroyed during the war will be replaced. In the next five years there is going to be a great world trade depression and the respective governments, to stave off trouble, must turn more and more into the markets of the world to get rid of their produce, and in fifteen years' time from the close of this war – I have pointed this out at all my meetings – we are into the next war if capitalism lasts; we cannot escape it.

He called for the Scottish working class to follow the example of their Russian comrades, thundering: 'The working class, when they rise for their own, are more dangerous to capitalists than even the German enemies at your gates.' Concluding his speech, he gave a final justification of his actions and statement of his principles:

I have taken up unconstitutional action at this time because of the abnormal circumstances and because precedent has been given by the British government. I am a socialist, and have been fighting and will fight for an absolute reconstruction of society for the benefit of all. I am proud of my conduct. I have squared my conduct with my intellect, and if everyone had done so this war would not have taken place. I act square and clean for my principles ... No matter what your accusations against me may be, no matter what reservations you keep at the back of your head, my appeal is to the working class. I appeal exclusively to them because they and they only can bring about the time when the whole world will be in one brotherhood, on a sound economic foundation. That, and that alone, can be the means of bringing about a re-organisation of society. That can only be obtained when the people of the world get the world, and retain the world.

Maclean's oration was over, but it was met with a stony silence in the court. The judge then turned to address the jury, pointing out that he was responsible for decisions on the law, but that it was for them to decide on the evidence whether the facts had been proven. His direction to them was that it was simply a question of fact that was before them and it was whether on the eleven different occasions that had been libelled the accused had made the statements. Going over the evidence that the jury had heard, he referenced the witnesses led by the Crown and then reminded them that no attempt had been made in defence to deny that the statements had been made. Finally, he pointed out that it was for them to decide, and he narrated the available verdicts.

It was as clear a steer as could legitimately be given by the court without demanding it, that a guilty verdict should be brought back.

However, that was no doubt of the intention of the jury as they didn't even retire to consider their verdicts as would be the normal action, but simply advised that they found the accused guilty. The Lord Justice General, having heard the perfunctory response from the jury, turned to the accused and asked if he had anything more to say. However, doubtless physically and mentally drained, Maclean declined. All eyes in the court the turned to the Lord Justice General, who was to pronounce sentence.

Declaring that Maclean was obviously a highly educated and intelligent man, but one who equally appreciated the seriousness of the offences he had committed, the judge imposed a sentence of five years' penal servitude. It was a lengthy and harsh sentence, which must have filled even Maclean with dread given his past experiences in custody. He appeared shocked by its severity and everyone in the court, including those actively seeking his punishment, seemed taken aback by it. Gathering his wits about him, he shouted defiantly to comrades in the court 'Keep it going, boys; keep it going' as he was taken down to the cells below. However, it must have been with a sense of foreboding that he trudged down the steps for transportation back to Peterhead Prison.

The sentence was met with mixed emotions by press and public when it became known. Many papers highlighted the dangers of Bolshevism and the seditious statements made by Maclean whilst soldiers were giving their lives. One paper even described the sentence as lenient, and suggested that in many other countries the death penalty would have been applied. As well as showing scant sympathy for Maclean, the *Herald* raged against Bolshevism more widely, describing it as 'not only a disease, it is a crime, which like other forms of morbid or unnatural offences, invariably brings a host of weak-minded and degenerate imitators in its train'.[55]

On the left there was a mixture of sympathy and anger. Those close to him and the followers of the BSP decided to campaign for his release. A great deal of support was gained from trade union activists, and the Secretary of State for Scotland was deluged with demands for his release and requests for clemency. In Glasgow they organised a monthly march and meeting on Glasgow Green demanding his release, where the turnout was considerable given the sensitivity of the issue. In July a demonstration numbering several thousand saw a violent clash with police who drew batons and beat protestors as they processed from George Square to Glasgow Green, but still the opposition continued.

Others on the left who had neither shared his opinions on revolution nor endorsed his calls to end the war were still shocked at the harshness of the sentence. Five years was a long time and penal servitude a harsh sentence for what, after all, amounted to simply public utterances. Many did not share his opinions, but respected his integrity. 'Release Maclean' became a common call at left-wing and peace group meetings and was a growing demand amongst many. As with others, whether in Scotland or elsewhere, the authorities were to discover that his incarceration simply increased his profile.

By then, though, the German offensive had not only stalled, but been repulsed, and an Allied counter-offensive was underway. US troops were also spilling ashore onto the European Continent in their

55   Nan Milton, op. cit., p. 175.

hundreds of thousands. American muscle was adding to American industrial might and tilting the balance of the war heavily in favour of the Allies. Meanwhile, Germany was being bled dry; the transfer of troops from the Eastern Front had taken place, but had all been used up in the final do-or-die spring offensive. It was evident that Germany was going to lose the war, it was simply a matter of when.

The war continued on the Western Front and elsewhere, but eyes began to turn towards armistice, and the fights that then would need to be waged. Peace may have been coming, but new battles just about to start.

13

PEACE COMES BUT NEW BATTLES BEGIN

The war was nearing its end – its outcome inevitable – but the date of victory was still far harder to predict, and still seemingly a long way off. Summer 1918 saw the Allies launch a counter-offensive, and by October they had broken through in many areas. Then by November, with now battle-hardened American troops joining the field, France was almost entirely liberated. The end was nearing for Germany, as its allies deserted it and dissension and discord broke out at home.

Although their army continued fighting on the battle fronts, mutiny was breaking out as the state imploded. Defeat was inevitable, with civil unrest the alternative to surrender. Peace overtures were accordingly made and the Kaiser abdicated – going into exile, believing that his removal would assist in the peace process. And so, finally, on 11 November an armistice was signed as both military defeat and the collapse of civil society beckoned. Guns fell silent and peace finally reigned on the Western Front, where war had been waged for over four years and hundreds of thousands had died on all sides, and countless thousands lay buried across a very shallow battlefront.

The announcement of peace was met more with a sense of relief for an end to the horror than an outpouring of joy at victory achieved. This was perfectly understandable given the sacrifices made and the losses sustained. In many nations, hardly a community remained untouched, and in Glasgow and the west of Scotland there was hardly a household that had not suffered loss directly with the loss of a husband, son or father or through the death of family or friend. Thus, whilst the defeat of Germany was welcomed, it was muted by an appreciation of the enormous loss that had been endured, and the difficulties still to be faced. The *Glasgow Herald*'s comments were of biblical proportion when reporting the news the following day: 'Never in all reverence be it said, could the message of Calvary be apprehended with greater vividness than now when, grieving for the sacrifice, but rejoicing in the hope of the resurrection, the nations acclaim the conquest of the powers of darkness.'

Soldiers and civilians alike grieved for fallen comrades, sons and husbands, whilst all began to wonder what lay in store, when they returned home and life began of new. Meanwhile, in communities where conditions had worsened with rationing and poor housing and in factories where work had been plentiful, fears began to grow about the price to be paid for peace finally coming. Overcrowding and poor housing remained endemic and memories of worklessness and hunger haunted many. There was a deep desire to get loved ones home after what had often been a long parting, with danger for the soldiers and stress for all. Yet, it was tinged by not just nagging worries, but growing concern that their return would exacerbate existing problems or could even result in worsening conditions. A loving embrace on return from war could herald increased hardship for all, as peace brought new battles and probably worsening social conditions. Mixed emotions indeed, as there was a price to be paid for peace just as there had been a cost to war.

So, minds were already turning to the new battles to be fought, when rent restrictions would end and demobbed soldiers would return to their former place of employment or seek new work. In Glasgow, where so many jobs had been in munitions or military supplies, with peace reigning, there was understandable concern about where new orders would come from to replace military requirements.

As the new era of peace dawned, fresh challenges soon began, and first to be faced was an election in December 1918. Called by Lloyd George on 14 November just three days after the guns fell silent, it was the first general election since 1910. Parliament was to dissolve on 25 November with voting on 14 December, though counting and the declaration of the results would not begin until 28 December. Although an election had been anticipated after the cessation of the war and was required by law, its announcement still caught many off guard. Which was understandable, perhaps, given the focus on the war and the speed of the German collapse.

It was also a time of transition for politics in Britain and in Ireland. In the latter, Sinn Féin were challenging the Irish Parliamentary Party for the nationalist vote, as the reverberations from the Easter Rising continued to echo. Likewise, in Britain the war and the sheer length of time since the last election meant that old orders were fraying and new alliances had been forged. Labour voted shortly after the armistice to leave the coalition, though some would refuse to leave office or cease to support it. George Barnes, the Glasgow MP who had replaced Arthur Henderson in the Cabinet the year before, along with a handful of colleagues declined to resign and were expelled from the party.

The Liberals had already split when Lloyd George replaced Asquith as Prime Minister in 1916, and that divide was widened across the country with the election, when Lloyd George chose to run on a coalition platform continuing the wartime arrangement with the Tories. As with the coalition government, the new electoral platform would be dominated by the Tories, albeit under the leadership of Lloyd George. The Liberal Party under Asquith formally rejected the alliance, but many MPs and others chose to follow their Prime Minister and stand as National Liberals, and the party split irrevocably. A handful of Labour MPs including George Barnes in the Gorbals sought election as 'Coalition Labour', but overall Labour remained united. It was nicknamed the 'coupon election' as coalition coupons were given to candidates who were approved both by Lloyd George and the Tory leader Andrew Bonar Law.

The election offered hope for Labour and the wider socialist movement for several reasons. Firstly, there was the significantly extended franchise now available to men aged over twenty-one, which for the first time ever would allow the overwhelming majority of working-class males to vote. The ballot for women was less extensive, being restricted to those over thirty and who either had property or those whose husbands did, but it was still progress and provided grounds for optimism.

Secondly, those changes to the franchise were aided by the political circumstances at the time. In Parliament and in the country the profile of Labour had increased, as had the growth of trade union membership. The war years had seen the Labour Party go from being a fringe movement to a major political party, and even though industrial militancy had been defeated, there was a growing politicisation in many factories and workplaces. Trade union organisation had both increased and improved over the period.

Thirdly, Labour was broadly united and peace brought the divide over the war to a close, unlike with the Liberals, for whom division was exacerbated. The rift that had seen Ramsay MacDonald resign as leader in 1914 was all in the past. It even seemed that the public mood towards the war had changed, with hostility towards those opposing it apparently a thing of the past.

Finally, for some, it was also a continuation of the long and historical march to victory that had been interrupted, but not ended, by the conflict. The Bolshevik Revolution and the ongoing political turmoil in Europe were indicative for them of worldwide social transformation. The working class had mobilised in Russia, and so this could be emulated anywhere – especially in a well-developed industrial economy facing difficult social conditions like Clydeside. So, hopes were high.

However, there had been no election for eight years and society had changed markedly in that time. How that would impact on politics was unknown, as there were neither opinion polls nor any other way of discovering the mood of the country. Focus groups were unheard of and even basic political tools like canvassing had not been developed. All parties were, in many ways, entering into the contest blind and with their hopes based on anecdotal evidence or perceptions as they saw them.

So, although there were understandable reasons for the hopes and optimism on the left, there were also warning signs and major issues to overcome. Firstly, and perhaps most importantly, there was simply the compilation of the extended electoral register and the arrangements for voting. It would have been no easy task anyway, but it appears to have been compounded by considerable bureaucratic failings. Many returning soldiers and sailors found themselves excluded from it. Similarly, when it came to conducting the ballot for soldiers serving abroad or stationed in camps even where they were registered to vote, there were failures in the arrangements to allow for it.

Politically, peace, as with war, brought issues for the socialist movement. There was the political hangover from the position many especially in Glasgow had taken of being opposed to the conflict. Many voters welcomed peace, but were to remain just as sceptical, if not scathing, of those who had opposed the war as they had been during it. Attacks by the opposition and the press on the former pacifist line of many candidates would become relentless and often vitriolic. They were to hit home politically, and hurt electorally.

Likewise, as peace negotiations prepared to commence, many of the public wished to eschew any magnanimity or forgiveness in victory. They held Germany culpable for the war and wished to punish them for it – and their suffering (as they saw it). Demands for war compensation and actions against Germans ran high, as did feelings against them, which meant making Germany pay for the war became politically popular. On that issue, Labour and the left were again to be portrayed as weak and vacillating, whilst coalition candidates were strenuous in making demands that Germany should be held to account and that action should be taken against foreigners in the UK. All of this was dutifully echoed in reporting by the press, who were as hostile to the left in peace as they had been during the war. Calls for reparations were numerous in the papers, as were denunciations of those who wouldn't demand them.

The speed at which the election had been called also caught parties off balance, even though an early post-war election was a statutory requirement and must, therefore, have been known about. However, the speed of the announcement was as sudden as the German collapse. Whilst political campaigning had been ongoing during the war and preparations, such as the selection of candidates, had been happening, the announcement still caught many off guard. Labour and the left's funds were limited and their resources constrained, and so the short election period limited their ability to mobilise.

Coalition candidates were accordingly better prepared and resourced in so many ways. The combined political strength of the Tories and the Lloyd George-led National Liberals was a significant power base, with many candidates having been elected members and thus already possessing an existing profile and established political base. Financially they had far greater backing across the country and possessed widespread support in the press both nationally and locally. For Labour candidates there was the additional challenge that, as well as the formal coalition, there was also often widescale cooperation between the coalition and the Liberals to ensure only one candidate ran against the left.

Additionally, as in all elections, the incumbent government had not only the opportunity, but the resources to dispense largesse. Lloyd George's administration was not just able to bask in the reflected glory of having won the war, but could also set the agenda for the new society to follow, now that peace had arrived. That involved both making Germany pay for the cost of the conflict and also providing for citizens at home. As ever, pork barrel politics was involved, and in early December the coalition announced a 20 per cent rise in war pensions, an opportune time for the granting of what was a significant benefit to many.

They were also able to set the agenda and others were required to follow or answer, most especially over the war, where feelings were raw and the calls for punishment of Germany were great. As peace talks prepared to commence, discussions on the latter became the major topic of political debate. The government had not just the power, but the publicity that the opposition lacked, and the coalition were therefore able to dominate the campaign by initiating proposals, where (crucially) their demand for sanctions against Germany resonated with many members of the public. That agenda also had the benefit of allowing them to portray Labour as weak on making the defeated pay for the war, just as they had been weak in their support of it.

Notwithstanding that, hopes were still high on the left within the city of Glasgow – despite signs of a growing electoral juggernaut in the form of the coalition. Though it would also be fair to say that optimism was also reflected in fears that existed within the establishment about success for the left. It wasn't just papers that were supportive, such as *Forward*, who were tipping widespread Labour success, but even those of the right such as the *Glasgow Herald* were acknowledging likely Labour gains. *Forward* 'thought that five Labour gains were likely and two (Govan and Shettleston) almost certain'.[56] The *Herald*, meanwhile, had thought 'Govan, Shettleston and Bridgeton were certain and Springburn and Partick likely labour gains'.[57] Success was also anticipated by many for David Kirkwood, who was standing in Dumbarton Burghs, as well as other candidates including Manny Shinwell in Linlithgowshire.

Expectations also rose, as did morale, when John Maclean was released in early December 1918, just six months into his sentence of five years' penal servitude. The campaign to free him had continued with regular marches and demonstrations against his continued

---

56   Iain McLean, op. cit., p. 154.
57   Iain McLean, op. cit., p. 154.

incarceration. However, it was more the fear of him dying in prison through continued ill health that resulted in his release, than the ongoing protests. For, though he had recuperated slightly after being freed in the summer of 1917, he was still frail when reimprisoned in April 1918. His frailty was then compounded by his paranoia over his food being poisoned, which affected him both physically and mentally. There appears to have been no basis to his fears, but the concern most certainly plagued him. He had requested that his food be provided from outside, to which prison authorities had agreed, but he then refused this too, worried that it also was poisoned. His mental concerns played on his physical health and vice versa, in what was, in any event, already a very tough regime.

From July 1918 he had been refusing food and was being force-fed, the effect of which was to worsen his already poor general health. He seemed to have visibly aged and he appeared haggard to those who met him, including his wife. Concerns for his welfare exacerbated the anger that already existed at his detention. Not just the left, but many liberal and concerned citizens were protesting by writing to the government and further major demonstrations were planned. The Scottish Office had been monitoring the situation closely, with regular briefings being provided by the prison authorities. A report was eventually submitted to the War Cabinet where agreement was reached to release him, ostensibly under a general amnesty for political prisoners.

There were, though, only two such prisoners held in Scotland, the other being a rather obscure shop steward, so it is clear that the basis for the release was concerns related to Maclean's health and possible death in custody. Only the Home Secretary demurred, suggesting his liberation might give succour to revolutionaries, but the rest of the Cabinet argued that it was indeed quite the opposite and that his death in custody would do so. In that, they were most certainly correct, as his death would have transformed him into a political martyr and, as it was, upon his release his decline in stature and change in attitude (being physically weak and emotionally volatile) were already clearly visible to colleagues.

Released from HMP Peterhead on Monday 2 December, he was met at the prison gates by his wife. She accompanied him to Aberdeen where they spent the night after being greeted by friends and supporters and holding a public meeting in the evening. The following day they departed by train for Glasgow. Arriving at Buchanan Street Station in the late afternoon, he was warmly greeted on the station platform by Maxton, Gallacher and Neil Maclean and given a tumultuous reception by a crowd of thousands who thronged into the concourse and surrounded the station.

Many had taken time off work to welcome their hero home. Placing him in a carriage, they paraded him through the city-centre streets with the crowd following singing 'The Red Flag', as Maclean himself waved a red flag from the back of the vehicle. Working its way slowly through the city, the procession was followed by an exuberant crowd, whilst others simply lined the streets to pay tribute. This was a remarkable contrast to Lloyd George's visit the year before, when a police and military escort was required, and was the sort of welcome only accorded to favourite sons – an indication of the widespread sympathy and support for him. Passing through George Square, the procession eventually reached Carlton Place on the other side of the Clyde where brief speeches were made. After that Maclean headed to his house in Shawlands, accompanied by his wife and some others who continued to march with him for the final homecoming.

Speaking to press at the time, he pronounced himself fit for the election challenge that lay in wait for him in the Gorbals, and indicated that he was aware that his release had come about through a Cabinet decision because of fears for his health. However, it soon became clear to those about him that he had been badly affected by his repeated incarceration. Deranged he wasn't, but damaged he certainly was. Speeches could be rambling and his behaviour towards friends even confrontational, meaning for many a marked decline in his oratory. The change in his temperament also caused ructions as he became more demanding and sometimes erratic. This would soon lead to a split from Gallacher and a growing marginalisation for Maclean in coming years, even if his name still resonated.

Firstly though, as with others, he had to deal with the coming election for which he had been selected as the Labour candidate for the Gorbals constituency. Originally it had been held by George Barnes, who had been expelled for remaining in Lloyd George's Cabinet and who would be running on a Coalition Labour ticket. Despite that, Maclean's selection was not backed by the Labour Party nationally and attempts were made to have him removed as candidate. The objections were not based on his continued membership of the BSP, which, at that time, was an affiliated organisation, but simply to him and the views he espoused, and there was considerable resentment from senior members and trade union leaders towards him. Though keen to oust Barnes, senior Labour and trade union leaders were equally reluctant to see him replaced by Maclean. As late as November when Maclean was still in prison, Gallacher and Kirkwood had met with Labour Party leaders in London to seek to have endorsement given, but it was rejected out of hand. However, despite (or even perhaps because of) that, Maclean was strongly supported within the Gorbals constituency party by ordinary members, and his nomination remained, with the local organisation rallying around his selection. He would run as the Labour candidate in the election, albeit without official endorsement.

That show of support and those celebrations could only have further boosted hopes of victory at the coming elections for many on the left. However, as in subsequent elections ever since, there is a considerable difference between hype and reality, never mind the danger of speaking to your own people and believing your own rhetoric. It might have been wiser to have heeded the counsel of Tom Johnston, who wrote following Maclean's imprisonment, 'Alas, the bulk of the workers do not want a

Social Revolution by any method, but go on rivet-hammering compe-
titions, and scrambling for overtime, and regard the John Maclean's as
"decent enough, but a bit off".[58]

Or, as was recognised by characters in the novel *No Mean City*, written about Glasgow at that time, where reference was made to him being
'a saint and a martyr', he was also deemed too unpractical for everyday
life.[59] And so it was to be that thousands might have met and marched,
but that many more workers, whilst sympathetic to Maclean or even
supportive of his wider actions, still failed to vote for him or the other
socialist candidates. He was only to be the first of many left-wing idols
to suffer the pain of electoral failure.

For the election was a crushing victory for the coalition, sweeping
away opposition from both Labour and Asquith's Liberals. Bonar Law's
Coalition Conservatives were returned as the largest party within the
coalition with 382 seats, whilst Lloyd George presided over a Coalition
Liberal group of 127 members. Some who supported the coalition,
many from Ulster, and George Barnes with a handful of others were
returned as Coalition Labour. All this provided not just a healthy majority, but a commanding presence that dominated Parliament.

Labour became the official opposition, but had returned only forty-
two MPs across the entire country and the non-coalition Liberals under
Asquith were reduced to just thirty-six. Senior opposition leaders also
fell before the coalition electoral tidal wave, with Ramsay MacDonald
and Philip Snowden for Labour losing their seats, as did Asquith the
Liberal leader and most of the senior anti-coalition Liberals. However,
in Ireland it was an entirely different electoral machine that swept to
power with Sinn Féin obliterating its opponents, taking seventy-three
seats. They would decline to take them, though, or even come to Westminster as they prepared to establish the Dáil Éireann as the Irish War
of Independence was about to break out.

---

58   Iain McLean, op. cit., p. 151.
59   Iain McLean, op. cit., p. 153.

In Britain, however, it was a crushing victory for coalition candidates as their political juggernaut rode roughshod over opponents even in Glasgow, where some success for Labour had been anticipated. As it was, the coalition won fourteen out of fifteen constituencies in the city, with only Govan being a Labour gain. There Neil Maclean was elected, polling almost 48 per cent of the vote and winning by a majority of 815 over a Coalition Unionist, though a Liberal also ran polling 1,678 votes, which may have played a part in his election. It is certainly arguable that the split vote between coalition and Liberal allowed Labour in. In Shettleston, where there had been high hopes for John Wheatley, he missed out on election by just seventy-four votes to another Coalition Unionist. There he only faced a Coalition Unionist with no third party or Liberal candidate in the fray, and it may well have been that had there been any other nominees, it would have allowed him in, as just as likely absence of one would have ensured Maclean's defeat in Govan.

In Bridgeton, Maxton was defeated by a Coalition Liberal polling nearly 40 per cent. A third, female candidate had stood there, a suffragette standing as an independent. However, she only polled 991 votes, whilst the majority was over 3,000. Although her intervention undoubtedly did not help, it certainly didn't result in Maxton losing the election. In the Gorbals, George Barnes standing as Coalition Labour comfortably held off the challenge from John Maclean by 65.7 per cent to 34.3 per cent. Maclean ran on a revolutionary manifesto, but it seems defeat was more due to the strength of the coalition ticket allied to Barnes retaining the support of many in the Irish community. Having been the sitting MP and earning a reputation as a hard-working representative, Barnes had ensured that he allied closely with the influence-makers in the constituency, which included the Catholic Church. The strength of the Coalition Coupon vote, though, was perhaps best shown in the Glasgow Central constituency where the Tory leader Andrew Bonar Law was returned, polling almost 80 per cent of the vote.

Across the rest of Scotland, it was much the same, with only six Labour candidates returned. William Adamson, who had been acting Labour leader since Henderson, had stepped down the year before retaining his West Fife constituency and another seat in Dundee was held by the sitting Labour MP, Alexander Wilkie. Gains were also made in South Ayrshire where, as in Govan, the failure of the right to have a single candidate allowed the Labour candidate to win; in Edinburgh Central Labour won by a very narrow margin; in Aberdeen North an unofficial Labour candidate also just sneaked home by a handful of votes and also in Hamilton, where the intervention of another left candidate didn't stop there being a victory by the official Labour candidate. However, David Kirkwood lost to a Coalition Liberal in Dumbarton Burghs and Manny Shinwell was defeated by a Coalition Conservative in Linlithgowshire, adding to the long list of heavyweight candidates unable to make any impression against the immovable coalition machine.

Another of those who had been at the centre of events in the city during the war to contest a seat was Arthur MacManus, though he fought Halifax on a Socialist Labour Party ticket where he was comprehensively crushed. He had been advised against it, and in many ways the SLP did not seek the parliamentary road, preferring industrial organisation. However, he was one of the early revolutionary candidates to stand in an election, perhaps more to fly the flag than realistically expecting election. Many more would follow in subsequent elections, but each would suffer the same ignominious defeat. Gallacher, though, was active in giving support to John Maclean – even giving up his job to campaign full time for him.

All in all, in Scotland as all across Britain, Labour, the ILP and the left were simply overrun by the coalition electoral machine. James Stewart, an ILP councillor who had contested the St Rollox constituency and been comfortably defeated by a Coalition Unionist, made clear to the press that the reasons for the defeat were war-related with the indemnity to be paid by Germany and the demand for the expulsion of aliens the main factors. On both those issues, he argued, he and other ILP candidates had been seen as weak or vacillating, and press hostility had been huge with corrosive criticism seeping through to the public. They had been castigated for their apparently lacklustre demands for punishment of the defeated, which mirrored their lukewarm commitment – or even sometimes outright opposition – to the war. Public perception of Labour was therefore of a party failing to hold those responsible for the war to account, just as they had failed to support it in the first place, and it hurt them electorally.

Poor organisation was also lamented, as well as a lack of funds to fuel the electoral machine. As the reviews and assessment were conducted it became clear that Labour and the ILP both needed to raise more funds, as well as improve their political campaigning. But turnout also played a part, with only 57 per cent being recorded nationally, whereas future elections would see well over 70 per cent participation on a regular basis. The national turnout was somewhat reduced by there being quite a few uncontested seats; evidence of Labour's organisational difficulties in some areas. However, it was also reflected locally where, for example, in Bridgeton the turnout was 52 per cent in 1918, but would rise to 77 per cent in 1922. In Shettleston, the situation was likewise, and turnout rocketed from 63 per cent to 84 per cent. That undoubtedly would have impacted on the left vote though, given the public mood, it may have made less impact than might have been anticipated. But in light of the general trend, without the bureaucratic failures in allowing for the extended franchise, then Wheatley in particular, and perhaps even Maxton, would most likely have been elected.

Though for his part, whilst Maxton expressed satisfaction with the result, it must still have been tinged with some sadness at both his own and colleagues' failure to break through when there had been that mood of optimism. As in every election, defeat can be far harder to take when victory is anticipated or seems within grasp. However, though there was some despondency it was no doubt lessened by it being seen as a failure to break through, as opposed to an electoral reversal. In any event, seats had still been won across the country and the role of major opposition party secured. The coalition may have dominated the House of Commons, but the profile and effect of supplanting the Liberals as the principal opposition would have immediate benefits for Labour and the ILP. All of that helped cold analysis assuage the disappointment.

In Glasgow, Govan was a gain, even if the Gorbals remained as Coalition Labour. As the analysis from James Stewart and others showed, they reflected on their own failings and appreciated that other factors had played a significant part – from press to turnout – and realised that progress had been made, even if the results didn't reflect it. As with future electoral breakthroughs for many parties, it would take more than one election to achieve success, but the basis for it was laid.

In any event, there wasn't time for too much self-absorption or despondency, for the election would soon be overshadowed by a strike, and the battleground moved once again from the political campaign back to the industrial front, as the strike for a forty-hour week commenced.

14

THE FORTY-HOUR
WEEK STRIKE

Both the STUC and Labour Party had come out in support of a forty-hour week as the end of the war approached. However, the situation was complicated by the multiplicity of organisations involved and by changes that were already being implemented for a reduction in hours across some industries. Rather than there being any coordinated single discussion between trade unions and employers, it was left to individual unions and sectoral federations. Some deals had already been struck, and other negotiations were ongoing for changes to working hours though not to that extent. It resulted in a significant divide within the trade union movement and also in some instances between union leaderships and their members. That resulted in the miners for example continuing their own negotiations rather than joining in demands for the forty-hour week and in the west of Scotland the CWC having solid support amongst the engineering sector whilst many other industries didn't become involved.

In some ways the strike came about more by accident than design with those seeking it as surprised at their success as those opposing it were astounded that it had happened. Neither those desiring it nor indeed those against it had prepared for what happened or were ready for the consequences that then followed. Fervour and hope allied to opportunity swept aside doubts over both practicalities and readiness.

As with some future strikes, circumstances allowed for a small group determined to take industrial action to dictate the agenda and rhetoric overcame reality. Those involved and certainly in the vanguard of the dispute became caught up in the fervour of the situation without much consideration of the reality on the ground.

Political and trade union agitation for a reduction in hours had been almost universal and there was widespread support from the STUC, Labour Party and the trades councils. Forty hours had been called for by some and thirty hours by others in the CWC. Meanwhile union leaders were negotiating for a variety of different hours, from forty-seven to other amounts of hours depending on the sector. The momentum was therefore all for change, but given the complexity of the political and trade union landscape meetings were taking place where decisions were being taken that often conflicted with others.

Moreover, whilst negotiations were going on at union executive level with employers' representatives, shop stewards were agitating and militant in other areas. Threats of industrial action were discussed, but still seemed distant as discussions were ongoing within the labyrinthic structure. In any event, union leaders and political leaders were similarly opposed and neither anticipated any precipitate call to action.

That hiatus was compounded by circumstances in the engineering sector where a 47-hour week had been agreed between unions and employers' federations. However, the outcome for many was increased hours in the morning without a break as they worked from 7:30 a.m. until 12 p.m. before stopping. Previously, though starting earlier, they had a short breakfast break before continuing on again until lunch. Though welcoming the reduced hours, the additional period between breaks caused anger, not just with militants, but across much of the wider workforce, and especially in Glasgow. This resulted in a demand for yet shorter hours than those being proposed and led to the union leadership's recommendation to accept the offer, which, whilst being comfortably approved across the country in a national ballot, was rejected in the west of Scotland. Calls for action there were always going to find a more receptive audience.

Meanwhile, though, others demanded militant action for political reasons, and were eager to deliver it – and soon. The forty-hour week became the focus for the CWC, backing away from original demands for a thirty-hour week. Though John Maclean counselled that they should await the miners, who were negotiating their own deal on hours, but where there was the possibility they might strike if terms weren't agreed. However, as happened elsewhere, unplanned events occurred that created their own momentum.

On 18 January a meeting took place in Glasgow, ostensibly for shop stewards from all across the country but, in reality, attended mostly by engineers on Clydeside. Over 500 attended in total, but the representation was sparse from elsewhere and it was heavily skewed towards the CWC. That was perhaps understandable given the time of year, the distance people involved had to travel and also the fact that many seemed oblivious to the actions that were about to unfold, with neither immediate danger nor opportunity anticipated. Though the meeting had been called the week before by stewards and political activists with the remit of electing a committee and organising a strike, it must have seemed unlikely or at least not imminent to many. After all, these meetings were by the stewards and trade councils, not through the union leaderships, and whilst a strike was talked about many must thought it simply rhetoric that was unlikely to become reality.

As it was, the meeting took place and a strike committee was elected and, given the views of those attending, it was dominated by those demanding immediate strike action. Needless to say Gallacher was elected chair. Later that evening the strike committee met for the first time and voted for industrial action in support of a forty-hour week and for it to commence on Monday 27 January. Previous meetings had heard similar demands, but they had invariably been rejected. It seems that this was more a case of simply seizing the opportunity when it arose. Those demanding action almost certainly hadn't expected it as there were no preparations laid for such an immediate event. Nor had those who might not have been sympathetic anticipated the events now unfolding as, in all likelihood, they would have expressed caution. Likewise, not just trade union leaders, but Labour Party and STUC officials were also blind-sided by it, finding themselves with a strike that they hadn't called or prepared for and many didn't support. But, a strike there was now going to be.

At union leadership level the position was clearer. The ASE remained implacably opposed to a strike; the Dockers' Union initially agreed to it, but then withdrew to pursue their own 44-hour week negotiations and only the Electricians' Union supported it. The miners were pursuing their own 30-hour week campaign and viewed this as a deflection from their agenda and declined to become involved, though some local areas would later participate.

It also caused some consternation and confusion amongst the political leadership of the STUC and the Labour Party. They seemed at a loss to know what to do about it. Initially, there seemed to be almost an air of unreality about it with much press criticism and even some speculation as to whether it would actually proceed at all. That was presumably a view shared by many senior trade union and labour figures, but the CWC was now again in command.

Trade unions had lost control of the situation by this point, and some local officials appeared genuinely shocked at what had come about. But events had overtaken central control and the strike committee were now in charge and determined to proceed. They set to with a will, though that was indicative of the lack of preparation that had taken place beforehand and perhaps confirmation that, in many ways, the motion had been made more in hope than expectation. As the strike was unofficial, there would be no strike pay forthcoming and given that it hadn't been anticipated (as such), neither had funds been ingathered nor steps taken to seek financial backing. Those participating had also not had a chance to prepare by making savings or seeking support. The CWC had funds through its levies and would gather donations in the days to follow, but no financial preparation to support those striking had been made. Again, suggestive of the lack of planning with the actions occurring more by accident than design. But the die was cast and there were those who had been only too happy to roll it. The strike was proceeding irrespective of others' views or actions, and without ensuring widespread support.

Still somewhat bruised from the election, the ILP hadn't been involved in the calling of it, even though Kirkwood and a few others were prominent in the CWC. But, once it was called they were to be active in support of it. After all, it was a rallying for the cause and whether they had been involved in the planning of it or had time to reflect upon its wisdom, in many ways didn't matter. Stand with the strikers, the ILP leadership would.

As McKinlay and Morris perceptively note in *The ILP on Clydeside, 1893–1932*,

> The ILP leadership made it clear that their endorsement of the strike as a legitimate political act was not a reversal of their long-held belief in the separate spheres of economic and political mobilisation. To the contrary, the prime political use of industrial action was to check the excesses of particular governments, not to challenge the authority of parliament in principle. In this respect, industrial action was an extension of the rent strike, a desperate tactic of civil disobedience, a demonstration of Labour's political weakness rather than its industrial strength.[60]

John Maclean, who had thought it a tactical error to strike without the support of the miners, had sought to intercede to try to establish

---

60   Alan McKinlay and R. J. Morris, op. cit., p. 146.

unity, but it was too late and to no avail. Again, in spite of reservations, standing idly by was never an option and full support was given.

However, even if the political leaders were united, that did not mean that the labour movement or even all the workers would be fully supportive. Though it was meant to be a general strike across all sectors (and that was the desire of the engineering shop stewards and some others), it was far from a universal view and not simply one held amongst union leaderships, but across workforces. This wasn't just going to be primarily a strike in Glasgow and parts of the west of Scotland, but one that would be heavily concentrated in the engineering works and shipyards on the Clyde.

Dockers in Glasgow had voted against strike action and the bakers were likewise, even if sympathetic. Whilst at local level some other craft unions intimated support, other major unions such as the Municipal Employees' Association hadn't agreed to it and were unlikely to ever support it. Many workers themselves would also see it as a strike by the craft unions in those sectors and neither by them or for them, which would ultimately limit the action that was ultimately taken. They had their own hours to negotiate and battles to fight.

The lack of unity and limited support in Scotland was replicated across the country despite a call for revolutionary action being made by groups and militants. In many English cities, and in particular London and the north, attempts were made to bring workers out on strike despite the ongoing negotiations. Merseyside saw industrial action as did some Midland cities. Tube and transport workers struck in London, where the electricians were also involved in a dispute, and DORA was invoked there. Those disputes were significant and caused great concern for the government, and other English cities also saw industrial action, but still there was no general strike.

In London, where major challenges were being faced, the disputes were led by trade unions and negotiations were taking place with government and employers' federations. Negotiations with the miners were still ongoing at a national level and the government were striving to avoid any coordinated action by the triple alliance of miners, rail and transport workers that would have been the major threat. Those disputes lacked the co-coordination that had come about in Glasgow, and more importantly the same wider and political nature. So, whilst the alliance caused the government huge concern, the situation was being monitored and discussions were taking place.

Only in Glasgow and Belfast had the situation seemingly got out of control, and this was because the leadership in the dispute was at a local and far more revolutionary level. In Belfast, where 100,000 would soon come out to see the city grind to a halt, delegations from the Clyde, including Gallacher, had gone to visit and this continued during the strike. Likewise, attempts were made to link with kindred spirits south of the border but to little avail.

Neither the mood nor leadership existed in most other places to replicate what was happening on the Clyde. Edinburgh and Leith, in particular, initially had seen strike action taken and other areas, including Aberdeen, had seen a very limited involvement. Miners in Lanarkshire also joined in the strike despite the directions of their union leaders, throwing their weight behind the CWC. This saw confrontations between members and officials in Hamilton, but they too would ultimately return to work. London also saw settlements achieved and work resume.

Belfast would continue on after Glasgow and it came at a time when the labour movement was still managing to work around the sectarian divide. That would soon end, as the war of independence was about to break out and the sectarian virus would be injected into the city and its labour movement. And so, Belfast and Glasgow were largely on their own, and in many ways isolated from each other despite delegations crossing the North Channel. Despite all of this, the size and scale of the engineering and shipyard sectors and the importance of craft unions was still massive. Accordingly, a mighty struggle was about to commence in Glasgow.

This was the opportunity that some had been waiting on, and their chance to do what others were doing elsewhere – whether in Russia or beyond. The general election may have been a disappointment for some or a sideshow for others, but this was their chance to confront the government with industrial muscle, and for a few, was even a potentially revolutionary moment. It was, after all, part of their ideology to deliver socialist change through workplace organisation as well as to mobilise workers for political action. Gallacher was excited by it and, having given up his job to assist John Maclean in his Gorbals campaign, he was able to dedicate his full commitment to the strike. The ILP in Glasgow also rallied to the cause.

The committee and countless others set to with zeal. Posters and handbills were quickly printed and shop stewards briefed to ensure that their factory or yard would come out on strike that following Monday. Those involved in organising were energised by what was happening, and their enthusiasm was infectious across a far wider membership and support base. The network that had been created by the CWC swung into action. It may have been short notice, but the chain of command was short and lines of communication existed from the wartime period and, accordingly, those sectors operated with almost military efficiency. Whether through the experience of the previous years or the desire to deliver this time, the outcome was remarkably effective in the areas where organisation was strong.

Estimates of numbers vary from a more disparaging 30,000 to 35,000 put about by some of the established press, to higher numbers of 40,000 on the Monday rising to 70,000 the following day as the momentum began to grow and was claimed by the shop stewards. It is likely that the numbers were towards the higher side, as the effect on the major factories and yards was both immediate and considerable. Gallacher recalls that a mass meeting was called for the Monday morning at the St Andrew's Halls. Thousands turned out and many more were unable to gain access but simply stood about outside. Confidence was high and he recalled that 'fiery speeches were made and cheered to the echo inside and outside the hall'.[61] Thereafter a resolution was passed unanimously stating that there would be no resumption of work until the demand for a forty-hour week with no reduction in pay was conceded.

Thereafter the strikers lined up outside the St Andrew's Halls and marched through the streets of Glasgow to George Square where Gallacher and others addressed the crowd. It wasn't just strikers who had gathered, but many other supporters. Mrs Reid, the lady who had provided the red flag that was unfurled when Lloyd George had visited the city in June 1917, was also present once again with her huge standard. This was passed about the crowd before being hoisted up the municipal flag pole standing in front of the City Chambers, resulting in jubilation amongst those gathered with 'The Red Flag' being sung – not just flown.

It was a moment of celebration and revelry, but in some ways it also sent shock waves across the country. Pictures appeared in papers and news reports abounded. Glasgow seemed to be in quite some turmoil, just as other cities were around Europe. As Gallacher recalled, 'From Glasgow to London messages were flashing, suggesting possible happenings of all kinds. Red Flag hoisted on municipal flag-staff – what did it mean? Would we follow up with other action? This question was obviously agitating the minds of many people.'[62] The actions in Glasgow would not be without consequences as the authorities in London and elsewhere took note. In the interim, though, morale was high and the mood buoyant amongst the strikers.

As had happened elsewhere, the enthusiasm of those involved seemed to generate momentum. This feeling soon spread not only to those who converted to the cause willingly, but also to those who were persuaded, cajoled or even threatened to join. Stewards and strikers mobilised in what, in many ways, was the precursor to the flying pickets that would become infamous later in the century, especially with the miners' strike.

61   William Gallacher, op. cit., p. 219.
62   William Gallacher, op. cit., p. 220.

Picketing had previously taken place at especially large factories and at mines such as in the pre-war disputes, and this was a normal way then to conduct a strike, but this was perhaps its first major use on such a large scale. Groups sometimes in their hundreds went from yard to yard calling on the workforce to down tools and join them or not enter the workplace. Many did join, and accordingly numbers swelled and increased, often rolling in some areas from site to site. The concentration of factories made this easy, and a strike in one site often had an immediate knock-on effect on a neighbouring factory. Ironically, the very same proximity that had been useful for employers in production of goods was now equally helpful to strikers in organising direct action.

Most major shipyards and engineering works in the city were affected. They provided the core support for the actions and work there had soon ground to a standstill, which had perhaps been expected. However, there was growing anxiety about the power stations and the energy supply to the community. Port Dundas Power Station had come out on strike, but an undertaking had been given by the strike coordinators to continue to ensure supplies for public works and hospitals. A demand had been made to have the tramcars off the road within a week, and on the Wednesday a mass demonstration took place at the Pinkston Power Station from where there was then a march to George Square. There a huge crowd gathered and a delegation of strike leaders led by Shinwell went in to ask the Lord Provost to communicate with the government on their behalf. He agreed to do so and asked the deputation to return on the Friday, by which time he believed that he would have obtained a response. It was agreed that there would be another march and rally on that Friday, 31 January, to both hear the response and again demonstrate the strength of the strike.

The Municipal Employees' Association, meanwhile, had met and decided to ballot its members, who included tram workers. So far only workers at the Coplawhill works in the south side of the city, which dealt with repairs and maintenance, had become involved, but that didn't interfere with the running of the service. But its operation, however, was still a sore point for those already out on strike and their continued presence was causing concern on both sides. They were the life blood of the city, keeping it moving for those remaining in work and seen as vital by those opposed to the strike. If they went off then the disruption increased massively and the threat became even greater. Yet, their continued running was equally seen as a visible display of contempt by those agitating for a cessation of work. Confrontation was looming.

The concentration of the dispute within engineering and craft unions was causing frustration and anger amongst strikers and supporters. Demands for others and, in particular, municipal workers to join them and to shut down the tram system were being made. The regular meetings of those involved would have been a key factor in fuelling the agitation, as people supported each other and berated those who weren't with them. Though not yet bitterness, discussions most certainly would have been causing rancour as demonstrations took place in George Square but trams sidled by. Coming out on strike is never easy at any time or in any society, and was certainly hard in Glasgow in 1919 given low incomes and the housing market, to name but two ever-present hardships. Savings were limited, or non-existent for most, and the threat of eviction hung over many if rent arrears were accrued despite the success of the rent strikes.

People were paid weekly in those days, and the knowledge there would be no pay packet later that week would have caused concern at home, as well as with the usual breadwinners. It was also winter and heating a home cost money (especially without modern-day insulation techniques), meaning the absence of cash to pay for coal would also have been in the minds of many families. The strike had come about without any opportunity to set money aside and, with no official support from the trade union leaderships, there were limited funds – if any – to support those involved. Some were caught up in the political maelstrom of the time; seeing the opportunity for revolutionary change. Many more would have realised that there was a real cost to be paid in the current world in which they lived. It would be up to the individual to cope, and whilst the mood was determined, there must also have been a realisation that it couldn't last long, and time was therefore of the essence. Getting others out on strike was vital; and winning it quickly essential. Time and tempers were therefore growing short.

But anger and concern weren't just felt by the strikers and their supporters, but also by those either opposed to them or just concerned at what their actions might lead to. As Gallacher had correctly noted, the pictures and reports of the red flag being unveiled had sent tremors southwards to many areas of the establishment and the authorities. Those who had been outmanoeuvred or not involved began to realise the seriousness of the situation, and began to take action accordingly. The demonstration may have been a moment of celebration, but it was also to be the wake-up call for reaction.

The trade unions, side-lined by how the strike had come about (never mind by the leadership of the CWC in the city), were quickly taking steps to get organised and try to exercise some control. That was harder in Glasgow, where they had long since ceded influence to the CWC – especially in the shipyard and engineering sectors – though some steps could still be taken and ASE executives suspended their Glasgow district secretary, Harry Hopkins, for his participation in the strike committee. That was the immediate action in Glasgow in those craft areas as London sought to stop the situation escalating or being supported elsewhere. Meanwhile, other unions in different sectors sought to avoid their workforce coming out on strike or even showing solidarity.

Whilst for many of the craft unions there was a limit to what they could do at that time (other than punish those over whom they had some control), it was therefore elsewhere where their real efforts were made to rein in any solidarity or similar action. However, even in the major engineering and shipyard communities in England and Wales, little sympathy or support was forthcoming. Some of this was no doubt down to action by the union leadership, though it is also no doubt the case that many workers in other communities were either just not keen on striking or unwilling or not interested in becoming involved in a wider political struggle. Glasgow would therefore be fighting this battle mainly on its own.

But it was also the authorities, and not just in Glasgow itself, who were taking note as the red flag was unfurled and revolution called for. The War Cabinet had been keeping a watchful eye on the city, with regular briefings from political, legal and military figures. It was chaired by Prime Minister Lloyd George; it included Bonar Law, the Conservative leader and local MP, who was Lord Privy Seal and had, until a few weeks before, been Chancellor of the Exchequer. Other members included Winston Churchill, who was Secretary of State for War, and Robert Munro, who was the Secretary of State for Scotland, and a Liberal who sat for Roxburgh & Selkirk. The Lord Advocate (Scotland's most senior law officer), James Avon Clyde, who was the Coalition Unionist MP for Edinburgh North, was also a member. Reflecting the nature of a wartime Cabinet, Sir William Robertson, the military commander of Home Forces, was also in attendance.

They met on the afternoon of 30 January, days after the unfurling of Mrs Reid's red standard in George Square and on the eve of the next major demonstration. A report had been given on the situation as it was seen then, and it was clear that concern was growing about the effects of the strike and any escalation of it. With further strike ballots ongoing and as rolling mass picketing proved successful, anxieties increased and thoughts turned to preventative actions. According to the Cabinet minutes, Bonar Law

> thought it vital for the War Cabinet to be satisfied that there was a
> sufficient force in Glasgow to prevent disorder and protect those vol-
> unteers or others who could be made available to take the operation

of the generating stations and municipal services. It was certain that if the movement in Glasgow grew, it would spread all over the country.[63]

A discussion took place about the situation and the resources that the authorities had to meet the growing unrest. It was admitted that police ranks were reduced due to wartime service. Consideration was given to the mobilisation of special constables, who were warranted officers, but who were not full time and only served when required. It was thought there were 2,000 in Glasgow, but numbers might vary due to the wartime situation. Readying the special constabulary, though, was felt essential, and police and police horses were also mobilised and drafted into the city centre.

General Sir William Robertson provided a résumé of the military situation in Scotland. He stated that General McCracken was the commanding officer in charge in Scotland and pointed out that the military were subject to civilian authority and that they would need to be formally requested. It was also made clear that this wouldn't apply if martial law was declared. That was a different situation entirely and the military became the commanding power.

He then went on to outline the military strength in Scotland at that time, explaining that there were nineteen battalions present, all bar one of which were Scottish troops. One of the battalions was in Glasgow and twelve were in Edinburgh, with others at barracks elsewhere. There had obviously been prior consideration given to the use of Scottish troops within their own country and the potential consequences of it, namely the potential for mutiny and refusal to follow orders if conflict arose. This was understandable not just given the situation in Ireland and elsewhere in Europe, but given there had also been ructions and demonstrations from serving conscripted soldiers eager to be

---

63   War Cabinet papers, 8 January 1919 to 31 March 1919, pp. 514–52.

demobilised. Equally, there had been thought given to the alternative scenario of bringing soldiers north from England, where again, there could be issues with them being portrayed as an army of occupation and anger likely to flow from it. However, on balance, the War Cabinet came down on the side of using local troops, with Sir William Robertson adding that whilst there were 'certain disadvantages to using Scottish troops', it was, on the whole, 'safer than importing English Battalions.'

Churchill, though, was not one for overreacting and indicated that they had been through it all before. In this, he was no doubt referring to Ireland as well as to other industrial disputes, although this was on a larger scale than previous industrial unrest. He pointed out that the Defence of the Realm Act that had been brought in at the start of the war was still in force. Several of the leaders on the Clyde had already been incarcerated under it during the war and its powers were both wide-ranging and draconian. Whilst this seemed sufficient for him, clearly continued monitoring would be required.

Sir Robert Horne, who was the Minister of Labour and also the Unionist MP for Glasgow Hillhead, stated that 'if there was any possibility of seizing the leaders they should do so', going on to add that they were 'well-known extremists'. The Lord Advocate agreed to consider this and to see what might be also possible in terms of preventative actions against the strike leaders. After all, both arrest and deportation had been used a few years earlier with considerable effect.

Preparations for the strike were being made and further opposition to it being planned and not just by the War Cabinet, but within the city itself. Active support was being provided to those who wished to continue at work or to return to work having allegedly been brought out under duress or through intimidation. Some ex-servicemen's groups were whipped up to express their concern, and even to hold meetings and demonstrate against the strike, similar to actions they had taken against anti-war protestors. At a meeting just the night before,

Major V. L. Henderson, the Coalition Unionist MP for Glasgow Trade-ston, had stated that the strikers should go away and join the army, caustically suggesting that they hadn't stopped them winning the war or the election. Again evidence that many of the leading politicians from the establishment were eager that far more vigorous action be taken to defeat, if not crush, the strike. Those sentiments were echoed in *The Scotsman*'s editorial on 31 January, which stated that if 'workers [are] anxious for a fight to the finish, they should be given their desire'. Sadly, this was partly to be realised.

So, whilst support for the strike was growing, bitterness against it and opposition to it was equally rising. The mood began to change as the week progressed. The stakes for both sides were becoming much higher and the risks far greater for all. There had been some evidence of the tension that was increasing when, on Wednesday 29 January, a young striking apprentice had appeared in court charged with assault-ing a tramcar worker. As the vehicle had turned into St Enoch Square some demonstrators had jumped in front of it and the young man had assaulted the female operator in the mêlée that followed. He was fined for his actions, but it showed the pressures that were increasing across the city and it would only portend what was to come on Bloody Friday.

15

BLOODY FRIDAY

As 31 January dawned, tension hung in the damp city air. Demonstrators were gathering that Friday in George Square, as they had other days that week. George Square stands in the centre of Glasgow with the grand and impressive City Chambers taking up its entire east side, reflecting the wealth that had been accumulated as the second city of the empire.

Other important buildings surrounded the Square, from the Post Office on its south side to a station and large hotel on its north, with major offices sited to the west. Streets ran along its edges between the offices and buildings radiated off from it. Within it stood gardens and statues, the one of Gladstone a regular hang-out for speakers with its plinth providing a makeshift platform. It is much the same today, though the nature of the offices or buildings has changed, but now as then it lay at the very heart of the city.

Protestors were due to gather to listen to strike leaders about the latest news and, more importantly, to hear from the Lord Provost about his attempts to communicate with the government. The mood was convivial, even if determined, as meeting there was an opportunity to find out what was happening from strike leaders, as well as to meet with friends and comrades. This was long before the age of mass communication technologies, and meetings and leaflets were vital for garnering information. In addition, the press was almost uniformly hostile to their efforts, and to counter that the strike committee had their own regular bulletin available for those involved or supportive of their cause. It was being distributed along with other pamphlets and papers from numerous socialist groups.

Some suggested the crowd may have been as large as 60,000, others even suggested that figure was higher still, though no precise tally was ever taken. Most likely, it was somewhere between 20,000 and 40,000 and all agree that it was at least in that range. Significantly, however, it was growing by the minute as people were arriving to meet and await news from both their strike leaders and the Lord Provost.

People were coming by tramcars; many more on foot. Everyone dressed for the weather, wrapping up warmly with coats and jackets, many donning the flat caps worn by working men and with scarves wrapped around their necks. It wasn't just men, but women and children who were present. A few directly through being on strike, many more simply accompanying husbands and fathers, or supporting the industrial action and wider cause. They were equally dressed for the weather with coats, shawls and hats, as it was a cold day with light winds and mist expected. Adding to the crowds were office workers and members of the public simply going about their business, with it being a busy location for offices and other public buildings.

Compounding all that was the presence of 140 police officers lined up in two rows in front of the City Chambers. They were armed with batons and were mostly facing the backs of demonstrators who were listening to speakers or otherwise engaging in events in the Square. Police horses were also located at the back of the City Chambers, along with other officers, on hand and ready for any increased threat to civil order.

With trams passing and other vehicles moving on the road between the Square and the city buildings, space was limited as the area became congested. Tempers were growing short, and both police and strikers were on edge. Willie Gallacher arrived and prepared to speak at the Gladstone statue as others did on such occasions, given its central location and makeshift platform. There he was flanked by a few trusted comrades and others quickly began to crowd around to listen to him. Elsewhere, others were standing talking to old friends or discussing the situation with colleagues, but soon began to edge closer to where the speaker was located. Meanwhile, papers continued to be sold and other materials given to strikers and supporters, much as they had been all week.

Though they were about to listen to Gallacher, the principal reason for their attendance was to hear from the Lord Provost about his request to the government for them to intercede in the strike after he had been approached by the strike leaders on the Wednesday. This plan of action had been initiated by Shinwell at the conclusion of the demonstration without, it appears, prior discussion with Gallacher or others, who were considerably more sceptical about its merits.

However, the Lord Provost had agreed to communicate with the government – though had been heavily criticised for doing so by others, including the press, who perceived him as giving succour to a strike they vehemently opposed. The *Glasgow Herald* was stinging in its rebuke of him deigning to contact Bonar Law, the leader of the Conservative Party and the Lord Privy Seal, who was also the MP for Glasgow Central. To them it gave sustenance to the strikers, as well as placing the government in the spotlight when they sought to leave it as a dispute between the official trade union leaders and employers' representatives. Though it appears that the Lord Provost did little more than act as a conduit for the communication, with neither power nor intention to intercede himself. However, it offered some hope to those involved in the dispute that pressure might be put upon employers' federations and the government to settle the dispute.

As it was, Bonar Law had quickly rebuffed the request, stating that the strike was unofficial; that it remained the responsibility of employers and employees; that he condemned the anti-democratic actions and was opposed to their methods of picketing. He was absolutely unequivocal and gave no sign of any flexibility on demands or willingness to even enter into discussions. Given the stance that had been taken by the government, not just throughout the war but since its end, it is hardly likely that his response would have been otherwise. The government was preparing for confrontation, but with the approach having been made a response was awaited.

The news was still to be transmitted to the expectant crowd; meanwhile, within the City Chambers itself, a deputation from the workers was waiting to meet with the Lord Provost. Those attending included Manny Shinwell, David Kirkwood and Neil Maclean, the newly elected Govan MP. John Wheatley was also present, but as a councillor, and although in the building anyway, he no doubt intended to lend his support to the strikers. Maxton was out of town, but endeavouring to get back as soon as he could, though it would all be over by the time he arrived back.

For the authorities, the Lord Provost was joined in the City Chambers by the Sheriff of Lanarkshire (which then included the city of Glasgow) and the chief constable of the city police force, who was located outside the building with his men.

Just then, the fateful tramcar passed with the striker and soldier aboard. The vehicle was halted and the fight began. Whether the confrontation between the two men actually continued in the street is unknown, for it was immediately overtaken by events that either broke up their fight or possibly just swallowed it up in the general mêlée that followed.

As with all such incidents, working out later how and why a fracas started is almost impossible. Trying to discern who did what is equally difficult – often something happens and it all just kicks off from there. People get swept along and individuals get subsumed into the wider event. A common purpose can develop and equally individuals can perpetrate particular actions unbeknown to the wider grouping to which they belong. Just who struck the first blow after the incident on the tramcar, or what precisely happened is hard to be truly certain of.

Months later at the subsequent trial, two quite separate versions were given of the same event when witnesses from both sides testified. Police claimed that they were required to intercede with batons drawn to allow tramcars to move as the crowd surrounded them, and that missiles had then rained down upon them. Whilst strikers claimed that they were charged indiscriminately by baton-wielding officers who responded to an order to attack. In truth, it was probably a mixture of both, though the reality was probably much closer to the version of the strikers.

Certainly, the incident from the tramcar spilled onto the road and strikers would have moved towards the vehicle to see what was happening. Crowds had already been milling around, spilling into the path of the trams, making it harder for the vehicles to get past. And, as the number of demonstrators grew, that problem only increased.

It also appears to have been the cue for the chief constable to order his officers to attack the strikers, ostensibly to restore public order. Nerves would have been jangling and the disorder in front of them doubtless exacerbated that. At the trial, it was alleged by the authorities that trams were deliberately being held up. Though there was no real evidence of this, other than the general crowd obstruction that came about due to the sheer numbers present in what, after all, was a relatively confined space.

It was subsequently suggested by police that missiles were hurled indiscriminately at them whilst they were simply standing peacefully in front of the building. Officer after officer at the trial spoke of stones, bottles and other missiles, and one even described the air as being black with projectiles, which simply doesn't appear credible.

There is little evidence to support this account, other than the words of officers whose testimonies almost appeared scripted at the later hearing. Those on tramcars or on the street neither recall so many flying objects nor were injured by them. The windows of the municipal building lying directly behind the lines of police officers weren't broken, despite being large and running the full length of the Square. Nor were four ornate lampposts that stand in front of the building itself – each with seven globes arching out from them. They would have been hard to miss for a mob throwing missiles indiscriminately, if it had been as was suggested. Had such a hail of projectiles been flung it is impossible to believe that significant damage would not have been done to the surrounding buildings and lamps.

As Gallacher himself was to admit, missiles and objects were flung, but only after the police had charged and strikers had retaliated. They were also flung far further into the Square and away from the City Chambers. It is hard to come to any other conclusion than the order for the police to draw batons and charge the strikers lined in the Square was given when the fight from the tram spilled into the street. Whether that was due to overreaction, fear, or a mixture of both is unknown.

It was also later suggested at the trial that Gallacher had refused to get off the plinth at the Gladstone statue, and had to be pulled down by police officers, which implies that he started the riot by instigating the trouble there. Moreover, it was suggested that Kirkwood had shouted 'Rally round, boys' or something similar. Comments like this, it seems, were made to show the two of them as leaders and troublemakers, rabble-rousing amongst a mob, and to imply that the trouble was started by the strikers.

Though both Gallacher and Kirkwood were to be involved in the general fracas, the allegations that they were involved in instigating it or that it was a planned attack by strikers are absurd. Such claims seem simply to be an attempt to move the blame away from the police attack and to smear two of the principal leaders of the dispute. When the order came the police reacted with shocking brutality. Most in the crowd had their backs to the lines of officers, as they were mainly situated in the Square. After all, it was not the police they were interested in but the events there. Not only would the police have been intimidatory, but they weren't the focus of their interest. It was in the Square that their leaders would be addressing them from, and Gallacher was lining up to do just that. That was where their attention was drawn and hence why most would have been initially unsighted to the police actions. Kirkwood meanwhile was in the building and oblivious to what was happening outside.

No doubt some were spilling onto the road as they sought to make their way to the Square, and others may have been accidentally (or perhaps even deliberately) trying to restrict the tramcars given the antipathy about them running. The fight spilling from the tramcar onto the road would have exacerbated all that antagonism and made the situation more congested and confusing.

Then the order came for officers to move against the crowd. No attempt seems to have been made to call the crowd to order or simply push them back from the tramcars using their physical presence and lawful authority. Instead, officers wielding batons steamed into strikers irrespective of whether they had been blocking vehicles or not, charging at the crowd in front of or facing them, and clubbing them seemingly at random and without warning. This narrative appears to be confirmed by the fact that the direction of the police attack was across to the Square, rather than down streets perpendicular to it and where the trams ran. Also, rather than seeking to move the crowd from blocking the trams, the lines of officers moved against the demonstrators sited in the Square itself. This is also given credence by the fact that individuals a considerable distance away from the tramcars themselves were targeted and attacked.

Initially, total disarray occurred, with heads cracking and men and women running every which way, many having been caught entirely unawares. Police batons were made of solid wood, and when struck down they caused considerable injury. As the police charged many surged towards the west side of the Square and towards where the speakers had been addressing them from, which was the direction away from where the police were coming from and the way to escape. When the disturbance broke out, most were simply listening or standing in the Square and initially had no idea what was happening or why folk were running. They simply moved with the crowd to avoid the danger or, in many instances, were just swept along by the surge of people in such a confined space.

Others, whether strikers, demonstrators or just passers-by, sought to get away from the confusion and moved across the roads and out of the way. They were conscious of the dangers they now faced as officers flayed left and right with their batons and many, including women, fell to the ground. The blood began to flow from wounds to heads as the police moved across the Square, striking out indiscriminately at those in their way or simply beating those within range. A woman was seen on the ground with a boot mark on her face from an officer either kicking or trampling on her, and men lay dazed on the ground with blood streaming from their wounds.

However, soon the tide began to turn as the crowd steadied, partly through so many standing at the far side and partly through a growing anger and determination to fight back. The police surge ceased and officers sought to regroup, possibly because of the sheer size of the crowd, a wariness about venturing too far into it, or perhaps even exhaustion.

But there was to be no rest for the police, for others in the Square, having got over the initial shock and realising that they were being attacked, sought to fight back. Initially, men began striking out at officers with their feet and fists. Turf was then gathered up from the gardens in the Square by others and flung at the lines of officers, along with whatever other missiles could be acquired or were just lying about. It has also been suggested that even iron railings surrounding the grassy areas of the Square were ripped out and hurled at the lines of police, as the crowd mobilised for a counter-attack. The maelstrom continued, with police striking men and individual confrontations between police and strikers taking place across the east and centre of the Square. What had started with one punch was now descending into a major riot.

The tide then turned and surged back the way it had come and that included both officers and men. Those who had been swept into the fray and those who had been washed along with the rabble were quickly ebbing back from whence it had originated. Soon, massed ranks of strikers started to charge at the police who, by this time, had moved back to where they had been initially located in front of the City Chambers.

No doubt less coordinated than the police, the strikers still charged at the now static police lines massed in front of the City Chambers. It seems that thereafter charge and counter-charge followed as men attacked officers and officers sought to repel them by beating them back with their batons. The situation had well and truly deteriorated and it was only going to get worse as the minutes passed.

Leaders and organisers on both sides sought to try to rally their men and bring order to the chaos. Gallacher jumped from the plinth, having realised what was happening as the crowd surged past him pursued by baton-wielding officers. He ran towards the chief constable, who had followed his men and was soon approaching the centre of the Square where his men were headed. Gallacher's intention was to remonstrate with him and have the officers stop the attack upon his comrades.

As it was, he simply got caught up in the general mêlée himself. As he approached the chief constable, officers were striking out indiscriminately and, as he admitted in his memoirs, he became angered. Accordingly, he let fly with his fists and the surrounding officers sought to protect their chief. Gallacher attempted to punch the senior officer, and in his biography talked of landing an uppercut on the chief constable. It appears, though, from evidence at the trial, that he had embellished what happened and though he bravely (or stupidly) sought to strike out, it was far less effective as he was soon overpowered by other officers and forced to the ground.

Truncheons seemed set to batter him senseless when a comrade dived on top of Gallacher to protect him from further blows that were raining down. The striker who had flung himself on him took the full impact, saving Gallacher from more serious injury. He was Neil Alexander, who, as well as being bludgeoned that day, would soon find himself arrested and in the dock alongside the man he saved. However, other strikes still landed upon Gallacher, as officers laid into him. He lay beaten on the ground until he was lifted up with blood flowing from a serious gash to the head. Lying in the grass, the blood flowed from the wound, mixing with mud and caking his clothes. He was then lifted up and dragged away by other officers towards the main entrance to the City Chambers as battle raged elsewhere in the Square.

The noise was deafening as strikers and officers charged and counter-charged. Missiles and objects were flying through the air and crashing to the ground. Oaths were shouted and rallying calls made. Some were running away, others stampeding towards each other. It was total mayhem and there were no obvious signs of it coming to a conclusion any time soon. The chaos and cacophony quickly alerted the attention of all those already within the City Chambers. Moreover, as police retreated to reposition themselves and their prisoners (Gallacher amongst them) they found themselves almost directly in front of the entrance to the buildings and below windows that afforded a full vantage of the makeshift battlefield.

Those in the Chambers up above – including the deputation from the strikers waiting to see the Lord Provost – had rushed to look out and saw battle raging in the Square below and were horrified at what they saw below. Immediately they rushed down the stairs and out of the buildings, anxious to see what they could do to protect comrades and restore calm. Rather than succeeding in defusing the situation, they simply ran into the eye of the storm themselves. David Kirkwood was first out and was half way across the road in front of the Chambers when he saw a bloodied and beaten Gallacher being dragged away by officers. He sought to object to what was happening to his colleague, but before he could make any protest he was struck by a police sergeant, and was knocked unconscious.

Neil Maclean had rushed out immediately after and was only a yard or two behind Kirkwood when he saw him struck down. He started vehemently remonstrating with the officers who had done it and who then looked set to attack him. However, fortunately for Maclean, they seemed to appreciate who he was and recognised that attacking an elected Member of Parliament might have severe repercussions, and so they backed off, sparing him from injury.

Officers then dragged the unconscious Kirkwood, along with the injured Gallagher and arrested Alexander, into the City Chambers, then through to a quadrangle located at the back of the Square. The civic building soon began to more resemble a fort under siege than public offices. A phalanx of officers stood in front with more in the building and to the rear. Many had retreated to it under the sustained effort of the counter-charges that were taking place. The injured were being pulled there and those arrested dragged there, all to the alarm of those working in it.

Out in the Square total disarray continued. Police horses that had been at the back of the building were brought round to be used as a form of cavalry in the pandemonium that was playing out. Their size and weight were intimidating, as they sought to force their way through. Whilst other such disturbances in Glasgow and elsewhere had been speedily resolved simply by their appearance, with the size of this crowd there was limited room for them to manoeuvre. As police were pushed back by the volume of people in the Square (never mind the hail of missiles that were unleashed), the space for horses was limited. It seems that they failed to have the usual deterrent effect and their riders suffered the same torrent of missiles that their colleagues on foot also sustained.

The battlefield carnage accumulated as bodies lay all around, some wounded and others exhausted. Fights continued and blood, glass and objects were strewn about. The Square also became a sea of mud in what had been its grassy parts. It had rained the day before and though cold, it was not freezing. The constant movement and scuffling churned up the tended garden plots, but the conflict soon extended beyond the immediate site.

According to Gallacher, a lorry turned into George Square which was commandeered by strikers. Carrying boxes of aerated water, he described it as a 'gift from the gods' for the strikers. The lorry, he said, was driven round and into North Frederick Street, which lies on the north-east corner of the Square and which rises in an incline away from the City Chambers. There, the lorry was turned into a makeshift barricade and the boxes unloaded to be used as ammunition. Harry McShane, another organiser, recalls the water as having come from a pub that was situated on North Frederick Street, where strikers gathered bottles and pelted the police lines below. It seems most likely that as the riot moved, the lorry which was parked at the pub was simply commandeered. Moving it through the general mêlée was unlikely, given the difficulties not just people, but police horses, were having.

Irrespective of how it happened, mounted police and officers on foot sought to charge at the strikers and break through the makeshift barricade. As they neared, the unloaded boxes were lying open and the bottles were quickly launched upon the police below. With the strikers having the advantage of the higher ground, the lorry blocking the road and with bottles crashing down all around, the police were forced to beat a hasty retreat.

Back at the City Chambers the main battle had been ongoing in the Square, with charge and counter-charge by the police ranks and those of the strikers who, by this time, had become much more of an organised body. They were able to repulse the police thrusts and were making headway themselves. Others, as well as the strikers' deputation, had come out from the building when they saw the mêlée. They included the Sheriff of Lanarkshire, who appeared to quickly converse with the chief constable about the gravity of the situation that was unfolding. Fearing that control was being lost, he decided to read the Riot Act.

This was legislation was originally enacted in the early eighteenth century to deal with civil disturbance. As a formal declaration, it has to be read out by an authorised official and it requires individuals thereafter to remove from the area or face arrest. Given the circumstances in which it could plausibly be applied and the draconian powers it unleashed, it was rarely used. But its use in twentieth-century Glasgow proves the panic felt by the authorities as they lay besieged in the City Chambers.

Even the reading of the act, though, was not to be without its difficulties. It requires the proclamation to be read even if this might appear rather nonsensical, given the general disorder that usually requires the action. The sheriff started reading from the formal document that he held, despite the mayhem that was all around him. As he was reading it a striker either grabbed it from his hand or bumped into him, knocking it from his grasp, with even some suggestions that it might have been a bottle that was flung. Such was the chaos that it is hard to say what happened. Either way, it fell to the ground. At the subsequent trial the sheriff gave evidence that he thereafter gave the rest of the proclamation from memory. This is perhaps rather hard to believe, even from an officer of the law, given it is likely that he had never been required to read it before, nor was it something he would have committed to memory. However, whether it was or wasn't is irrelevant as the battle of George Square waged regardless.

By that time, the fracas had also spread well beyond the confines of George Square. The trouble in North Frederick Street continued, and after a short while, the strikers retreated further up the road as police efforts to both rush up it and go around it through adjacent streets continued. That confrontation moved to Cathedral Street, which lies at the top of North Frederick Street, running east to west. Officers had by then reassembled, but were faced by angry strikers who were determined to fight back.

According to McShane, first strikers charged at police and then retreated, followed by officers counter-charging. It continued that way for a while, with an impasse seemingly being reached and the police considering what their next move would be. It seems one older officer charged again, expecting to be flanked by colleagues, only to find that he was, in fact, alone and surrounded. Whether through being overwhelmed or simply retreating to escape, the police line broke. Officers began to run, fleeing up closes in Cathedral Street and escaping over back walls. Most no doubt wanting to get back to the City Chambers, where their main force would be. Others perhaps just running in any direction to avoid being captured by strikers, who now considerably outnumbered them. According to McShane, some officers were caught and given considerable beatings by workers, many of whom had themselves previously been struck or hit by police and who more than gave back what they had suffered.

Meanwhile, bedlam back at George Square. There the main body of strikers were now forcing the police back, not just towards, but into the City Chambers itself. Despite the sheriff reading – or attempting to read – the Riot Act, the forces of law and order were losing control and police casualties were rising. Initially it had been noticeable that the bulk of the injured were strikers, but as that began to change a sense of foreboding grew for the authorities, as they realised they faced being overwhelmed. The sheriff accordingly put in a telephone call for military assistance.

As officers retreated into the besieged building, the authorities also felt it necessary to seek the support of the strike's leaders to try to bring about some calm. Discussions took place about dispersing to Glasgow Green, where a more orderly meeting could be held. Members of the strikers' delegation who were also there thought the suggestion sensible. Order had broken down and they feared for their comrades, and for the safety of the constabulary – and what their enraged colleagues might do to them. The police also hoped it would be the strike leaders who would speak to the crowd, presumably fearing that any requests they made themselves would either have no effect or inflame the situation further still.

Neil Maclean, who had rushed out with Kirkwood when he had

been knocked down to the ground, had sought to defuse matters. He had remonstrated with the sheriff and the chief constable and had already suggested that the police should be withdrawn as they were exacerbating matters rather than pacifying the situation. However, he was initially no more able to achieve that than he had been able to stop Kirkwood being bludgeoned to the ground.

It was becoming recognised by all that moving the crowd away might allow calm to develop and avoid possible serious injury or loss of life. For, by now, both injured police and civilians were streaming into the building to be out of harm's way and to receive treatment. Men with blood wounds, cuts and concussion were all around. They made their way – or were taken – through the building and into a corridor where others, including the wounded Gallacher, were already lying. Gallacher, however, was soon moved up to a secure room where he was guarded by nervous police officers (though he sensed they were happier to be inside with him than out in the tumult).

John Wheatley had already tried to go out onto one of the balconies at the City Chambers and call for order to be restored, but without any obvious success. It may just have been the timing of his attempt, with the violence at its height and pandemonium down below resulting in no one having the ability or inclination to listen. Or it could have been that he had less authority with the strikers as, though a respected figure, he wasn't a leader of the movement.

Kirkwood and Gallacher, however, were generally perceived to have the authority of office and, more importantly, the respect amongst the men to be listened to. There is also some suggestion that those gathered around outside were demanding to hear from them. Whether that was to ensure themselves of their safety or to be satisfied that moving off to the Green was actually what they wanted is not known, but was perhaps a mixture of both. Neil Maclean, in discussion with the chief constable and sheriff, speedily arranged for them to address the crowd from a balcony.

Gallacher and Kirkwood were, of course, by that point under arrest and within the building. However, another member of the deputation went in search of them to explain what was happening and to get their agreement to address the crowd and have them disperse to Glasgow Green. They were located in the corridor where they were ostensibly under arrest, but were sitting with police officers, some of whom were also injured and clearly glad to be away from the affray. They had also been visited shortly before that by John Wheatley and Rosslyn Mitchell, who had gone to see that they were okay and advise them that legal representation would be provided for them.

Accordingly, a now conscious David Kirkwood, along with Willie Gallacher, with a now bandaged head wound, was asked to speak to the crowd below from one of the balconies in the City Chambers. Flanked by colleagues, they called on the crowd to stop the fighting and to then move in an orderly fashion down to Glasgow Green, where they could reassemble. The Lord Provost would later be vehemently criticised by some of the press for appearing to indulge the rabble-rousers. However, it seems to have been merited, given the critical situation and, more importantly, it seems to have worked.

Though the anger within the main body was still evident, the crowd were prepared to listen to their leaders. Simultaneously, other strike organisers were going around the crowd seeking to quieten dissenting voices and bring some calm to the situation. The police had also moved back, aware that they were simply exacerbating the situation (not to mention the fact that they had lost control of the Square).

Soon, the strikers began to line up in an orderly fashion and prepare to march the short journey to Glasgow Green. It brought a sense of relief to those from all sides in the City Chambers who had grown increasingly concerned about the loss of control and the mounting disorder. Some, like Kirkwood, Gallacher and Alexander, were by then under arrest, and would continue to be detained. Others though, such as Maclean and Wheatley, would be free to go and join the crowd, where it was expected that they would address the strikers.

Peace had been restored to George Square and the running fights in Cathedral Street had ended. However, whilst it brought an end to the riot it wasn't to be the end of the trouble in the city. Violence and disorder continued elsewhere in the city centre, as it would through the night, as the George Square Riot turned into Bloody Friday.

At the City Chambers, treatment of the wounded continued; many had been lying in the corridors and were receiving basic first aid from council staff. Both police and strikers lay together, largely peaceably, though a few cast withering glances at the erstwhile opposition, but were either too sore or exhausted to continue the fight. Some had head wounds, whether from police batons or objects flung, and were bandaged up to stem the flow of blood. Others had makeshift slings for broken or badly bruised arms and shoulders. Rudimentary ambulances had been pulling into the building from the rear or side streets to avoid the trouble raging, and taking the wounded to the Royal Infirmary. A constant procession streamed in and out from there to the hospital for quite a while thereafter – a telling indication of the numbers hurt in the fray. The following day the papers recorded the tally of wounded taken to hospital as fifty-three, but many more would have made their way separately, or perhaps lying or failing to declare how they had been injured when they attended. Some would also have sought treatment elsewhere or simply gone home to lick their wounds. Despite the number of injured being so considerable, thankfully there were no fatalities.

Other vehicles also came to the City Chambers, not on a mission of mercy but instead to take away prisoners. Four were noted in the press as having been arrested at the time, including Gallacher and Alexander. They were taken to Duke Street Prison, again only a mile or so to the east, but which, at that time, was the main prison for the city. Those vehicles, though marked, were more discreet, given the hostility many wandering about felt towards them. Others detained also began to be taken to Duke Street or to police stations in the city, as a general round-up of the leaders of the strike was beginning.

The main body now sought to move off towards Glasgow Green in an orderly fashion. Lined up by stewards, and led by the strike leaders, they processed in an almost military fashion to Glasgow Green. The military formation was organised by some ex-servicemen within the wider strike movement who had been working with the CWC. Though many of the organisations for those who had served in the forces supported the government or the right, there was also a grouping for the left. They had been involved in a variety of ways with the strike, including no doubt providing some protection on occasion.

The ex-servicemen, numbering several hundred, then sought to organise the march into a more coherent order and prepared to lead off. Their leaders included J. R. Campbell from Paisley, who had served in the Royal Navy where he'd been wounded, but had also won the Military Medal for bravery in battle. On discharge, he had returned to Glasgow, where he'd become active in the CWC and in forming the ex-servicemen's organisation. After a few years, he would become editor of the Communist Party paper, *Workers' Weekly*.

Meanwhile, a piper also appeared and led the crowds off down the relatively short distance towards Glasgow Green. The mood was mixed, with those angered by the violence willing, if not anxious, to continue the struggle with the police. Others were more sombre and reflective, worried about the events that had happened and concerned about what might lie ahead. But, off they set marching in order together, watched by wary crowds that still mingled about the city centre and along the route to the Green.

However, it was not to be the end of the violence and disorder, and incidents occurred en route as events, though calmed by the tempering of the crowd by Kirkwood, once again flared up. At Glasgow Cross, half way between the Square and the Green, some minor skirmishing took place as further clashes between marchers and police erupted. As the marching workers then neared Glasgow Green, another battle broke out, this time at Jail Square, just opposite the entrance to Glasgow Green and in front of the High Court. Windows in the building were broken when fighting between strikers and police flared up. It continued on to Albert Bridge, which crosses over the River Clyde into the Gorbals and the south side, lying beyond the court building and the entrance to the Green. Given the proximity of all those areas from the Saltmarket down to the bridge (which is a distance of less than half a mile), it was, in all likelihood, just a continuing running fight between police and strikers that took place.

McShane narrated that an incident perhaps en route to (or somewhere around) Albert Bridge had occurred in the nearby Saltmarket, when strikers clashed with two police officers. They overpowered them and, stripping them of their uniforms, forced them to flee semi-naked. He also said that groups of strikers went around cutting the trolley ropes, bringing the tramcars to a halt and blocking the roads. Hundreds of vehicles lay idle, unable to move, causing their passengers to disembark whilst other vehicles were forced to try to meander around them. This then increased the numbers in the crowd just swirling about, unsure what was going on or what they should do about it. All of this further added not just to the tension in the air, but to the overall chaos in the city.

It is uncertain just precisely what triggered the violence, though incidents appear to have been occurring all along the way to the Green. The following day the press reported that it may have again been tramcars that were the cause. With passions inflamed, strikers sought to hinder or stop them, with a consequent reaction from police. Nine tramcars were reported as being attacked, and a pitched battle between police and strikers apparently lasted a quarter of an hour.

Though some semi-formal event does appear to have taken place in the Green as groups moved on into it and away from the ongoing trouble, it seems that many more simply began to drift away when they reached it, rather than listening to speakers. Perhaps they were just eager to get away from the trouble they had seen and could sense was still brewing. After all, not just on the route, but thereafter clashes were occurring, and there must have been an atmosphere of tension, if not malice, in the air.

As people made their way home, though, trouble continued and indeed others sadly sought to capitalise on the general disorder. Both in the city centre and in areas away from it, windows were smashed and some looting took place. According to the following days' papers, Cathedral Street and North Frederick Street were badly damaged, which is understandable given the violence that took place there. Argyle Street and Queen Street were also badly damaged given their proximity to George Square and how people would have flowed from it. However, windows were also damaged on the south side of the city and trouble raged elsewhere, with Bridge Street and Adelphi Street suffering damage as people dispersed, no doubt after the trouble at Albert Bridge continued across and onto the south side of the river.

Looting took place later that night by those who simply sought to exploit the general chaos. There were reports of a jeweller's shop in Paisley Road West and a tobacconist in Renfield Street having been looted, with random violence recorded and a few other such incidents also taking place overnight. However, by the following day, the disorder had ceased and an element of eerie calm descended.

The effects of the strike alongside the events in George Square affected the city that day, adding to the tension and foreboding. The ongoing industrial action and continued picketing was beginning to cause issues at power stations and, in particular, Port Dundas in the north of the city, which had been the major concern to the authorities that week. Electric lighting was interrupted during the early evening and some of the main streets in the city centre were in darkness until 8 p.m. With it being winter, the sun had set in the late afternoon and, accordingly, the streets must have been unnervingly dark, compounding the problem of debris and glass strewn about.

Meanwhile, strike leaders quickly met up again later in the day, some sporting their battle wounds, some knowing that arrest would likely follow for them as it had already for some of their comrades. The leaders realised it was essential to get their story out, which was why they had been printing their own strike bulletin throughout the week. They knew the papers would be uniformly hostile and it would be more necessary than ever to put their version of events across to the public. Moreover, there was an air of uncertainty hanging around, given what had happened, and spirits needed reviving.

Accordingly, a bulletin was speedily prepared for distribution. Headlined a 'Dastardly Attempt to Smash Trade Unionism' it read:

Fellow workers,

Ever since the Armistice was signed it has been evident that a big unemployment crisis was imminent unless steps were taken to absorb into industry the demobilised men of the Army and Navy. Over a hundred thousand workers in Scotland have been dismissed from civil employment. There is only one remedy, reduce the hours of Labour. The Joint Committee representing the STUC parliamentary Committee, the Glasgow Trades and labour Council, and a number of other important Unions initiated the movement for a 40 hours week with a view to absorbing the unemployed. A strike for this object began on 27 January. This has the support of Trade Unionists all over the British Isles.

On the 29th a huge demonstration was held and a deputation from the strikers who offered to approach the government on the matter and arrangements were made for another demonstration on Friday to receive the reply. On that day, many thousands of strikers marched in orderly procession to George Square for this purpose. There was no disorder. The demonstrators were, however, met by a vicious bludgeoning attack by the police. The authorities had evidently determined to break the strike by force, and had made their plans accordingly. With such ferocity did the police make their attack that even the members of our deputation, who were there by arrangement with the Lord Provost, were attacked and one of them – D. Kirkwood – was brutally bludgeoned from behind as he was leaving the Council Chambers. Remember that was a peaceful and orderly demonstration of workers from all districts of the Clyde area. It was met by police batons, which were used indiscriminately upon men, women and children.

Since then the authorities have imported thousands of troops into the city with machine guns and tanks for the purpose of breaking the spirit of the strikers and forcing them back to work.

On the following day the offices of the Glasgow Trades and Labour Council, the centre of Scottish Trade Unionism were forcibly raided by the police.

Three years ago, we were told by spokesmen of the Employers that, after the war, the workers would have to be content with longer hours. Here then is the secret of the determination to crush by any and every means attempts to secure shorter hours.

The organised workers of Scotland put forward an orderly and legitimate demand for Forty Hours. The government's reply is bludgeons, machine-guns, bayonets and tanks. In one word, the institution of a Reign of terror.

Fellow Workers!

Railwaymen, Miners and all Workers of Scotland, England and Wales, Rally to the support of your comrades on the Clyde.

Are you prepared to support us in the struggle of organised labour to obtain better conditions and to decrease unemployment! Or are you prepared to see your organisations broken and terrorised, your Council Chambers raided, your own elected spokesmen insulted, bludgeoned and imprisoned!

Stand, then, shoulder to shoulder with us on the Clyde, and prove that organised labour is a force to be reckoned with, not something to be despised or broke,

Every man, therefore, to his Trade Union Branch–

Protest, Agitate and Organise

That leaflet was to be distributed as widely as possible to counteract the interpretation that strike leaders knew would be put upon the events by the press, not just in the city but beyond. Indeed, the propaganda effort to demonise them went into overdrive, with papers lambasting the strike and its leaders. The *Herald* headlined with 'Unparalleled Scenes of Disorder' and other banner lines reading 'Glasgow Street Fighting', 'The Riot Act Read' and the 'Aftermath of War', but all carried wide-ranging reports on the events in the city. Other papers were likewise condemnatory and almost apocalyptic in their description of the scenes.

The *Herald* editorial fulminated, 'It's impossible to repress indignant comment. Those primarily responsible are those who from the outset flouted law and democracy to paralyse the functions of the community.' They continued by criticising the Lord Provost for listening to them and communicating with Bonar Law. They considered that it was an 'insolent demand' by the workforce that should have been rejected out of hand by the council's political leader. Accusing strike leaders of 'trying to bring the government down', and referring to the 'malevolent activities of its Bolsheviks', the paper emphasised the 'need to maintain law and order', and demanded action to quell the unrest and address strike leaders.

That demand was to be swiftly delivered and, indeed, had been on-going as it was penned and went to press. For troops began entering the city that very night, and tanks arrived the following day. Quick action was taken, not simply due to the seriousness of the situation, but down to the fact that the authorities had been preparing for it. Plans approved by the War Cabinet were quickly implemented, as the panicked call came in from the besieged sheriff. Moreover, a round-up of strikers also began as the authorities sought to bring to account those they held responsible for the events that had unfolded.

When the call came in soldiers quickly sprang to attention in camps across the country, though not in the city of Glasgow itself, as local soldiers from Glasgow and its environs were not to be trusted. Maryhill

Barracks in the north of the city was the base not just for troops but families, as married quarters were also located on the thirty-acre site. The Highland Light Infantry was based there and was the regiment that recruited mainly in the Glasgow area (despite its name). The barracks would be sealed and soldiers confined – not sent to quell the disorder in their home city. The authorities sensed danger in allowing them to even meet or mingle with friends or family, let alone engage with strikers or political agitators, lest they be persuaded to refuse orders, or worse still, mutiny. Scots from elsewhere were one thing, but not from the city or its surrounding communities.

No attempts were made to go the barracks by strikers, which was something that Gallacher would later rue in his biography, believing that a revolutionary moment had been missed. However, whether battle-hardened troops would have listened or been sympathetic to strikers, many of whom they would have seen as having been anti-war, is highly debatable. The authorities, though, were taking no chances, and the Glasgow troops were detained in their barracks as other soldiers arrived and the round-up of strike leaders began.

16

TROOPS ARRIVE AND
A ROUND-UP BEGINS

Troops began entering Glasgow that very evening as trains arrived, bringing soldiers from near and far across Scotland. The city was still in a state of shock, with citizens trying to fully comprehend the day's events, as fully armed soldiers began disembarking to head for the City Chambers. This must have been as frightening for many as it was reassuring for the beleaguered police and authorities.

Whilst troops on the street had been commonplace during the war, it had always been part of a parade or when heading to or from barracks. The days of suppressing civil revolt had long since passed into history. However, now they were combat-ready and on duty in the streets of the city. Reports and photographs had been seen of Dublin in 1916 and elsewhere around the world, but this was the first time in living memory that soldiers were appearing in this capacity on the streets of Glasgow. It was not just unusual, but unprecedented, and indicative of the fact that the civilian authority had been overwhelmed – and how concerned the government was of any escalation.

As the *Herald* was to comment later in the week when the troops took over the city, 'the panic of the civic and national authorities can only be explained thus. They actually believed a Spartacus coup was planned to start in Glasgow, and they were prepared to suppress it at all costs.' That feeling wasn't just held in Scotland, but in London, from where reporters were despatched north to cover events. One young member of the press corps was to be a young Siegfried Sassoon, the poet and erstwhile war correspondent. He seemed as supportive of the actions of the strikers as he had been hostile to the war, later even dropping a note to Gallacher in Duke Street Prison regretting that he hadn't been able to meet him, but wishing him well.

Meanwhile, the soldiers were marched to George Square to be billeted at the City Chambers. Barbed wire was uncoiled and rolled out, machine gun nests appeared on the roof and a howitzer was brought in and positioned menacingly over the Square. The City Chambers was transformed into a fortress from which the military presence could guard the city centre and patrol surrounding areas.

Other buildings in George Square were also utilised for military purposes. Machine guns were placed on the roof of the Post Office on the south side, and buildings on the north side similarly had armed soldiers positioned there. Soon that all-encompassing presence in the city centre would be added to by the tanks arriving as they made their way from the north of England. Six tanks and dozens of motor lorries had also been despatched when the call came in from the sheriff and the military was mobilised.

The military presence wasn't just in the city centre, but spread throughout it. Soldiers were deployed at power stations and other critical infrastructure sites, doubtless to protect from potential damage being inflicted, but equally no doubt deterring picketers and protestors from continuing their agitation. Soldiers were on other central streets carrying carbines, and tanks were likewise positioned, adding to an air of military occupation that would exist for a week. The tanks were quartered at the cattle market in Bellgrove Street in the city's East End that was requisitioned for the struggle.

The soldiers must have thought they were entering a war zone given the debris and detritus from the battle that lay all around. Broken glass and ripped-up gardens and fencing were strewn around George Square, which was no longer the central ornate setting it once was. Both there and in other streets, shop windows were boarded up and others were closed. It was a Saturday so many offices were shut, which meant less hustle and bustle than normal. However, those who might normally have been expected to wander up into town were staying away, fearful of what might happen.

The War Cabinet had also met on Saturday 1 February, not a normal day for the leading forum of government to meet, but indicative of the concerns they had about the situation. They were apprised of the events and discussed action to be taken. Robert Munro, the Secretary of State for Scotland, was recorded as stating that 'it was a misnomer to call it a strike – it was a Bolshevist rising'. He went on to add that it was primarily caused by 10,000 malcontents but overall, he thought that public opinion supported the government not the strikers.

General Sir Charles Harington Harington, attending on behalf of the military, provided a situation report giving an assessment of readiness and action. Stating that they could send in up to 12,000 troops if required, he also confirmed that six tanks supported by 100 motor lorries were heading north. The Lord Advocate provided an update on the situation with regard to those strike leaders who had been arrested or detained: they had been held under the Defence of the Realm Act and he advised that they also had powers to deport individuals from the city which, after all, they had done before and with effect. It seemed to him that sufficient powers existed and no further action beyond that was needed.

The soldiers came from near and far. Bringing them across from Edinburgh or Stirling was relatively simple, but coming down from the Highlands was slightly more complicated. However, it was done with military precision, with troops arriving from Redford Barracks, Edinburgh and Stirling Castle, as well as Fort George and Cromarty Barracks in the north. The soldiers were from various regiments, but included the Argyll and Sutherland Highlanders, Gordon Highlanders and Seaforth Highlanders. English regiments stationed in Scotland and English soldiers serving with Scottish regiments were also sent. That the troops were ready to be deployed so quickly was shown by reports in the *Edinburgh Evening News* on the very day of the riot, which noted that 'long columns of khaki-clad men who belonged to the Seaforth Highlanders, the Gordons and other Highland Regiments' were already heading west to deal with civil unrest.

An army veteran was to recall the events that day for the Seaforth Highlanders in the Cromarty Barracks, located in the Highland town of that name. Detailing how soldiers were called to parade in the central square when they had been lined up, all men from Glasgow and surrounding areas were ordered to take a step forward. Once identified, those men were told to stand down. Many mistakenly assumed that they were to be demobbed and returned to their rooms delighted. However, the reality was that they were being confined to barracks and their comrades were ordered to mobilise, though the precise nature of their destination was not given. Those mustered, however, were taken to a train to embark for Glasgow, whilst it was believed that their erstwhile colleagues back at the barracks could not be relied on to follow orders. All those heading south were advised that they were going into a serious situation and were under orders to shoot if required.

News of the arrival of soldiers began to spread and some of the strike leaders who weren't already detained by then sought to see if they could intercede and speak to them. McShane recalled going to Buchanan Street Station late at night when he heard that soldiers from the north of Scotland were coming in, and how he had wanted to try to explain to them what the strike was about and why they were taking action. As an anti-war activist, he had experience of speaking to soldiers and trying to get them to consider their actions and change their minds. When he reached the station, he discovered that others had thought similarly and were there to help him try and convert the troops to the cause.

It was all to no avail though, as the soldiers disembarking from the train were simply not interested. Perhaps it was exacerbated by their journey and knowing little of where they were going or what they were doing, but they were tetchy and irritable. Being approached by working men who they didn't know seemed to anger rather than appease them, and doubtless they were also frightened and a bit bewildered by it all. McShane and others walked alongside the young soldiers as they marched down to George Square seeking to tell them what it was they were doing and why they were striking in the hope of persuading them to desist. Officers kept seeking to intercede, and physically stood between the strikers and their young recruits, barking out orders to keep marching and ignore the men.

In the end, the soldiers weren't for being persuaded anyway. They were, after all, as McShane recalled, young recruits with little knowledge or involvement with the labour movement, and perhaps even less sympathy for it. Whilst the soldiers locked in at Maryhill Barracks were battle-hardened and from the city, many of these arriving were more like young boys, and Glasgow was a strange and alien place for them. It would be a frightening situation for many, some of whom would have had little or no combat experience, let alone training to deal with civil unrest.

They viewed those seeking to lobby them as the enemy, not comrades. McShane recalled one young recruit they spoke to pointing at his rifle and stating that it was better than bottles. So obviously some indication (albeit one-sided) had been given to them of what had happened, and which would only have predisposed them to be wary of the strikers. They were going there, they believed, to restore order, perhaps even quell a Bolshevist rising, and weren't going to be dissuaded by strikers lobbying then. The message was therefore clear to McShane and other strikers that the troops meant business and orders would be followed, no matter how severe.

As the troops arrived the beleaguered authorities breathed a sigh of relief as they looked around and contemplated what might have been.

It also gave them a second wind, and they were revived both by the chance for officers to catch some rest and by the overwhelming military resources now to hand. Accordingly, reaction and retribution were also to be swift, and a round-up of strike leaders began as the darkness of the evening descended. Some, of course, like Kirkwood and Gallacher, had already been arrested at the City Chambers. Whilst they had been allowed to address the crowd from the balcony they were immediately thereafter taken back into police custody and found themselves heading to Duke Street Prison, Gallacher still sporting a bandage that had been wrapped around his head when struck by a baton at the Square.

The strike headquarters were visited by police seeking to see who was there and what was ongoing, no doubt also to intimidate the strikers and make it clear who was now in charge. One of the first to be detained under the more general round-up of leaders was Manny Shinwell, who was the chairman of the strike committee. He was arrested at his home in Govan and reports of his arrest appeared in the papers on the Saturday along with details of the events. Gallacher, Kirkwood and Shinwell all appeared in court that day along with others who had been arrested and were detained for further procedure and committed to Duke Street Prison. They were soon joined by George Ebury, and a few days later by Harry Hopkins, along with others who continued to be arrested or were brought in from other police stations. All appeared in court that Saturday morning, the day after the battle, and all were further detained in custody.

By this point Glasgow was a city firmly under military command. Troops were stationed throughout the city centre, tanks were on the streets and power stations and tram depots were patrolled by soldiers with guns and bayonets. It was a city under military occupation, very much highlighted in the newspaper reports with the *Herald*'s headlines on Monday 3 February including 'Glasgow Occupied by Military Forces', 'Order Restored', 'Strike Leaders in Court' and 'Police Visit Strike HQ'.

It was the desired outcome for the establishment, who were incandescent at the events that had occurred and which seemed to confirm the fears they had earlier held. The *Herald* editorial on Saturday 1 February had fulminated, 'It is impossible to repress indignant comment. Those primarily responsible are those who from the outset flouted law and democracy to paralyse the functions of the community.' It went on to mention that they had been 'trying to bring the government down' and that it was simply 'malevolent activities of its Bolshevists'.

Reports narrated how soldiers from both English and Scottish regiments had arrived to quell the disorder. They had started arriving on the Friday night and some Highland regiments had been led by a piper to their temporary HQ at the City Chambers. They also narrated how machine guns and coils of barbed wire now adorned the building and that large numbers of troops were quartered there. Other aspects of the events were also covered. Twenty-three tramcars were noted as being damaged with fifteen needing to go to the depot for repair. As well as the strike leaders, some who had been involved in looting had also been charged.

The events also had an effect in dissipating the strike. It would run on for over a week but already it seemed that the battle had knocked the stuffing out of many, as well as taking the leadership out of circulation. The strike leaders and wider participants continued to meet, but they were fewer in number and met in smaller local halls. The mass meetings that had taken place in George Square were now a thing of the past. Whilst then it been taken over by jubilant strikers it was now watched over by scowling soldiers; the red flags and singing replaced by a howitzer and barbed wire.

The mood in the city was tense and that anxiety was exacerbated by if not a growing hostility towards the strike, then most certainly a desire for it to all be over and the city to be back to normal. Whilst many had supported it, many more had either only accepted it reluctantly or were now turning against it. The military presence hardened the opposition to the cause, and persuaded many who had half-heartedly acceded to it that it was time to call a halt. With no strike pay and little savings, many would also be conscious of debt, something that could be risked if there was the likelihood of success but a gargantuan waste if not. With troops in situ and their leaders in jail, many must have decided it simply was not worth continuing. By this time there was little revolutionary fervour remaining, other than perhaps in the hearts and minds of a few diehards.

With it being the weekend, a drift back to work couldn't really commence until the Monday, and even then it would take time, as many still remained on strike or were awaiting a formal decision to return to work. The leadership of the CWC initially tried to keep the dispute going, but soon became aware of the change in mood and atmosphere across the city. Numbers were diminishing before their very eyes and with the leadership team incarcerated and the threat of action against others, the pressure was mounting. This had no doubt been part of the plan by the authorities who, after all, had considered pre-emptive arrest and were now imposing detention on the leaders after Friday's events.

With Shinwell, Kirkwood, Gallacher, Hopkins, Ebury and other senior representatives all in prison, the leadership had effectively been decapitated. Others did try to step into the breach, but either lacked the experience or the presence of their erstwhile colleagues. The likes of Gallacher, Shinwell and Kirkwood had been leading disputes both before and during the war; they were used to threats and intimidation and, in some cases, even to the privation of jail. They were, in many ways, as battle-hardened as the troops confined to barracks in Maryhill or elsewhere.

However, they weren't there to assist, and though the likes of Muir and MacManus had been through similar privations, others were far less experienced. It was not just that much of the motivational rhetoric was now silenced by the imprisonment of the former leaders, but their incarceration must have been a salutary lesson about the potential risks of fighting on to others.

Press reports from that week confirmed the gradual return to work and the slippage in the strike's coverage and effect. The *Herald*, in its editorial on Monday 3 February, stated that the dispute was 'a minor grievance being abused by a minority'. It also demanded 'greater protection of workers' and action by union leaders who, they stated, 'need to defeat the revolutionary movement within'. The strike committee, though, still called on workers to remain on strike, but it was clear that they were looking for a way out and that it was just a matter of time before a halt would be called.

By Tuesday 4 February the *Herald* editorial was stating that 'order had been restored after the Friday riot' and the 'city was fully occupied by the military'. Tanks had arrived and they advised that 'the military occupation continues and will be maintained as long as needed'. They also added that they 'were fully armed for all emergencies', which apparently 'caused great interest amongst the population' – perhaps an understatement!

The paper went on to comment on the industrial situation, writing that arrangements were being made for those who wished to return to work. But still they added it had been a 'poor start in the return to work but full resumption was expected tomorrow'. However, they did detail that there were 'no massed pickets at shipyards, engineering shops or other major industrial sites'. These had been the major power base of the strike and mass picketing had been the basis of much of the workers' success. There were still individual pickets, but these were a far cry from the huge numbers that, either encouraging or intimidating, certainly proved highly effective. It is doubtful whether as effective a strike could have been obtained without the use of picketing to bring workers out – willingly or otherwise – and in its absence a drift, if not a torrent, of returning could be expected.

The strike began to fragment. Miners in Hamilton and Blantyre, who had joined in and ignored the directions of the Miners' Federation, decided to resume work. In Edinburgh, where some had joined in and especially in the port of Leith, a drift back was reported. Though by this time, the drift was turning into a steady stream. More worryingly, unity was fragmenting. By the Friday the *Herald* was reporting that the Glasgow city employees' ballot had shown a substantial majority against the strike. However, shipyard workers in Glasgow, Partick and Clydebank had voted to remain on strike in support of the forty-hour week.

By the end of the week it was becoming clear that more were marching with their feet, and the fragmentation in many parts was in danger of becoming a full-scale collapse. Accordingly, a tactical retreat was agreed upon, and it was decided to call for a return to work. The joint committee representing the shop stewards and political supporters met on Monday 10 February and agreed to recommend a return to work. Though there may have been some who were reluctant, the overwhelming mood was that as much as could be achieved had been and to continue it would be to court a full-scale rout now that the military were involved. That decision, though, would still have to be approved by mass meetings at the workplaces.

But papers were able to report the following day that it was anticipated that it would be ratified, with many meetings taking place later that afternoon and some having already decided to return. Most engineers were beginning to return and Singer's in Clydebank would be going back the following day. The Wednesday saw a general resumption of work, with only Parkhead Forge of the major industrial sites still not back (but their return was imminent and the delay technical rather than political). To all intents and purposes, the strike was now over.

However, it was not a cowed or submissive retreat, but a return to work where strikers went back with their heads held high. They may not have achieved what they had set out to, but in the circumstances they doubtless felt that the defeat was honourable. They had made their point and were going back on their own terms. Those involved in the riot in George Square must have felt they gave as good as they got.

Simmering anger and a feeling of justification would likely have been the mood of many.

It was also tempered for some by returning not to the 54-hour week that had once been operated, but to the 47-hour week that was now in place. Discussions between shipyard and engineering federations and unions had continued and delivered the new weekly regime whilst the strike was ongoing, and many of the strikers were in those very sectors. Though not at that stage applicable to many other trades, negotiations were underway and progress was being made with the expectation that it was coming.

That was something McShane years later recalled in his biography: enjoying a longer lie-in, able for the first time to start at 8 a.m. rather than 6 a.m. Previously it had meant a rise at five and a breakfast break mid-morning. Now no such breakfast break was included; the later start allowed for it to be had at home, with the routine now being working through until lunch with a brief mid-morning tea break; a much more civilised lifestyle than the long day and hard slog that had preceded it. Others must have equally welcomed the change, even if they had initially rejected it in a ballot. It was still a significant reduction from what had been the norm, and from before the war especially.

Normality also began to return to other areas as industrial disputes settled, though Belfast continued on for a week or so after. British troops were also called in and ultimately the strike, which had been for a 44-hour week, collapsed. The virus of sectarianism was also injected through the Orange Order into what had been a labour dispute to seek to divide the working class, as Ireland faced the backdrop of the War of Independence and the ultimate partition of the country. The unity of the workforce was undermined by religious divisions, and though some of this may have been inevitable given the political backdrop, it was still used by the authorities to break the strike along with their military muscle.

Elsewhere, in most of the major disputes that had been threatening the government, settlement was also reached in the weeks following Bloody Friday. A strike by electricians in London had resulted in it being made a criminal offence to deny the supply of electricity. Tube workers also struck, but both disputes were settled quite speedily with DORA invoked. More worrying for the government was the danger of a triple alliance strike by rail, transport and mine workers, hence why, unlike in Glasgow, there were direct negotiations with unions to avoid a united front and to bring about settlements.

By the end of March settlement with the big unions had been achieved and the possibility of a major confrontation averted. A commission had been set up to investigate the claims by miners and the Prime Minister even met with them, such was their potential threat. Hours had been reduced, with the miners going down to seven hours per day for those working underground with the agreement also including that they would decrease further to six hours in 1921 if economic circumstances allowed it. For surface workers it was to be 46.5 hours exclusive of meal breaks. Other major unions and sectors including the National Union of Railwaymen negotiated similar reductions and resolved their disputes. McShane would not be alone in welcoming a later start and a shorter week.

The cessation of the strike was also matched by a reduction in the military presence, and Glasgow began to return to normal as troops were stood down. Soldiers guarding the power stations and factories were withdrawn, tanks and military vehicles returned to their bases and the City Chambers began to become a municipal building again, rather than an army garrison. The visible sight of a city under siege was gone, and all the troops removed from the city by 17 February. Though some tensions still remained and no doubt some animosity lingered. However, that was further reduced by the release of the strike leaders on bail pending trial. Their fears no doubt assuaged that the Bolshevik Revolution wasn't happening, the authorities felt it was safe to release them and show some magnanimity, if not generate some goodwill.

Gallacher and others had appeared in court for a procedural hearing on the Monday following the riot and all were refused bail. That was a cursory hearing and Gallacher represented himself, rejecting the services of Rosslyn Mitchell, although Gallacher did use another solicitor, Walter C. Leechman, known on left circles in the city. That was probably inspired by his then closeness to John Maclean and memories of his speech from the dock as much as a disdain for lawyers and the legal system. He took the opportunity to complain about the conditions of his imprisonment, though it received short shrift from the magistrate.

All accused appeared once again on 20 February when bail was again refused, and reference was made to one of the strike leaders as being 'political', no doubt Willie Gallacher. The sheriff was reported in the *Herald* the following day as saying 'Tut-tut, a political character', the mask perhaps slipping from the veneer of a supposedly impartial member of the judiciary.

An appeal was made to the High Court, though, and on Saturday 22 February all were granted bail. The defence made it clear that there was no danger of them absconding pending trial and all were willing to give an undertaking to attend further proceedings. The Lord Advocate opposed the application on the basis that he could see no grounds for it and given the seriousness of the offences. Having retired to consider its position, the court returned to grant bail in each case. Shinwell, Hopkins, Gallacher and Kirkwood were then released on £300 bail, the others on bail of £120 and £80. Most were released that Saturday night from Duke Street Prison, though for some reason Shinwell was detained until the Sunday morning. Their detention was over, but their trial still had to take place.

This was quick in coming around, and it seemed as if the authorities wanted it over and done with so that all could move on. The charges were laid against the accused as quickly as Saturday 8 March at a preliminary diet with the trial commencing before a jury the following month on 7 April. It took place at the High Court in Edinburgh once again and, as with Maclean, it was moved east and away from Glasgow. There Lord Justice Clerk Dickson presided, the second most senior judge in the country, who, before the war, had been Lord Advocate in the Unionist government. The Lord Advocate was prosecuting and there were counsel for the accused, other than Gallacher who was representing himself. Over 190 witnesses had been listed by the prosecution and several hundred for the defence. The court room itself was packed with press, supporters and interested members of the public. A huge police presence was also present to ensure that there was no disorder.

The twelve accused were Shinwell, Gallacher and Kirkwood along with Joseph Brennan, George Ebury, Harry Hopkins, David McKenzie, Robert Loudon, Neil Alexander, James Murray, David Oliver and William McCartney. The charges against them were laid in legal language and alleged that Shinwell, Gallacher, Kirkwood, Brennan, Ebury and Hopkins had, between 27 and 30 January 1919, planned and then incited the mob in George Square on 31 January with the intention of overwhelming the police and taking over the municipal buildings and the North British Station Hotel. The charge then went on to allege that the mob including Shinwell, Gallacher, Kirkwood, Brennan, Ebury, Hopkins and McKenzie, Loudon, Alexander and Murray had conducted itself in a riotous manner, stopped tramcars, smashed windows and assaulted people including the sheriff and police officers. Then finally narrating that the mob or part of it, consisting of Oliver and McCartney and a large number of others, had surrounded and robbed a shopkeeper in Paisley Road West of rings and jewellery and assaulted the police.

The political leaders were being targeted and the entire catalogue of events that had thereafter unfolded were being laid at their door. Initial legal points relating to the relevance of aspects of the charges were rejected and they all then pled not guilty. In Scotland, unlike some other jurisdictions particularly in England and the USA, there are no preliminary speeches to the jury by either prosecutors or defence to set the scene for them and give them an indication of what they intend to show. Instead the evidence is allowed to unfold and it is the witness's testimony itself that provides the information to the jury, for them to then decide upon. Though, there are closing speeches to allow prosecution and defence to remind the jury of points they consider critical.

The first person called, therefore, into the witness box by the Lord Advocate and doubtless to try to make an early impression upon the jury was a police officer, Lieutenant Gray. The following day he was followed by more police colleagues and the town clerk, with the Lord Provost and further officers appearing on the third day. All began to outline the attacks that they said they had endured from the crowd. By the Thursday, police officers were still being called to give evidence – all speaking to a fairly standard script about being attacked and almost overwhelmed with missiles and bottles raining down upon them.

They were followed by the chief constable and the sheriff. The chief constable stated that his instructions had been to have a large force present and to be well disposed to the crowd. But he went on to narrate that he had been struck by a man when near to the Gladstone statue. Though the senior officer himself did not identify his assailant, other officers had said it was Gallacher. Under cross-examination the chief constable admitted that there had been no sign of any intention by the crowd to attack the tramcars, but proceeded on to defend his officers with regard to the baton charges that had taken place.

When he gave evidence Sheriff MacKenzie said that the crowd had deliberately held up tramcars and that a police baton charge was needed otherwise officers would have been overwhelmed. He continued by adding that it was his duty to read the Riot Act and he was satisfied that an appeal to the military authorities had been required. Other police officers giving evidence that day not only identified Gallacher as the perpetrator of the assault on the chief constable, but also stated that the strike leader had refused to get off the plinth at the Gladstone statue when asked and had to be pulled down. Another went on to state that they had heard Kirkwood call for 'boys to rally round'.

On the Friday the case for the prosecution was concluded and the case for the accused opened. Rosslyn Mitchell, both a lawyer and an elected councillor, was called first for the defence; he was also the instructing solicitor for several of the accused. He was called, no doubt, to try to give a favourable impression to the jury with his articulacy and demeanour, and to speak of the good character of the accused. When questioned by counsel he gave glowing references for the other clients, though, as Gallacher was to recall in his biography, he proved to be somewhat less than helpful to him.

This appears to have been unintentional, and came out in cross-examination by the Lord Advocate – though it did no doubt paint a picture for the jury of Gallacher being a rabble rouser and hothead. During questioning Mitchell had referred to earlier meetings, giving the impression of Gallacher as angry and impetuous. In later years Gallacher would laugh about it with John Wheatley, who had, after all, wanted him to take Mitchell as his lawyer. However, Mitchell did also give evidence in which he was clear that he'd had a good sight of the events from the City Chambers and that it was the police who were responsible for what had happened.

Mitchell was followed by the leader of the Labour group on the council, again no doubt to try to impress the jury with the respectability of those supporting the accused and the strike. Another defence witness stated that two trams had been held up by the crowd but that the police had baton-charged them. As a consequence, he said the crowd had surged towards the Square to get away from it all, but that the police had charged them once again. He was in no doubt that it was police brutality that was the cause of the riot.

The following week witnesses for the defence continued to be called and were as adamant that it had been police actions that caused the riot as the officers had been that it was all the responsibility of demonstrators. Testimony was heard which denied that there had been any attempt to stop tramcars and others spoke of an unprovoked attack by the police. Any interference with tramcars, they stated, was not deliberate, but for the safety of those around them that might be struck.

It wasn't just strikers and protestors who were called to give evidence by the defence but others who had been in the area for work or other reasons and had simply got caught up in it. A man from Denny (then part of Stirlingshire) said that he had been in the Square, though had no connection with the strike. Yet, notwithstanding this, he had been struck by a police baton. His clear impression was that the police had looked as if they were going to do something.

In all, over fifty witnesses were called for the defence before their case was finally concluded on the Wednesday. All spoke to much the same story, whether they had been participants in the demonstration or just innocent bystanders before the riot subsumed them. Under some intense cross-examination by the Lord Advocate all denied that there had been any stoning of the police or missiles flung before the riot broke out. Some were also pushed on the political nature of the strike, with one witness making it clear that nobody with any authority in the strike had anything to do with the red flag being passed around and hoisted up the flagpole at the City Chambers earlier in the week. Another made it clear that the reason for the strike was the forty-hour week claim, and was adamant that Shinwell had emphasised that. As well as disputing the denials of violent actions by the accused, some spoke of Gallacher being struck down by police officers.

There was even one light-hearted moment when a witness who was asked to take the oath and 'swear to God to tell the truth', responded, 'Which God are you referring to?' The bewigged judge retorted that the witness wasn't there to ask questions, which only elicited the cheeky reply, 'The reason I am asking is that you appear to be a Handy Andy in a pantomime.' Needless to say, the defence counsel speedily indicated that they were dispensing with his evidence, to the general mirth of all those watching.

With the evidence of both prosecution and defence concluded it was then time for speeches to the jury. In his address on the Thursday the Lord Advocate sought not just convictions against those accused of the violent actions that had followed, but against those who, he argued, had incited them, though he withdrew that aspect of the complaint against Kirkwood, recognising that there was no evidence that he'd been involved. However, he certainly didn't seek to either underplay the seriousness of the situation or minimise the actions of those he held culpable for it. According to the *Glasgow Herald*'s report on 18 April 1919, Scotland's senior prosecutor even ended his oration by stating with a theatrical flourish that an 'act of revolution was in progress and could be traced to the previous incitement'.

He was followed by defence counsel, where several initially focused on the failure of the prosecution to prove any intention by their clients to incite the crowd, before moving on to address the jury more widely on the case and most referring to the good character of their clients. That final aspect somewhat irked Gallacher, who would follow them in addressing the jury. He had been fully participating in the proceedings and from his memoirs seemed to be enjoying himself, cross-examining prosecution witnesses and obviously feeling at liberty to be more robust than the learned counsel had been, and especially with some police officers who he challenged quite forcibly.

However, he also believed that the nature of the defence being put forward by the King's Counsel for many of the others about their outstanding good character meant that by implication blame would fall upon him. They were being portrayed as being fine upstanding men and solid citizens, whereas it was common knowledge that he was the leader of the dispute with a fairly wild reputation. In that he was probably right, but it seems he equally contributed to it by the nature of his defence. According to his biography, his speech to the jury was an impassioned call for justice in which he told them, 'I am accused of having struck certain policemen. This part of the evidence is true. I struck out, I struck hard. My only regret is that I didn't have greater strength, so that I could have struck harder.' It may have been said passionately and with all sincerity, but it was not necessarily likely to impress the jury. He concluded with the melodramatic ending, 'Gentlemen, it is for you to decide. You can decide that I'll sleep tonight in my own home or in a prison cell, but believe me, whichever it is, I'll sleep with an easy conscience.'[64]

After that the Lord Justice Clerk concluded proceedings for the day, stating that he would give his charge to the jury the following day. The charge being the directions on points of law that the judge provides and also any comments that he may have on particular parts of the evidence that the jury may wish to consider, though always qualified by pointing out that it is for them as jurors to ultimately decide on the evidence as they saw it.

The following day Lord Dickson returned once again to a packed and expectant court. He started by dismissing the charge of incitement before Wednesday 29 January as he said no evidence of any kind had been led and it was clear that at that time a meeting on the 31st hadn't even been thought of. It had followed, after all, from the march to the City Chambers and the rally on the 29th when the request to the Lord Provost had been made. The judge's summation on other aspects of evidence led was also notably balanced, stating that the 'evidence of the town clerk and of Neil Maclean conflicted as to whether the strikers' promise to "stop the cars" was a threat of violence, or merely a promise that the tramway men would be brought out on strike'. He left that for the jury to decide but by raising it most certainly would have got them thinking about it. 'He further pointed out that it was a question of fact for the jury whether the stoppage of cars on the south side of the Square was deliberate or merely the result of the pressure of the crowd.'[65] The balance contained in the judge's address to the jury was acknowledged by Gallacher, who felt that it almost certainly cleared most of his colleagues.

---

64 William Gallacher, op. cit., p. 241.
65 Iain McLean, op. cit., p. 128.

Two of the accused were acquitted as no evidence had been led against them and with that it was over to the jury for their deliberation. They were away for two hours but returned thereafter to announce that by a verdict of fourteen to one (a Scottish jury comprises fifteen) they found Shinwell and Gallacher guilty of incitement and Murray and McCartney guilty of mobbing and rioting. All eight other accused were acquitted. A later news report in *Forward* suggested that the jury had been influenced by evidence of the actions of some of the accused in seeking to protect police from serious assault and that most certainly applied to Kirkwood, but the culpability for the wider actions still fell upon Shinwell and Gallacher.

Those acquitted were dismissed from the dock and Lord Dickson proceeded to sentence the four convicted. Before a deathly silent court, he sent Shinwell to jail for five months and Gallacher, Murray and Mc-Cartney for three months before rising from the bench and departing the court. The sentences seemed remarkably light in comparison with what had been dispensed during the war to the likes of John Maclean, never mind the huge violence and disorder that had occurred on this occasion. After all, Gallacher had been sentenced to a far longer period in prison for what was a far less serious incident several years before. Moreover, wartime conditions were still prevailing: DORA still applied and it was the worst civil unrest for generations, where a very lengthy sentence could normally have been anticipated.

Whether Lord Dickson, having heard the evidence, was minded that it had either been caused by the police actions or that they had hugely overreacted isn't known. He most likely was not persuaded by the police evidence or prosecution case (though he never criticised the police or the authorities in his summation to the jury or in passing sentence), as, if he had been, several years' hard labour would most likely have been imposed.

Of course, the authorities were initially seeking to calm the situation down by restoring order through the military, but as soon as possible equally trying to return to an air of normality in the city and country. Whilst it may have been felt that a heavy sentence could have worsened that or inflamed passions, there is no suggestion that this feeling was communicated to Lord Dickson or that it interfered in the trial in any way. It appears that even he could see from the evidence that had come before him that it had not been planned as a revolution and that the cause had primarily been the actions of the police. For that he deserves some credit, appearing to be prepared to mitigate the sentences despite a wider clamour from establishment circles.

That is given credence by the fact that the Lord Advocate had not only prosecuted the case, showing how importantly it was viewed by the authorities, but, in his speech to the jury, had sought to portray the accused as instigating revolution and being responsible for the riot. That view was, after all, the prevailing opinion of the establishment – not just from the Secretary of State for Scotland who had described it as a 'Bolshevist Revolution', but in the newspapers which, having condemned the strike throughout, were scathing in the comments on the outcome of the court case.

The *Herald*, as with many other establishment newspapers, was out-raged by the leniency shown by the judge and the acquittals brought in by the jury. They accused the strike leaders of having 'levelled a pistol at the heart of society' and having used unconstitutional methods. Their editorial the following day described the outcome as an anti-climax given the sinister purpose and calamitous possibilities, dismayed that the punishments – especially against Shinwell – had not been more severe. With reference to the Bolsheviks they opined, 'We trust that the plight of Central and Eastern Europe has made them realise the horrors of the abyss to whose edge they dragged the community.'

However, the sentence had been imposed, and though appeals were intimated by counsel for the accused, they didn't subsequently proceed. Gallacher turned and shook hands with his former co-accused who were, by then, sitting behind him, and waved to his wife in the crowd before being taken to the cells along with the other three. Meanwhile, the other eight left the court, where a large crowd had gathered, before heading back to Glasgow where they were met by friends as they arrived off the train. A significant police presence was on hand in case of any trouble but, as it was, Kirkwood and his colleagues were greeted warmly by supporters before being accompanied to the station. Arriving by train back in Glasgow they were again met by friends who had been advised of the outcome in the High Court and had hurried to meet them.

It wasn't the only trial relating to the events of 31 January, though it was the major one and captured the attention of the nation, with so many leaders involved and the threat they had posed to the state through potential revolution. Others, though, had also been arrested and charged with incidents both in the city centre and across the wider region as trouble had flared. The end of April saw a trial at the High Court in Glasgow, which was not moved to Edinburgh, no doubt as the five accused were not political in character and were without any public support.

They were charged with rioting and looting in George Square, Argyle Street and Queen Street, causing extensive damage and the theft of goods. Police evidence detailed the extensive disorder that took place as a crowd of 500 or so proceeded down from Queen Street. One of the accused was identified as having a piece of wood and breaking shop windows, another was accused of kicking them in. Perfume, bedding, boots and shoes were all stolen as a trail of carnage was left as a section of the crowd rampaged. Officers also spoke of having had to shelter from missiles in a stairway after they had detained one of the rioters. The defence had been that they had simply been in the area when they came across a crowd throwing missiles at the police. There seems to be no suggestion that they were involved in the strike or had even been attending the demonstration in George Square.

Two were convicted by the jury, two found not proven (a Scottish verdict which is an acquittal, though often seen as indicating some suspicion but which acknowledges insufficient proof) and one was found not guilty. However, in sentencing them to three months' imprisonment each Lord Dickson, who was once more presiding, again exercised considerable leniency given the damage, theft and flagrant criminality involved. He did, though, make it clear that he hoped that the sentences would be a lesson but that they 'shouldn't be taken as a precedent – as [they] would be severely dealt with in future'.

A trial also concluded then of nine miners charged with rioting near Bothwell and Blantyre on 31 January. That had been a related strike in the pits as part of the wider campaign, even though it lacked the support of the miners' leadership. Disorder had broken out and damage to colliery equipment was alleged to have taken place. The jury returned a verdict of guilty for most, though under considerable deletion of many of the allegations and also making a request for leniency due to the age of the accused who were all young men. One was sentenced to six months, another three months and five received a period of just ten days. That seemed to bring the events of 31 January to a conclusion.

The riot had obviously cast a shadow over the city but the mood was also made more sombre by other factors. Spanish flu was beginning to take effect and the death toll was rising and noticeably so. The widespread sickness must have been evident. By the end of February, the *Herald* was reporting that the city death rate was the highest for twenty-five years, with flu and pneumonia the major killers. By March, reports were stating that the numbers were still continuing to rise.

Similarly, the unemployment and increased poverty that had been the driver for the strike also began to manifest. The *Herald* reported that month that there had been a 50 per cent increase in the number of 'necessitous children' reported to the school board. There were 11,133 as opposed to 7,870 just the previous session, and the increase almost entirely due to army and navy cases. The article pointed out that previously it had been 70 per cent military and 30 per cent civilian, but that had now grown to 80 per cent and 20 per cent respectively and was based on the conscription from the summer of 1918. It appeared that even having a father or son in the army was insufficient to avoid penury.

All of this was occurring in a city and a country that was licking its grievous wounds and assessing the sacrifice it had made in the war. As T. C. Smout wrote about the death toll, the numbers were never entirely precise, but

> one well-argued estimate put the figure at 110,000, equivalent to about 10 per cent of the Scottish male population aged between sixteen and fifty, and probably about 15 per cent of the total British War dead – the sacrifice was higher in proportionate terms than for any other country in the Empire. Thirteen out of fourteen were privates and non-commissioned officers from the working classes.[66]

Later figures have suggested that it was as high as 148,000 with the National War Memorial that stands in Edinburgh Castle recording over 150,000. It depends on dates and various classifications given for the dead, but however it is calculated it was a huge loss for a nation where the population in 1914 was estimated to be only 4,747,000. Over 18,000 of those who fell came from Glasgow alone, and it is reckoned that nearly 200,000 had gone off to war from the city. No wonder it had such a sobering effect immediately after the war, and had significant ramifications for generations to follow.

Those statistics showed that hardly a family in Glasgow was unaffected, and loss was often most deeply felt in the poorest areas. The war fervour of 1914 had been replaced by the grim reality of the Somme in 1916, and in the aftermath there was an opportunity to finally measure the loss and try as best to come to terms with it. The War Graves

---

66   T. C. Smout, op. cit., p. 267.

Commission, which had been established in 1917, was hard at work in graveyards in foreign fields to repatriate a few to their native land. Thoughts were turning to the memorials, which were soon to spring up in every community across the land commemorating those who would never make it home, even just to be buried.

That sombre atmosphere must also have impacted on attitudes to the strike and its aftermath. For many there would be reluctance for any further confrontation and certainly not at home; war had long since lost its glory and revolution wouldn't be for them. For families who had lost loved ones and were coming to terms with their grief again some normality would have been sought. In a city still shrouded in sadness and suffering with poverty and unemployment, the last thing many would have sought was further turmoil.

Events abroad would also have been noticed and added to the concerns that many would have had. Fighting continued with the Bolsheviks in eastern Europe and some sporadic clashes still occurred in Germany, tension mounted in Ireland and martial law was even declared in Spain. 'Red Terror' featured in reports as war waged in and with Russia, exacerbated by the execution of the Tsar and his family the year before.

So, there were some like John Maclean who were committed to the Bolshevik cause, and he had a hard core of support in Glasgow that was greater than in most areas in the country. Many more, though, must simply have been concerned about further conflict and feared that it might escalate and end in a return to war. It was no doubt why the ILP concentrated on housing and living standards rather than revolution and foreign affairs. The prioritisation of those bread-and-butter issues had begun before the war's conclusion, but the outcome of the election in 1918 would also have been a salutary lesson. Having focused on the constitutional route to power they now concentred on the issues they knew mattered, as they prepared for the next election.

As well as the overall public mood, the authorities and the wider establishment were taking steps to both calm the political situation down, as well as reassert control and authority. Troops in Glasgow may have been the starkest image of demonstrating their control, but negotiations also took place with unions to settle industrial confrontations, whilst pressure mounted on union leaders to exercise control over their own membership and confront shop stewards and other radicals.

Negotiations with the miners saw a deal concluded and a commission established. Putting troops on the streets of the second city was one thing, confronting the most powerful section of the workers quite another. The government was anxious to avoid confrontation with them, and the agreement was not so much reflective of their willingness to negotiate, but of the power and indeed fear the miners could induce. From the workers' perspective it might not have been everything that they wanted, but there was enough there to satisfy most, and a reduction in hours had been won. Later in the year, a strike in the railways began, which was again settled by the government and saw an eight-hour day introduced. The 47-hour week was being settled on by the unions as the demand across most sectors for a forty-hour week was further marginalised and, by implication, was no doubt seen as far too radical.

The government was managing to calm the situation and ward off further disputes through ceding claims for a reduction in hours and other benefits for workers. A position that, whilst viewed as right and sensible, was still lamented for interfering with what was seen as the sole domain of management and workers. The *Herald* leader reflected the views of many in agreeing with the appropriateness of the terms decided upon by government, but still regretting their involvement at all.

However, whilst government intervention might not have been wanted by some, action by trade unions in taking control of their memberships most certainly was. It was not just getting a grip of their members but, more importantly, addressing the militant minority within them that was demanded. It was even stated by the monarch in his King's Speech at the opening of the newly elected Parliament in February, who gave a warning to revolutionaries. The sentiment was similarly echoed by the powers that be in politics and in the press. Leaders railed against unions that didn't rein in their members, and even the parliamentary committee of the TUC warned about attempts by minorities to undermine and circumvent entire memberships, not just elected leaders.

That did not, of course, mean that morale was low or that the campaigning for social change had ceased. Appalling social conditions that had been the driver for change over generations still remained. A war had been fought and huge sacrifices made, but with little discernible benefit for so many in the city. Some as stark and tragic as the war's toll and the statistics on poverty every bit as sad as those of the war dead. As Maggie Craig details in her evocative book on Red Clydeside, 'In the years immediately following the First World War, 40 per cent more babies died in infancy in Glasgow than in the rest of Britain as a whole. One in every seven children in the city did not reach their first birthdays.'[67] Tuberculosis also stalked the overcrowded slums, with a recorded 1,000 adults lost every year to it, leading James Stewart the ILP councillor and leading activist to describe the city as 'earth's nearest suburb to hell'.[68] The issues that motivated had not been resolved by war, and were only going to worsen as the economy faltered. Anger and determination remained.

So, May Day 1919, a Thursday and a work day, saw over 100,000 process through the city with floats and banners. Not just workers marched, but their families, with bands playing and streamers billowing, and it took over an hour to pass as it made its way from George Square to Glasgow Green. Reports detailed over 250 organisations involved, though it was noticeable that the ILP had the largest representation.

At the Green and later in the evening at the St Andrew's Halls speakers addressed the crowds. Countess Markievicz, a heroine of the Easter Rising and a newly appointed Minister for Labour in the Irish

---

67   Maggie Craig, *When the Clyde Ran Red* (Mainstream, 2011), p. 53.
68   Maggie Craig, op. cit., p. 54.

Republican government, was one of the principal stars. Another large crowd was drawn for Neil Maclean, the newly elected Govan MP; John Maclean also spoke and was warmly received. A resolution was passed in favour of the overthrow of capitalism and the establishment of a cooperative commonwealth. Fraternal greetings were sent to the Soviet Republic and all workers' organisations worldwide, whilst the four imprisoned colleagues weren't forgotten, and their release was demanded. The day was hailed a great success – spirits remained undaunted, but the way of expressing it and the method of delivering it were changing as influence moved from those advocating revolution to those pursuing the electoral path.

For, whilst the city was returning to normal, the political situation was about to change. The CWC was moving out of the picture and the ILP were coming to the fore. Shop stewards were being pushed aside as the trade union leadership reasserted control. Activism would continue in the community as rents and housing would once again become major issues, but electoral politics were about to replace strikes or community action as the battlefield.

A new party was to be formed in the wake of the Bolshevik Revolution to give support to it, as opinion on the left began to divide. Most, though, would remain with the ILP, which was to transform from the umbrella organisation encompassing social and educational aspects including a wide spectrum of political views, into a formidable electoral machine.

For, despite the election outcome in 1918, the tide was turning and notwithstanding the events of 31 January radicalism was still on the march. The means for attaining socialism and the new society that was dreamed of were changing from direct action to the electoral route. A Bolshevik Rising there had not been, but politically, Red Clydeside was about to rise.

17

THE POLITICAL RISE
OF RED CLYDESIDE

Red Clydeside had been on a long slow march for many years, firstly gaining representation in the city council and then a tenuous foothold in Parliament. Disappointment at the outcome of the 1918 general election was offset by a belief and understanding that victory could still be had. The reasons for defeat had been analysed and taken on board, and the events of Bloody Friday had not crushed the desire for social and economic transformation, though it would result in a change in how it would be delivered.

Those changes were brought about not so much by the events of 31 January, though they undoubtedly focused some issues and accelerated others. Rather, they were brought about by wider social, political and economic changes, all within a changed atmosphere in a city that had been tempered by the war, but energised by the widening of the democratic franchise.

As well as the changes that saw power and control swing back to the union leaderships, a firming up in political thinking and organisation was taking place. Political thought was further evolving following the Bolshevik Revolution, both due to support for it and opposition to it, as well as a growing appreciation by many that radical change could be won through the ballot box.

The political pendulum swung away from the CWC, which,

although it continued to exist for some time to come, was a shell of an organisation from what had existed before the war and even earlier in the year. That transformation occurred everywhere to some extent, but was perhaps most marked in Glasgow where the power and organisation of the CWC had been unique. Union leaders were eager to reassert control, and in that they were supported by government and employers' organisations. Moreover, recent deals negotiated nationally on hours by the major unions had been appreciated by most workers, and doubtless contrasted in the eyes of many with the unsuccessful localised strikes in the likes of Glasgow and Belfast.

Union leaderships did just that, negotiating nationally and seeking to take back control from local militants in Glasgow or elsewhere who had both outflanked them and undermined them – as they saw it. There had often been little love lost between the two, despite a shared membership. The position not just of the union leaders but of local officials was reasserted. They not only had the resources and the mechanism to do so, but were being encouraged and facilitated in that by the government and employers.

All this was compounded by the craft base of so much of the skilled engineering sector, which allowed employers to divide unions and play off worker against worker. Collective bargaining that was rightly welcomed by unions also undermined the ability of shop stewards to lead or act independently. Employers and union officials also sometimes even connived to restrict the rights and influence of the stewards, having negotiations and agreements struck at a level ensuring the exclusion of any say or influence from the factory floor.

Moreover, it appeared to be successful, as deals were struck and hours reduced. Not only were the shop stewards and radicals being punished, but the more moderate faction was being rewarded. Consciously or subconsciously it must have begun to seem to many that the more moderate route was more successful than the revolutionary road. That would also have played into the mood in the city. In many ways, January 1919 was the zenith of shop steward power such that by 1920, leading Marxist Robin Page Arnot was able to comment that he 'was bemused by Moscow's desire to win the movement for the fledgling Communist Party: "it no longer exists. One might as well try and recruit the Chartists!"'[69]

But, consideration of the political changes that took place after the Bloody Friday events requires reflection on the nature of what the ILP had been both before and especially during the war. It had evolved and grown, but it was considerably wider in influence than simply being a political party with a few councillors and an MP. It was steeped in the community and drawn from it, in the tenements and slums as well as in the factories and shipyards. Its strength was its grassroots campaigning, whether on housing, work or war, and it exerted an influence that was far beyond its membership base.

After all, it was from and through the ILP that most radical campaigning took place, and it was the forum for both social and political meeting and networking. It was astutely commented on by historian Alan McKinlay that 'before 1914 the ILP had become the organisational intersection of a series of progressive social networks, the hub of radical activity from the shop floor, the teeming tenements of the Glasgow communities, to the council chambers'.[70] The war greatly increased that profile and status, and the ILP further came to prominence with anti-war agitation, rent strikes and industrial involvement where, even if the bulk of the CWC leadership were BSP members, they orbited in a political environment largely created by the ILP.

For at that stage, with electioneering secondary in many ways, there was a far wider political spectrum within the organisation, again astutely referred to as 'an ever-increasing political eclecticism; between 1914–18 the party became host to every shade of radical thinking, from

---

69 Alan McKinlay and R. J. Morris, op. cit., p. 143.
70 Alan McKinlay and R. J. Morris, op. cit., p. 123.

advanced liberalism to doctrinaire Marxism'.[71] It was for that reason that the party had members from the liberal lawyer Rosslyn Mitchell through to the radical shop steward David Kirkwood, from the Irish catholic Wheatley through to radical socialist Maxton, and even Maclean and Gallacher ventured with ease in and out of its orbit.

It again also explains why more normal political descriptions of a party did not apply for the organisation that provided an umbrella for all to operate under within the city. Again, it was perceptively described by Alan McKinlay as being 'best understood not as a conventional political party but as a loosely organised democratic movement whose primary political terrain was the factory floor and the street corner'.[72] For it lived and breathed in the city and it was from there it grew.

Definition of individuals or the party as social reformers or revolutionaries during the war period are hard to make as they were often one and the same. Ideologies were still more flexible and party structures less well defined. The ILP had members from both factions and allowed for many others as political thought evolved. It allowed a forum and space and covered the entire range of socialist views and convictions. Debate and discourse flowed from it, into it and within it. People constantly interacted and views crossed over: some individuals may always have been classified in one section or another, from the revolutionary Maclean to the more pragmatic Dollan, and issues could divide as Maxton was vehemently anti-war, yet Kirkwood felt the solution was to be found in ending it quickly and working towards that. But, work together they did, and with a common purpose (even if slightly different in perception).

However, this could never be sustained, and the changed social political and economic situation after the war both necessitated and ensured that. The new opportunities that existed with the wider franchise and the requirement for political parties to focus on that was a

71   Alan McKinlay and R. J. Morris, op. cit., p. 123.
72   Alan McKinlay and R. J. Morris, op. cit., p. 123.

critical factor. Electoral programmes needed devising, and support for them was required. Moreover, one political party had never managed to reflect all the views or ideologies, but the arrival of electoral politics made the continuation of such a wide-ranging umbrella-type organisation unsustainable.

Likewise, the Bolshevik Revolution was a catalyst for the left with the formation of a party to support it and a firming up of political positions with regard to the movement. Added to that was the shift of political power that had taken place from the CWC and factory representatives to the political arena and those who dominated there. Politics would also begin to change from a much wider social base to a far narrower electoral role. All those shifts impacted on the ILP, which transformed from a broader democratic movement into a more focused political party.

The trajectory for the party was upwards, with the extension of the franchise and the underlying reasons for the lack of success in 1918 analysed. But, it still had to be worked for and won. Whilst success was still likely and believed in by many, it was still far from assured, and many even doubted that the ultimate victors would be the ILP. For its primacy was also to be challenged both from within by the Labour Party, to which it was affiliated, and from without by a new party on the left.

However, morale was given a fillip as early as July 1919 with a by-election victory in nearby Bothwell. There John Robertson, the Labour candidate who was also president of the Scottish Miners' Federation, romped home with nearly 70 per cent of the vote, having lost by just over 300 in December. Clear evidence that changes were afoot, and giving an impetus to the push to organise and adapt for political success. Though outside the city of Glasgow itself, it was a boost to those campaigning within it. They were revitalised by the win, and further success beckoned for the ILP as council elections were set for the November, though the situation in Glasgow was more complicated with a boundary review and further elections planned for 1920.

It was not all plain sailing for the ILP, rather they would still be facing some major headwinds and other challenges. When the local election came, gains were made across the country – though it was far from an electoral landslide:

> Labour did less well in Edinburgh than in the industrial west and in Fife. In a number of burghs Labour swept the board, all its candidates heading the polls at Cowdenbeath, Irvine, Lerwick and Kilsyth. In Aberdeen, labour made five gains, in Dundee no less than eight and in Clydebank five. 119 gains were claimed in all.[73]

In Glasgow five gains were made, which was solid progress even with the election being muted by the changes set for the following year. It must, though, have been a morale boost and an encouragement to increase the focus and the efforts on the electoral front.

Moreover, by the following year when the new boundaries were contested it was a huge success in Glasgow, even if elsewhere in the country it seemed to be a consolidation of the gains the year before. The ILP, under the direction of Patrick Dollan, who was becoming the electoral strategist and architect of the council campaigns, stormed home in many parts of the city. Forty-four seats were won in what were then multi-member wards, as they once again are now, and eleven saw a complete wipe out with Labour taking all of them, including one by Mary Barbour in the Fairfield ward in Govan. Though not enough to give them electoral power it was a huge jolt to the political establishment, with the tallied results in parliamentary constituencies pointing to many likely gains when a general election was next called.

Further local elections in 1921 in the city saw Labour suffer a slight setback, though that seemed to reflect the vagaries of the local electoral system as in the wards they lost, 'the candidate with the fewest votes of

---

73   Iain McLean, op. cit., p. 161.

the previous year's three successful candidates stood for re-election, so that in wards where Labour scraped in in third place in 1920 it would have had to improve its position to keep the seat'.[74] That didn't deflect from the growing power of Labour in the city and of the ILP, in particular, even though the relationship between two was about to change.

Labour had historically been a very loose umbrella organisation where trade unions and political groups came together to push for legislation and representation in Parliament. Campaigning in the main came from other groups or parties within it, rather than by the Labour Party itself. In Glasgow it was the ILP who dominated; direct membership didn't matter as representation was through unions or affiliated organisations. People stood under the Labour ticket if they were selected and were either members directly or belonged to an affiliated organisation. It was on that basis that John Maclean had contested the Gorbals parliamentary seat, as a member of the BSP, even if ultimately denied formal recognition by the party nationally.

However, changes to the Labour Party constitution were made in 1918. Several committees had been established by the CWC's hate figure Arthur Henderson in September 1917 when he had left the Cabinet and was still leader of the Labour Party. It afforded an opportunity for him to try to reunite the parliamentary group following the deep divisions over the war by seeking to modernise the party and change its structures and operation. The final proposals also established Clause IV with the commitment to public ownership – the source of argument in later years – but which was widely welcomed at the time. It provided a radical political programme that afforded an opportunity to bring radical groupings together but would also be a challenge to the distinct identity of the ILP.

It meant that the delineation between the ILP and Labour would grow more marked nationally. Again, though, given its history and

---

74   Iain McLean, op. cit., p. 162.

local strength, it was the ILP who would continue to dominate in Glasgow for some time to come. They possessed the membership and the campaigners on the ground, with almost all the then senior figures aligned to it, with activism and campaigning even more dominated by their rank and file members: 'The ILP completely dominated the executive of the Glasgow Labour Party: in 1920, 14 of the 18 members were ILP nominees.'[75] In many ways Labour was the ILP, and the ILP was Labour – and it would be many years before that would alter in the city.

But, the decision by Labour to recruit locally did still have consequences for the ILP, as it signalled an expansion of membership predicated around local constituency parties. Membership at a shilling a year was cheaper than the ILP and the expectations of activism significantly less. The ILP remained an affiliated organisation, but could now be challenged within constituencies by direct membership in a parallel structure.

For some, including amongst most of the party leadership, it was thought it might encourage political awareness and increase support on the left, and even provide a gateway for those less persuaded by the more radical vision of the ILP. For many activists, where commitment was expected if not demanded, armchair or notional members were frowned upon or disdained. For Maxton and some others, Labour's radical programme was also an opportunity for the ILP, whereby they could use the alliance as the vehicle to deliver their ultimate socialist goals working within the wider umbrella organisation, but with the clear intention of delivering their much more left-wing agenda.

Some ILP members, however, sought to sever formal links with the Labour Party and the Scottish conference in 1920 saw several west of Scotland branches push for just that, arguing that they would be damaged by the association and faced being challenged from the left by other parties. They sought a distinctive and entirely separate political party that would be to the left of Labour and in competition with them.

---

75   Alan McKinlay and R. J. Morris, op. cit., p. 129.

The party leadership was firmly opposed to that and the opposition to it was led by John Wheatley, who argued for the preservation of the distinctive nature of the ILP, but within the wider Labour Party, and accused the left-wing activists of seeking to create a situation that would demand that 'Workers of the World Divide and not workers of the world Unite'. When it came to the vote, continued Labour affiliation was comfortably carried and the party chose to remain an affiliated organisation but distinct within it, through its more radical and left-wing views.

The Communist Party of Great Britain (CPGB) was also to be established in 1920. The Bolshevik Revolution was the precursor for its creation, as efforts were made to unite the revolutionary left within a new party. The Comintern (or Communist International) had been established in March 1919 and was intent on seeking to establish revolutionary parties around the world. The purpose being to provide support for revolutionary aims abroad but, more importantly, to give support to the Bolshevik regime in Russia.

Initially, it was thought that the BSP and the ILP would provide the nucleus for membership. However, relationships between the Comintern and the latter were never good and soon broke down. The CPGB was formed without them, and any lingering hopes that they might thereafter join were soon killed off by the clandestine nature of the new party and its commitment to parallel underground networks, both of which were an anathema to the ILP. John Maclean had split from the BSP the year before and opposed the establishment of the new party, seeking his own Scottish one instead, but which was not countenanced by Moscow. Though it seems it required the full weight of Moscow influence, including that of Lenin himself, to offset the hold that the local hero had over the revolutionary left in Scotland.

Some of the minority ILP activists from the left defected to these new parties, including a few entire branches, though few leading figures. Helen Crawfurd, one of the leading lights of the rent strike, and

Walton Newbold (soon to be elected as a Communist MP) were the only senior members to do so. The CPGB also provided the political home to a minority from the SLP, including Arthur MacManus and Tom Bell. Both were well known in the CWC, MacManus from Weirs and Bell, originally from Parkhead, involved in the Foundry Workers' Union. They were also soon joined by Willie Gallacher who had initially declined, disparaging the parliamentarism and Labour Party affiliation, until lectured by Lenin himself on a visit to Moscow. The BSP, which many in the Clyde Co-ordinating Committee leadership during the strike had been members of, also merged into the newly established Communist Party.

When the CPGB was established in London in the summer of 1920, MacManus was elected its first chairman and Bell became national organiser. J. R. Campbell, who had organised the military veterans during the forty-hour dispute and marshalled the strikers to march to the Green on Bloody Friday, was also a founding member. However, other than these, few Scots were initially involved with the launch, and meetings were dominated by individuals and organisations from England and Wales. This was probably indicative of the absence not just of the ILP, but also Maclean. Further meetings saw the party established north of the border to become one of the largest and most influential sections within it, though still considerably smaller than the ILP.

However, the loss of many from that section of the left did have an effect upon the ILP in terms of its positioning and activity. Many of the left members had been at the forefront of positioning the party as a much wider political vehicle than simply an electoral force. Some were those most active in social and educational activities, and had sought to maintain that position for the party rather than concentrating on the electoral force that Dollan and others were creating. Though many who remained were equally committed to a party operating much more broadly, the removal of critical allies would swing the balance and affect the nature of the ILP over the coming years.

Membership of the party had also exploded, increasing by a quarter in Glasgow between November 1918 and January 1919 as part of a concerted membership drive. That had been driven at community rather than factory level, where the experience of the rent strikes had shown the possibilities of community activism, and in many ways was much more of a driver for the increase than the industrial activities. The politicisation of the city saw many signing up almost as a declaration of faith and commitment to a shared cause, whether as a consequence of the rent strikes, industrial disputes or anti-war agitation.

That was reflected in the nature of the membership, which was much more working class than the party nationally and, significantly, was based on the skilled engineering and shipyard workers and within the communities in which they lived; hence why growth and membership remained highest in the areas such as Govan and Partick. Added to them were the teachers such as Maxton, and others from middle-class occupations who were ideologically driven, along with women, who made up 20 per cent of the membership. In many other parts of the country, though, the increase had more been driven by disaffected liberals or pacifists joining without the socialist commitment and working-class roots of their Glasgow comrades. That would make the city party much more radical than the party nationally as a whole.

However, as the economy deteriorated and unemployment worsened in 1921, the industrial sectors of engineering and the shipyards suffered in particular, and accordingly, so did the core base of ILP membership: 'By late 1921 over one third of the Glasgow membership were unable to pay their contributions and the party was forced to appeal for the assistance of middle class sympathisers.'[76] That had been compounded by an increase in membership fees, not just greater than the Labour Party, but even more than the newly formed Communist Party. It had a knock-on effect of 'wiping out many east end branches and increasing

---

76   Alan McKinlay and R. J. Morris, op. cit., p. 139.

the relative importance of Patrick Dollan's power base in the Govan and Partick areas'.[77]

The membership decline also played a part in changing the nature of the party's activities, and moved them to become much more focused on election activities. That was probably inevitable, as politics transformed though the ILP remained a much more ideological party than the wider Labour Party, and social and educational aspects remained in many branches. However, from the perspective of the ILP leadership, the loss of members to the Communist Party (as Patrick Dollan wrote in the Glasgow ILP Federation annual report for 1920–21) allowed the party to be 'united in aim and purpose',[78] which no doubt meant focusing on electoral power.

The leadership of the ILP at the start of the third decade of the twentieth century remained primarily the same as it had been before the start of the First World War. Patrick Dollan, John Wheatley, James Maxton and Tom Johnston amongst many others, and though having different personalities and differing views on some issues, were united in their views on the direction that the party required to take. Although they disagreed with those now in the Communist Party, they most certainly remained passionately committed to the cause of socialism.

All had campaigned publicly and bravely during the war, some even going to prison as a consequence. They had supported the forty-hour week strike when it had occurred and had been the principal backers of the rent strikes. The views they had held before and during the war were unaltered, their principles unbroken, they simply saw the need for the party to take a different direction from those who left.

Moreover, there was good reason for taking that view. The battlefield was moving from the industrial and community front to the ballot box. An umbrella organisation was no longer sustainable as a coherent political programme and an election manifesto needed to be set, as

---

77   Alan McKinlay and R. J. Morris, op. cit., p. 139.
78   Alan McKinlay and R. J. Morris, op. cit., p. 146.

challenges were faced from Labour on the right and the Communist Party on the left.

There was a historic opportunity afforded by the franchise, which they realised could be achieved. The chance hadn't been taken in 1918, but the lessons that had been learned needed to be implemented. The election campaign had been shambolic with poor preparation and often even worse organisation. Yet, it was also realised that support existed and, properly managed, success could be achieved. The prize was great and the price was low, the loss of some former colleagues offset by the need to win over many more voters.

It didn't involve any changes to the values of the party or a ceding of any principles held by the individuals – it was a continuation of the old political philosophy, but within the new social setting after the war. It was essential for campaigns to become tighter and more focused in the new political world that was arising. Winning wasn't going to be easy, with finance and membership issues within and electoral challenges from without, but it could be done if the changes were made and the leadership knew that.

There were other factors that also assisted in their rise. Importantly, there was the Irish vote, which moved over from its historic allegiance to the Liberals and was driven not just by Gladstone's support for Irish Home Rule, but antipathy to the Tories and landlordism. It had been ongoing for a while, but was to become quite marked. The early cooperation on the council at the turn of the century between Labour and Irish representatives had laid the foundations, but there had been some issues that caused rancour and turbulence along the way. Though many in the community had been supportive and some were even leading party members like Wheatley and Dollan, a solid endorsement did not exist. But that was about to change with the community moving almost en bloc, and there were several reasons for that including prohibition, education and Ireland itself.

Not just the ILP, but even the Labour Party and the STUC had historically shown support for prohibition. It sprang from the deep moral basis that forged the socialism of many, and was not just a religious commitment for some, but a belief that the working class were harmed by the widespread availability of alcohol. Allied to that was antipathy to wealthy brewers who were often prominent supporters of the Tories. The ILP, in particular, had a streak that cleaved strongly to temperance and many senior members including Maxton, Johnston and many others were lifelong teetotallers.

The Irish community, on the other hand, had many senior members who were publicans and involved in the licensed trade. Prejudice and discrimination restricted career opportunities for them with many of the craft occupations, especially in the shipyards and engineering where jobs were either closed to them or very difficult to gain entry. Accordingly, the pub trade offered opportunities denied elsewhere, and pubs became a place where the Irish community could meet and socialise. It wasn't that they liked alcohol any more than the resident Scottish community, simply that circumstances brought them together in Scotland, as indeed happened around the world with Irish emigration.

Many of the poorest areas such as the Gorbals and Hutchesontown had large Irish communities and the publicans were influential in them, with Wheatley himself having briefly been in the trade. Prohibition was an anathema to them and they opposed candidates who supported it, sometimes with the effect of harming Labour candidates. The abandonment of prohibition killed off lingering hostility from some influential members of the community and, more importantly, brought them on board as supporters and activists. This would prove critical in many areas where the Irish community was large and the premises themselves almost became campaign rooms for Labour.

Education was another area that was to see the community move over to supporting Labour. Public schools had been funded, but not those that operated voluntarily and that primarily meant Catholic schools. They had been started largely by the Church, but funding was limited

and provision and premises often poor. The 1918 Education Act legis-
lated to bring schools within the ambit of the local authority for them
to be funded and supported. Although this was strongly supported by
the Catholic Church and welcomed by the Irish community, Labour
was ambivalent on the issue, but the political opposition was hostile.
Moreover, with many senior Catholics within the ILP it is easy to see
why backing would be given. Dollan may have been only notionally
of the faith, but he was from the community, whilst Wheatley most
certainly was, having set up the Catholic Socialist Society. With local
government becoming critical to the operation of schools, ensuring
influence on the council mattered and political activism in support of
Labour and within the party itself grew. This wasn't just supported by
the community, but by the Church hierarchy as well.

Lastly, there was the Irish war of independence. Home Rule had
always been supported within the Irish community in the city, even
if the Easter Rising had initially been disdained by most, mirroring
the then sentiment in Ireland. That had also been the position of the
ILP, where *Forward* had initially condemned it. However, after the 1918
election and support for Sinn Féin was manifest, and following an escalation in the war, Labour opinion changed. The behaviour of the Black
and Tans and the Auxiliaries drafted in by the British authorities caused
outrage in the Irish community and evoked widescale sympathy on
the left. A Labour commission on Ireland in 1921 roundly condemned
the activities of the British Army and trade union opinion was similarly hostile to their actions. Political support couldn't be provided
to Sinn Féin, but could be given to those who supported the cause.
John Maclean was vehement in his support for Ireland's struggle, as
were others from revolutionary groups. However, along with Asquith's
Liberals, who also opposed the British government's actions, they were
now marginal forces. Political influence on education locally and the
issue of Ireland nationally were to be exercised through Labour and in
Glasgow the ILP.

The Irish community was to move over, almost as a bloc vote, to supporting Labour and to great effect. They had influence not just in the pubs but from the pulpit, with the Church giving clear support. Added to that was the wide network of papers and other groups that existed within the community, many becoming partisan for Labour. The ILP could only benefit as elections approached.

Housing was also to return as an issue before the election, and the ILP would once again politically gain from it. Though, they would achieve success in a different manner than before, indicative in some ways of the party's changing focus. Rent restrictions that had been imposed by the wartime legislation following the rent strikes were coming to an end. Yet, other recommendations that had been made by the commission established to consider the housing situation had not been implemented, most importantly, the building of more available housing. Rents accordingly began to rise at the same time as the recession struck, with unemployment also increasing.

It was a recipe for hardship in the community, and also created a feeling of bad faith, with the view that promises had not been kept, going against if not formal commitments, then at least general intentions. Anger rose in the community and agitation for rent strikes increased within the ILP as rises started in 1920 and continued during the following years. However, neither the organisation nor the community support that had existed during the war could be repeated on this occasion. Efforts were made and strikes did take place, but they tended to be intermittent and localised, and enjoyed neither the scale nor the success that there had previously been. Many started but fizzled out, and cross-city unity was never established. Ultimately it was only in Clydebank that a rent strike held out for a significant period of time.

Why that was the case is hard to pinpoint. Essentially, the mood of the people was more accepting and less willing to confront the authorities. The rises were most certainly unpopular, but people were willing to accept them in the main, even if they complained. This was perhaps reflective of a more stoic and sombre mood in society at the time. The ILP did seek to campaign on the issue and were active in trying to generate community support. However, with less success and perhaps also with reduced efforts. Housing remained the major focus for the party and Wheatley was loud in his denunciation of the rent rises and support for strikes. Locally, activists sought to mobilise, and the Labour Housing Association agitated more widely. But the Labour group in Parliament was far less committed, despite the best efforts of Neil Maclean. There, rent rises were conceded as being inevitable, even though Maclean and a colleague dissented.

With national political support missing and local organisation largely absent, there was never the likelihood of replicating 1915. This was likely due to a growing shift towards Parliament from community campaigning – something that was consciously or subconsciously shared by ILP members and the general public. Housing remained a key ILP platform, but delivering and achieving it was moving towards political power and away from other activities, even though grassroots actions like rent strikes would continue to be supported. When elected, Wheatley would make radical progress on housing that would benefit generations to come.

The ILP would still gain from the housing issue – and not just from the legacy of the strike and loyalties won in 1915, but from events in 1922. A court case had been pursued, supported by Kirkwood and funded by the Labour Housing Association on behalf of tenants in Clydebank. The Kerr vs. Bryden case related to a technical aspect on how rent rises could be imposed. A strict interpretation of the legislation required that a notice of removal had to be given before any increase could be sought. Obviously, in practice, that had not been happening and both landlords and tenants had simply assumed that notification of an increase was enough. The case went all the way to the House of Lords where the judges ruled by a majority in favour of a strict interpretation, even although it was conceded that it was neither what had been intended or what was implemented in practice. The majority in the House of Lords supported an earlier Court of Session decision, where the Lord President confessed that although rather perverse, he could see no alternative interpretation.

That meant that increases that had been imposed and the rent rises paid were technically illegal and could end up being revoked. That would, of course, be of benefit not just to the particular Clydebank tenants but to thousands more across the entire country. The overpayments may have been a significant sum to tenants, but were a similar loss to landlords. The ILP was quick to capitalise on it as the government had threatened that the legislation could be changed to address the unintended consequence with the benefits for tenants lost. Support was offered by the ILP to help tenants reclaim potential reimbursement. Meanwhile, in Glasgow and no doubt elsewhere, the ILP's right-wing opponents were seen to be supporting the landlords. Writing in *Forward* on 18 November Tom Johnston stated that the court case was 'a gift from the gods'.

Other factors were also at play in wider society that would give rise to increased political support. As 1922 progressed the recession was biting with industrial production dropping and unemployment rising; figures for those out of work in 1920–21 rose markedly from 2 per cent to 18 per cent, with wages also beginning to plummet for those still in work.

Industrial disputes also mounted, though led by the national union leaderships, rather than by shop stewards. Tension increased as many of the disputes that had been avoided or resolved in 1919 came back onto the agenda. Days lost through strike action continued to increase substantially and were the highest since before the war. However, Black Friday, 15 April 1921, saw the proposed triple alliance between railwaymen, transport workers and miners fall apart, not to be revived again until the general strike in years to come. The miners fought alone but were defeated after several months and forced to return on worse conditions. There had been considerable public sympathy for them and the consequences of their defeat could only have increased that.

The government was seen to be faltering abroad with conflict in Russia, as well as issues arising in India and Turkey, whilst the thought of a return to war was viewed with horror by most. A peace treaty in Ireland establishing the Free State was signed in December 1921 and it prepared to leave the United Kingdom and become a self-governing dominion within the empire the following year.

Domestically, the administration was also seen to be failing as rent rises and increased poverty were being faced by many. Divisions were emerging in the coalition between Conservatives and National Liberals, and distrust in the premiership of Lloyd George growing. The Conservatives were themselves at loggerheads as to what to do, but eventually a majority moved to end the coalition as political tensions boiled over. And so, in October, Bonar Law removed Lloyd George as Prime Minister, forming a majority Conservative government, but quickly calling an election which was set for 15 November 1922.

18

THE NOVEMBER
1922 ELECTION

The general mood and how politics was conducted had changed in Glasgow since January 1919, but prospects looked good for the ILP. Despite financial and organisational challenges that had been endured and still existed given the troubled economic climate, the party had steadied and was prepared for an election. It was now better equipped and better focused for the campaign, possessing both experienced and credible candidates, as well as being a party much more adept at electioneering.

The prevailing circumstances also benefited them, and with issues over the electoral register now resolved, they could be assured that all potential supporters would be registered and able to vote. Unlike municipal elections there weren't multiple votes available for business owners or restrictions on tenants, which could only limit the opposition's support and maximise their own vote. With housing issues continuing to benefit them and with the Irish vote solidified, their political base had also expanded. Added to that was the overall dismal economic situation and grinding poverty afflicting so many in the city.

Nationally the Conservatives fought on a platform of continuity and stability under Bonar Law, who was once again standing in Glasgow Central. The Liberals remained divided between those who had supported Lloyd George and the coalition and those who had remained with Asquith and separated. However, the Asquith Liberals were becoming further marginalised across the country and were caught in a pincer between Labour and the electoral pact of Conservatives and National Liberals.

The main contest was perceived as being between the Conservatives with their National Liberal allies and the Labour Party, already the official opposition in Parliament. J. R. Clynes, the Labour leader, had supported the war and even served in the coalition government, though the policy platform was radical – being based on the new constitution and including commitments for nationalisation of mines and railways.

The ILP were equally radical in their demands, despite fighting on the common platform. They also had a commitment to a Scottish parliament, both through their candidates such as Maxton in his own local manifesto, and through the party generally. The nature of the parliament was never properly defined and was equally obscure in later years when bills in support of Scottish Home Rule were lodged at Westminster but, given the context of the time and references made, it is hard to see it as anything other than akin to the Irish Free State, a self-governing institution but which remained within the empire.

In Glasgow, though, it is clear that housing, and rents in particular, were to be the dominating issues for both sides, with the ILP having been actively involved in the rents campaign as well as offering support in obtaining reimbursement of overpayment. Meanwhile, the Unionists were considered to be supporting the landlords and their interests and had been seen as openly championing them.

Changes to the Labour constitution hadn't altered the almost total dominance of the ILP in the city, and challenges from without were limited. Across Scotland the ILP provided twenty-one of the forty candidates in the seats Labour contested. The CPGB were newly formed and were significantly smaller in comparison and influence. They were also affiliated to Labour, and Communist candidates would stand with Labour backing in Motherwell and Greenock, contesting the elections as Communists, but with the support of the ILP and other Labour-affiliated organisations. However, in Glasgow, power remained with the ILP and candidates selected to stand under the Labour ticket reflected that control.

Against the ILP was ranged the combined might of the Conservatives and National Liberals, where again a pact was largely in operation, despite the formal ending of the coalition in Parliament. In the 1918 election, ten of the fifteen MPs elected had been Conservatives supported by three National Liberals, George Barnes as Coalition Labour and only Neil Maclean providing any opposition. The ten Conservative seats faced no National Liberal challenges and that was likewise in Bridgeton and Partick where National Liberal candidates sought re-election. In Cathcart the sitting National Liberal wasn't seeking re-election and there was to be a three-way contest involving National Liberals and Conservatives, as well as Labour (for whom the seat would potentially be open to claim).

George Barnes was also not seeking re-election, leaving that contest for the ILP candidate there, although John Maclean would also stand as an independent Communist. Labour would also contest the Central and Pollok seats along with Asquith Liberal candidates. In Partick, where the National Liberal MP was seeking re-election, as in Kelvingrove and Hillhead, where there were sitting Conservative MPs, the competition was provided by a Liberal and Labour didn't stand.

On the revolutionary left, John Maclean had continued campaigning after the strike ended and had been further imprisoned for his activities as he sought to rally the unemployed and win support for the Irish struggle. Jailed for three months in May 1921 for sedition, he'd been convicted again and sentenced to twelve months in the October. Despite this both voluble support for him and threats by him of a hunger strike resulted in him being treated as a political prisoner, but even he was conscious of a changed mood when released just weeks before the 1922 election.

Acknowledging that the revolutionary road had been supplanted by the constitutional one, he found himself increasingly politically and personally isolated. Standing in the election as an independent Communist against an ILP candidate running on the Labour ticket, he was on the margins. He had a loyal band of supporters and still commanded great respect amongst many, and even some reverence. But, as the *Herald* reported during the campaign he continued to 'plough his lonely furrow', drawing large audiences, though not all would apparently 'accept the gospel', and they could see little prospect of success for him.

The ILP candidates were mainly drawn from those that had not just contested in 1918 but had been involved in the leadership of the party before and during the war. Neil Maclean was once again seeking re-election in Govan. Hoping to join him were Maxton, standing once again in Bridgeton, as was Wheatley in Shettleston, Johnny Muir standing in Maryhill, and Kirkwood once again contesting the nearby Dumbarton Burghs from the CWC leadership.

Other ILP candidates reflected the varied roots of the party across community and industrial activism. In the Gorbals, George Buchanan, a patternmaker by trade who had been vice chair of the City Trades Council, was contesting the seat; Barnes was standing down though Maclean was also seeking election. In Springburn, George Hardie, who was the younger brother of Keir Hardie, was again standing as in 1918. Tradeston had Thomas Henderson, who had worked in shipyards on the Clyde and in Belfast, as well as being elected an ILP councillor in the city in 1919. The candidate in Camlachie was Campbell Stephen, who had been a United Free Church minister until he had stood down to contest the 1918 elections. In St Rollox, it was James Stewart, who was a hairdresser and local ILP councillor and activist. Cathcart had Captain John Primrose Hay standing; slightly less well known, he was perhaps reflective of the more limited organisation there.

In his later biography Kirkwood provided a pen picture of his colleagues:

John Wheatley, cool and calculating and fearless; James Maxton, whose wooing speaking and utter selflessness made people regard him as a saint and martyr; wee Jimmie Stewart, so small, so sober and yet so determined; Neil Maclean, full of fire without fury; Thomas Johnston, with a head as full of facts as an egg's full o' meat; George Hardie, engineer and chemist and brother of Keir Hardie; George Buchanan, patternmaker who knew the human side of poverty better than any of us.[79]

In other constituencies, Tom Johnston was again contesting West Stirlingshire and Manny Shinwell Linlithgowshire. Rosslyn Mitchell, the lawyer, was standing in Glasgow Central against Prime Minister Bonar Law, and Walton Newbold, who had defected from the ILP to the newly formed Communist Party, was the Labour-supported candidate in Motherwell.

Council elections gave an early indication of the political temperature in the city, as they took place just the week before the national poll. The *Herald* leader indicated the growing concerns in the city by the establishment about possible Labour progress in an editorial in early November. The municipal contest approached, calling on moderate opinion to express itself 'against public extravagance and penalising private thrift', similar to comments that can be heard in local elections to this day. Fears of Labour progress were offset in some ways by a belief that it would not, at least, be compounded by a Labour government nationally, where there could be then be no checks upon it.

Though the number of wards fought was limited with contests in just twenty-five of thirty-seven wards, it was still an opportunity to test the mood of the city. The actual outcome of three gains and two losses for Labour looked at first glance like limited progress, if not a poor result. Indeed, initial comment in the papers was of Labour being roundly

---

79   David Kirkwood, op. cit.

beaten, and the final tally on the council saw seventy-four moderates (as the right were defined) and thirty-nine Labour.

However, as deeper analysis of the polling was made, it was recognised that it was far from the dismal display originally purported. In the following days, it was acknowledged that there had been a significant rise of 7 per cent in the Labour vote across the city, despite the loss of seats and the limited contests. Clear majorities were now evidenced in many parliamentary constituencies soon to be contested.

Such was the concern that the *Herald* editorial on 8 November, just a week before the election, was describing it as a wake-up call for the main event. Labour, far from being checked, was on the march and it was affecting not just those on the right but on the left, as voters got behind the movement. John Maclean contested a local ward; though polling well he was unsuccessful and probably obtained a considerably lower vote than might have been achieved as part of the wider Labour banner.

As political campaigning intensified as polling day drew near, crowds at meetings and rallies were increasing. Both hustings involving all candidates and those for individual contenders or specific parties were attracting big crowds. Many were raucous as the audiences grew more partisan and tensions mounted. There was a distinct drift to the left that the press, and even papers that weren't supportive, such as the *Herald*, couldn't help but notice. A reporter commenting on a hustings in Motherwell noted increasing support for the Communist Newbold not just in a younger section of the audience but amongst women, describing the votes as 'piling up' for him, and listing poverty, not just rent, as the reason. In the city, though, rents remained the predominant issue and the ILP were hammering it for all it was worth, condemning the rise and offering to assist in seeking reimbursement. A vote for Labour was portrayed as a vote for lower rents and repayment. It was hugely popular, striking a raw nerve in the city.

It was a hugely complex issue as a *Herald* editorial had commented on the Saturday before polling, when it had called for a commission to be established. Just who was affected by it, how it applied, whether it fell to be repaid and even in what way it could be reclaimed was uncertain. However, as they also noted it was 'understood by the mass of people only in its crudest terms that the rent increase paid were illegal'. Moderates on the council including Unionists and Liberals – both National and Asquith supporters – were siding with landlords. On the other side, the ILP had sided with the tenants and said they would seek to help get their money back. Never mind historic antagonisms to the Unionists and landlords, it was a great motivator in many working-class areas. The issue had a clear party divide and the ILP were not going to let it pass them by. Campaigners in Bridgeton were heard to have been calling out 'Vote for Jimmy Maxton and get your money back'.

By the Monday consideration in the *Herald* was turning to the possible outcome later in the week when polling would take place. Labour's increase in the council polls had changed expectations and it was also acknowledged that the parliamentary roll was far wider than the municipal franchise. That would only be of benefit to Labour, they surmised, as they gave their electoral prediction. Prime Minister Bonar Law had a fight on in his hands in his Glasgow Central constituency, but they thought he'd be safe. Likewise, Hillhead, Pollok and Kelvingrove were viewed as safe seats for the Unionists. Maryhill, St Rollox and Tradeston, whilst viewed as being close, were still, they thought, likely to be retained by the Unionists. Labour, it was said, would probably have to be content with just four seats in Govan, Shettleston, Springburn and the Gorbals. Dumbarton Burghs, where David Kirkwood was standing, was thought to be a close contest, though West Stirlingshire where Tom Johnston was fighting was viewed as being safe for the government. The paper also noted that the Orange Order was running a slate of endorsed candidates and needless to say, none included an ILP or Communist.

Polling day, 15 November, saw the paper launch a blistering attack on

Labour and the rents issue, no doubt a final effort to try to motivate its readers to vote. Other establishment papers were likewise worked up. Turnout had risen from 1918 to 73 per cent across the UK and to over 70 per cent in Scotland, but the question remained: who was going to benefit from it?

Counting took place immediately following the closing of polls, then as now, and expectant crowds gathered to hear the results. The *Herald* had arranged for a screen to be placed outside its offices to display the results as they were declared. Accordingly, St Enoch Square and St Vincent Street adjacent to their offices were described as being 'joined by caps' as thousands of primarily working men, but also working women, gathered to watch. As Labour gains were announced there was a crescendo of noise, though the largest shout was for a recount announced in the Prime Minister's Glasgow Central constituency.

Across the country it was a clear victory for Bonar Law and his Conservatives, who took 38.51 per cent of the vote and won 344 seats. But, Labour came second nationally with 29.65 per cent and 142 seats, the Liberals trailing in third on 18.92 per cent and sixty-two seats and the National Liberals following them on 9.86 per cent and fifty-three seats.

In Scotland, though, it was Labour who dominated, winning over half a million votes with 32.2 per cent of the vote and twenty-nine seats. The Liberals were in second place having polled only 21.5 per cent, but winning fifteen seats mostly in rural constituencies – partly explaining the lower vote but higher seat return. The Unionists actually polled 25.1 per cent, but only won thirteen seats, although they were still ahead of the National Liberals who polled 17.7 per cent and won twelve seats. The Communist Party also won in Motherwell, where Walton Newbold was successful, and there was an independent, Edwin Scrymgeour, elected in Dundee on a prohibition ticket and who actually defeated Winston Churchill, standing then as a National Liberal.

It was a good outcome across the UK for Labour with an increase in votes and seats and clear consolidation as the official opposition, likewise in Scotland, where it became the largest party in seats and votes. However, in Glasgow the result was quite outstanding with the ILP taking one in three votes and winning ten out of the fifteen constituencies with comfortable majorities. Bridgeton, Camlachie, Cathcart, Gorbals, Maryhill, St Rollox, Shettleston, Springburn and Tradeston all fell to be added to the Govan seat that was already held by Neil Maclean. In most the majorities were resounding, and only in the three-way fight in Cathcart was the result close. The Unionists only held on in Central and in Hillhead, Kelvingrove and Pollock, with the National Liberals retaining Partick; three of those seats were not even contested by the ILP.

Those winning seats that election included Jimmy Maxton in Bridgeton, John Muir in Maryhill and John Wheatley in Shettleston. David Kirkwood was successful in Dumbarton Burghs and they were also joined by Manny Shinwell in Linlithgow and Tom Johnston in West Stirlingshire. The ILP leadership before and during the war had won out, and spectacularly so.

Bonar Law was returned in his Glasgow Central seat for the Conservatives but with a hugely reduced majority. Asquith was also returned for nearby Paisley but only by holding Labour off by just over 300 votes. Even in Greenock the Communist candidate only missed out by around 750 votes. John Maclean standing as an independent Communist in the Gorbals had polled over 4,000 votes but was comfortably defeated by the ILP's George Buchanan with nearly 16,500. Willie Gallacher also contested the election, standing as an official Communist candidate in Dundee which was a multi-member ward returning two MPs. As indicated the prohibitionist Scrymgeour won one and the Labour candidate the other, with Gallacher polling almost 6,000 votes but falling well short of being elected. (The Glasgow results are attached in Appendix A and other notable ones in Appendix B).

It was a great night for the ILP and the celebrations continued the following day and into the weekend. As crowds had once gathered in support of the forty-hour week strike and for their industrial champions, so they did once again, but this time for their political champions. Rallies and celebrations were held all over the city with even a service of dedication being conducted at the St Andrew's Halls on Sunday 20 November. There those congregated sang the 124th Psalm:

If the Lord had not been on our side, Let Israel say,
If the Lord had not been on our side, when people attacked us,
They would have swallowed us alive, when their anger flared against us,
The flood would have engulfed us, the torrent would have swept over us,
The raging waters would have swept us away.

Indicating the deeply moral and religious roots of the socialism of so many, including Campbell Stephen the newly elected MP for Camlachie and former Church minister.

Even more gathered on the Sunday night when the newly elected MPs prepared to embark for London from St Enoch Station to take their seats. Some estimates have suggested that as many as a quarter of a million people may have been involved in the celebrations. This may well have been possible given the number of send-offs and victory parties that were taking place in many parts of the city and beyond.

The *Herald* on Monday 20 November noted that a crowd of 50,000 had gathered at the station a full two hours before their scheduled departure at 10:45 p.m., filling not just St Enoch Square but adjoining streets as they sought to catch a glimpse of their heroes. In the end, it wasn't just at the station that they gathered, but across the city and in other communities where there had been ILP victories. As the paper noted, 'Processions reached the centre of the city from Govan, Springburn, Bridgeton and other districts and parties in charabancs from Kirkintilloch, Clydebank and other outlying towns.' Several of the processions were led by brass bands and 'The Red Flag' was sung with gusto.

Before heading to the station for their departure the newly elected MPs addressed a packed meeting of party members at the Metropole Theatre, where the audience were again singing and cheering. 'The Red Flag' and 'The Internationale' were sung, along with Scots songs and even the hymn 'Jerusalem'. The newly elected MPs were rousing in their cries and commitment to the cause of socialism and Neil Maclean concluded by thanking them on behalf of the group. They then proceeded to a hotel where they were this time entertained by the executive of the ILP, before finally being able to try to make their way to the station concourse. Even that wasn't without its difficulties given the denseness of the crowd packed together, and according to police reports some people fainted due to the pressure, but there were no serious injuries and they were well behaved other than one attempt to force entry into the station. As the MPs made their way through a path cleared for them to the platform, they were cheered as they were individually recognised. Around 200 supporters were allowed onto the platform for one final gathering and farewell with Maxton commenting that it was 'harder to get into the station than the House of Commons'. As the train steamed out of the station 'The Red Flag' was again sung, as the Red Clydeside MPs departed for Westminster, taking with them their brand of radical socialism and firm commitment to a Scottish parliament.

A remarkable chapter in the history of both Glasgow and Scotland was closing, though another equally important one was about to open. The Red Clydesiders were to become legendary; they would be revered in many ways, not just by Scottish Labour and nationalist movements, but greatly respected within wider society. Whilst some would depart others would arrive to join them, though always at the central core were Maxton, Wheatley, Kirkwood, Stephen and Buchanan. They impacted on Parliament in a variety of ways, with Maxton becoming a noted orator and Wheatley and Johnston remarkably constructive ministers. Hugely progressive housing legislation was implemented by Wheatley and Johnston was acknowledged by many as Scotland's greatest ever

Secretary of State. Several attempts were made to legislate for a Scottish parliament by members including Buchanan. They weren't just political comrades, but also close personal friends. Several of them shared flats as well as socialising together, though almost all were teetotal and tea rooms rather than bars were their venues of choice.

In the city itself Patrick Dollan came to even greater prominence when, several years later, Labour finally took political control of the city. The drift apart though from both the ILP and the Red Clydeside group of other individuals from 1919 continued, with John Maclean and Willie Gallacher going their own separate directions. Following ructions within the Parliamentary Labour Group and the wider Labour Party in 1932, ILP voted to disaffiliate from Labour. As a result, the ILP split with both MPs and branches either joining a fully autonomous ILP or joining the Labour Party. The Red Clydeside group was no more, even though individuals continued in Parliament and served in elected office thereafter. It is not for this book to narrate the history of that period or what happened thereafter. (Though a brief synopsis is given in Appendix C of what became of the main characters from 1919.)

But, the Bolshevik Revolution that the Secretary of State had feared in January 1919 had not come to pass. Instead, it had been replaced by democratic socialism through an electoral process that was finally available. This brand of socialism was of course forged through generations by the appalling poverty and housing conditions endured by so many, and moulded by a radical history of individuals who bravely strove to build a better society. The year 1919 was a momentous one for Glasgow, and though the strike was defeated, it was the precursor for a historic political victory in 1922.

EPILOGUE

Was there a Scottish Bolshevik revolution in January 1919? Most certainly not, there was neither the planning nor intention to achieve it. Armed insurrection was never considered and violence never sought. The events of Bloody Friday came about as a result of police brutality where the authorities overreacted and were subsumed in the chaos of their own making.

Though troops and even tanks arrived, it was not as some have suggested an invasion by an English Army, but the deployment of British troops, most of whom were young Scottish conscripts. Preparation had been made and following the call for military assistance, aid was speedily implemented. However, the troops did not stay for long and the city soon returned to normal – even if the events have entered into folklore and remain crucial to the city's history. Nor, though, should the events be downplayed, given the scale of the dispute and the extent of the state's reaction.

As with all such incidents, though, the political intentions of most were also used as an opportunity for the criminal actions of a few. That was not supported by the organisers or the general public, and those charged with such behaviour enjoyed no support. The conviction, though, of Shinwell, Gallacher and others was rightly condemned by many, just as the criminal actions of a few were abjured by all. The lenient sentences, though, seemingly indicated not just the authorities' desire to draw a line under events, but a recognition of what really happened.

In many ways, events had simply overtaken those involved. However, it has to be seen in the context of times that were indeed turbulent and the concerns the authorities had about what was happening, not just in Glasgow but around the world. Planning for the action seemed remiss to say the least, and when the vote in favour of a strike was achieved many seemed genuinely surprised, if not shocked. Lacking support from the top in the national union leaderships and even across wider sectors than shipyards and engineering, the strike was almost doomed from the outset.

The seeds had, however, been sown years before when the CWC was formed to deal with the protection of workers' rights and trade union leaders had been sadly lacking, if not openly conniving with government and employers. This had seen a shift in power from officials in London to shop stewards on the Clyde. Such was the perceived threat that draconian action was taken by the government, but it delayed rather than deterred those leading the campaigns.

Allied to that were the appalling housing and social conditions that working people in the second city of the empire were forced to endure. They were the breeding ground for political agitation that would be arguably even more important in the political future of the city. But, with battles being waged on both the factory and housing fronts, it was also a deeply political city where the left was better and more powerfully organised than arguably anywhere else in the UK. As the Great War ended and the effects of the Bolshevik Revolution reverberated, Glasgow was bound to be more affected than most.

Though some momentum was generated during the early days, support was slow in coming and wasn't matched in other areas beyond Belfast and a few sympathetic communities. Irrespective of Bloody Friday it is hard to see how the strike would not have folded anyway, through lack of funds and wider support. It never managed to become a general strike across the city, nor linked up with others elsewhere, and significant opposition existed amongst other sections of workers – never mind the authorities.

There were those who hoped that a revolution might have sprung from it, but it did not arrive. Even the regrets espoused by Willie Gallacher that a moment had been missed when the soldiers in Maryhill Barracks had not been approached are questionable. Whether they might have made common cause is debatable, but given the British Army's ruthlessness during the Easter Rising in Dublin it is certain any rising in Glasgow would have been crushed. For sure, those driving it were in the main more committed to direct action than political campaigning, but that also has to be seen in the industrial setting in which they operated and when the full political franchise was still in its infancy. As a consequence, their focus was in the yards and factories, not in elections and Parliament.

That said, the strike cannot be underplayed given the numbers and the wider support it mobilised across a wide political spectrum. Those involved were not unbowed by what happened, and in many ways, the event marks a watershed as the power and influence moved from the CWC and industrial struggles to the ILP and the ballot box. Some alliances were to fracture as the Communist Party was formed, and others like John Maclean moved to the margins.

As the economy deteriorated and unemployment worsened, the conditions for political success still existed and were now matched by the franchise being available for working-class voters, though not yet all women. That would result in the historic breakthrough in 1922 and the political arrival of the Red Clydesiders.

However, their origins lay not just in the events of the First World War or that last week in January 1919 but long before. Arguably, rent strikes and the community activism laid the foundations for the election victory in 1922, as much if not more so than the forty-hour week strike. The legacy of that, together with the other factors of endemic

poverty, poor and overcrowded housing and the spectre of mass unemployment returning, contributed much more to the victory of the
socialist campaigners.

A commitment was forged through those events and inspired by
preceding generations from Thomas Muir and the Friends of the
People, through the Calton weavers and 1820 martyrs, to the Chartists
and pre-war militants. The causes of the struggles were the same, it was
simply the times they lived in and the manner that they attempted to
achieve their goals that were different.

In Scotland, much of the socialist folklore and especially songs have
revered the more revolutionary John Maclean, Willie Gallacher and
even Jimmy Maxton. Neither their contribution should be underestimated nor their courage forgotten. They most certainly were brave and
suffered for their efforts, Maclean in particular. Given that a century
on poverty still stalks their land and parliamentary reform is struggling
to address it, many may well see their ideology as still being the right
approach.

Yet there is also an element of the Scottish psyche that seeks to
venerate the gallant underdog and loser over those who temper their
views but deliver success. The huge influence of the likes of Wheatley,
Dollan and especially Johnston should not be ignored, even if it is often
less trumpeted. Their radicalism was equally as passionate and their
influence on modern Scotland arguably far greater, even if the progress
they hoped for has not been achieved and some successes even sadly
undermined. In the end, they did deliver a better land.

However, it was never quite reformist versus revolutionary during
those formative years before, during and just after the Great War. Political party structures were far less constrained and ideological views
far more fluid. In later years, as political parties evolved and rivalries
on the left exacerbated, harsh words were often said about one another.
Gallacher was often disparaging of Maclean and caustic about Kirkwood. The ILP rent asunder, Maxton was denigrated and Gallacher

condemned as political sectarianism grew and deep divides opened on the left. But that reflected the tension at that time in Britain and across the world, rather than the reality of the comradeship that had previously existed. Rent strikes and the struggle of 1919 were superseded by the Great Depression and the collapse of a Labour government, as well the rise of fascism and the Soviet Union. Whatever they said or felt afterwards was not how they had felt or acted when it mattered. For whilst they may have had different views on some issues, they were united in the common struggle and invariably came to each other's aid, as Gallacher did for Kirkwood on Bloody Friday.

Many politicians and political parties have sought to lay claim to being the heirs or successors to Red Clydeside. Whether they are is for individuals to decide, but what is certain is that both those involved in 1919 and those elected in 1922 were worthy heirs to those who had carried the radical banner before them. It was a titanic struggle and it continues to this day, as the dreams of a better and fairer society burn deep in a city and country still scarred by poverty and inequality.

To paraphrase Maclean, they 'stand not as the accused, but as the accusers of capitalism'. Or, as Thomas Muir said long before him, 'It is good cause. It shall ultimately prevail. It shall finally triumph.' They all rightly deserve the recognition and respect that Glasgow and Scotland pay to them, long may their legacy continue to inspire.

Tanks were despatched to the city after the Bloody Friday riot in January 1919.

APPENDIX A

The battle in 1919 may have been lost, but the election in 1922 was convincingly won.
These are the results for Glasgow.

General Election 1922: Glasgow Bridgeton				
Party	**Candidate**	**Votes**	**%**	**±**
Labour	James Maxton	17,890	63.7	+23.9
National Liberal	Alexander MacCallum Scott	10,198	36.3	-18.9
	Majority:	7692	27.4	n/a
	Turnout:	28,088	76.7	+24.7
Registered electors:		36,627		
Labour **gain** from Liberal		**Swing:**	+21.4	

General Election 1922: Glasgow Camlachie				
Party	**Candidate**	**Votes**	**%**	**±**
Labour	Campbell Stephen	15,181	53.2	+20.1
Unionist	Halford Mackinder	11,439	40.2	-22.7
Liberal	Walter Crawford Smith	1896	6.6	+2.6
	Majority:	3742	13.1	n/a
	Turnout:	28,516	81.0	+22.9
	Registered electors:	35,249		
Labour **gain** from Unionist		**Swing:**	+21.4	

General Election 1922: Glasgow Cathcart				
Party	**Candidate**	**Votes**	**%**	**±**
Labour	John Primrose Hay	9137	34.0	+10.9
National Liberal	Andrew Rae Duncan	9104	33.8	-43.1
Unionist	Robert MacDonald	8661	32.2	n/a
	Majority:	33	0.2	n/a
	Turnout:	26,902	81.0	n/a
	Registered electors:	33,198		
Labour **gain** from Liberal		**Swing:**	+27.0	

General Election 1922: Glasgow Central

Party	Candidate	Votes	%	±
Unionist	Bonar Law	15,437	49.9	-28.9
Labour	Edward Mitchell	12,923	41.9	+20.7
Liberal	George Paish	2518	8.2	n/a
	Majority:	2514	8.0	-49.6
	Turnout:	30,878	71.2	+18.3
	Registered electors:	43,351		
Unionist **hold**		**Swing:**	-24.8	

General Election 1922: Glasgow Gorbals

Party	Candidate	Votes	%	±
Labour	George Buchanan	16,478	54.5	+20.2
National Liberal	J. E. Harper	8276	27.4	n/a
Independent Communist	John Maclean	4027	13.3	n/a
Liberal	Francis John Robertson	1456	4.8	n/a
	Majority:	8202	27.1	n/a
	Turnout:	30,237	75.1	+21.9
	Registered electors:	40,251		
Labour **gain** from Coalition Labour		**Swing:**	n/a	

General Election 1922: Glasgow Govan

Party	Candidate	Votes	%	±
Labour	Neil Maclean	15,441	62.3	+14.5
National Liberal	Helen Fraser	9336	37.7	+29.3
	Majority:	6105	24.6	+20.6
	Turnout:	24,777	81.1	+17.9
	Registered electors:	30,539		
Labour **hold**		**Swing:**	-7.4	

General Election 1922: Glasgow Hillhead

Party	Candidate	Votes	%	±
Unionist	Robert Horne	12,272	62.7	-12.7
Liberal	Edwin James Donaldson	7313	37.3	n/a
	Majority:	4959	25.4	-25.4
	Turnout:	19,585	75.5	+12.1
	Registered electors:	25,951		
Unionist **hold**		**Swing:**	n/a	

General Election 1922: Glasgow Kelvingrove

Party	Candidate	Votes	%	±
Unionist	William Hutchinson	13,442	54.8	-9.4
Liberal	Robert Roxburgh	11,094	45.2	+33.0
	Majority:	2348	9.6	-31.0
	Turnout:	24,536	64.5	+11.0
	Registered electors:	38,031		
Unionist **hold**		**Swing:**	-21.2	

General Election 1922: Glasgow Maryhill

Party	Candidate	Votes	%	±
Labour	John Muir	13,058	47.3	+19.4
Unionist	William Mitchell-Thomson	10,951	39.6	-20.6
Liberal	Annie S. Swan	3617	13.1	+1.2
	Majority:	2107	7.7	n/a
	Turnout:	27,626	81.3	+24.1
	Registered electors:	33,991		
Labour **gain** from Unionist		**Swing:**	+20.0	

General Election 1922: Glasgow Partick

Party	Candidate	Votes	%	±
National Liberal	Robert John Collie	11,754	65.17	-4.98
Liberal	Daniel Macaulay Stevenson	6282	34.83	n/a
	Majority:	5472	30.34	-9.96
	Turnout:	18,036	66.68	+5.61
	Registered electors:	27,048		
National Liberal **hold**		**Swing:**	-4.98	

General Election 1922: Glasgow Pollok

Party	Candidate	Votes	%	±
Unionist	John Gilmour	14,920	63.9	n/a
Labour	Alexander Burns Mackay	5759	24.7	n/a
Liberal	T. R. Anderson	2658	11.4	n/a
	Majority:	9161	39.2	n/a
	Turnout:	23,337	78.7	n/a
	Registered electors:	29,670		
Unionist **hold**		**Swing:**	n/a	

General Election 1922: Glasgow St Rollox

Party	Candidate	Votes	%	±
Labour	James Stewart	16,114	56.58	+23.37
Unionist	James Brown Couper	10,343	36.31	-22.27
Liberal	James Alexander Fleming	2025	7.11	-1.11
	Majority:	5771	20.26	n/a
	Turnout:	28,482	76.68	+28.52
	Registered electors:	37,145		
Labour **gain** from Unionist		**Swing:**	+22.82	

General Election 1922: Glasgow Shettleston

Party	Candidate	Votes	%	±
Labour	John Wheatley	14,695	59.1	+9.3
National Liberal	Thomas Ramsay	9704	39.0	n/a
Anti-Parliamentary Communist	Guy Aldred	470	1.9	n/a
	Majority:	4991	20.1	n/a
	Turnout:	24,869	83.9	+21.2
	Registered electors:	29,639		
Labour **gain** from Unionist		**Swing:**	n/a	

General Election 1922: Glasgow Springburn

Party	Candidate	Votes	%	±
Labour	George Hardie	15,771	60.5	+21.4
Unionist	Frederick Alexander Macquisten	10,311	39.5	-13.2
	Majority:	5460	21.0	34.6
	Turnout:	26,082	78.5	+17.6
	Registered electors:	33,230		
Labour **gain** from Unionist		**Swing:**	+17.3	

General Election 1922: Glasgow Tradeston

Party	Candidate	Votes	%	±
Labour Co-op	Thomas Henderson	14,190	55.7	n/a
Unionist	Vivian Henderson	9977	39.2	-24.2
Liberal	Charles de Bois Murray	1310	5.1	-12.3
	Majority:	4213	16.5	n/a
	Turnout:	25,477	75.4	+21.5
	Registered electors:	33,792		
Labour Co-op **gain** from Unionist		**Swing:**	n/a	

APPENDIX B

The battle in 1919 may have been lost, but the election in 1922 was convincingly won. These are the results for other key constituencies.

General Election 1922: Dumbarton Burghs				
Party	**Candidate**	**Votes**	**%**	**±**
Labour	David Kirkwood	16,397	64.29	+16.91
National Liberal	John Taylor	9107	35.71	-16.91
	Majority:	7290	28.58	n/a
	Turnout:	25,504	76.22	+5.82
	Registered electors:	33,463		
Labour **gain** from Liberal		**Swing:**	+16.91	

General Election 1922: West Stirlingshire				
Party	**Candidate**	**Votes**	**%**	**±**
Labour	Tom Johnston	8919	52.4	+23.7
Unionist	Harry Hope	8104	47.6	-4.3
	Majority:	815	4.8	28.0
	Turnout:	17, 023	74.1	+15.0
	Registered electors:	22,974		
Labour **gain** from Unionist		**Swing:**	n/a	

General Election 1922: Linlithgowshire				
Party	**Candidate**	**Votes**	**%**	**±**
Labour	Manny Shinwell	12,625	46.4	+6.1
Unionist	James Kidd	8993	33.0	-29.7
Liberal	John Fraser Orr	5605	20.6	n/a
	Majority:	3632	13.4	n/a
	Turnout:	27,223	76.5	+9.1
	Registered electors:	35,582		
Labour **gain** from Unionist		**Swing:**	+17.9	

General Election 1922: Motherwell

Party	Candidate	Votes	%	±
Communist	Walton Newbold	8262	33.3	n/a
Independent Unionist	Hugh Ferguson	7214	29.1	+18.3
Liberal	John Maxwell	5359	21.6	-1.6
National Liberal	John Colville	3966	16.0	n/a
	Majority:	1048	10.2	n/a
	Turnout:	24,801	81.5	+17.3
	Registered electors:	30,443		
Communist **gain** from Unionist		**Swing:**	n/a	

General Election 1922: Greenock

Party	Candidate	Votes	%	±
Liberal	Godfrey Collins	10,520	36.6	-11.4
Communist	Alec Geddes	9776	34.1	n/a
Unionist	John Denholm	8404	29.3	-2.5
	Majority:	744	2.5	-13.7
	Turnout:	28,700	84.8	+18.2
	Registered electors:	33,835		
Liberal **hold**		**Swing:**	-4.5	

General Election 1922: Paisley

Party	Candidate	Votes	%	±
Liberal	H. H. Asquith	15,005	50.5	+16.5
Labour Co-op	John Biggar	14,689	49.5	+16.0
	Majority:	316	1.0	+0.5
	Turnout:	26,694	78.0	+22.4
	Registered electors:	38,093		
Liberal **hold**		**Swing:**	+0.3	

General Election 1922: Dundee (2 seats)

Party	Candidate	Votes	%	±
Scottish Prohibition	Edwin Scrymgeour	32,578	27.6	+12.5
Labour	E. D. Morel	30,292	25.6	-10.5
National Liberal	David Johnstone MacDonald	22,244	18.8	n/a
National Liberal	Winston Churchill	20,466	17.3	-20.2
Liberal	Robert Pilkington	6681	5.7	n/a
Communist	Willie Gallacher	5906	5.0	n/a
	Majority:	10,334	8.8	
	Majority:	8048	6.8	
	Turnout:	121,167	80.5	
Scottish Prohibition **gain** from National Liberal				
Labour **hold**				

APPENDIX C

James Maxton (1885–1946)

Maintained his fiery orator and charisma, even being excluded from Parliament on occasions for his vehement denunciations of Toryism. Pivotal in the disaffiliation of the ILP from Labour as he sought to maintain a left-wing agenda. He held his Bridgeton constituency, leading the small ILP group in Westminster, until his sudden death in 1946.

Willie Gallacher (1881–1965)

Became a leading member of the Communist Party of Great Britain and was imprisoned for twelve months again along with others under the Incitement to Mutiny Act in 1925. In 1935 he was elected to Parliament for West Fife which he represented until 1950, thereafter serving as president of the CPGB from 1956–63.

David Kirkwood (1872–1955)

Remained a member of the ILP until its disaffiliation in 1932 when he joined Labour. Served as MP for Dumbarton Burghs then East Dunbartonshire until 1951. Given life peerage and sat in House of Lords as Baron Kirkwood of Bearsden until his death.

John Wheatley (1869–1930)

Became Minister of Health in the first Labour government under Ramsay MacDonald in 1924 and brought in the Housing Act that saw a massive social housing building programme undertaken. Opposed MacDonald's drift to the right, he was excluded from the next Labour government in 1929. Along with Maxton was a leading left-wing critic of the administration until his sudden death in 1930.

John Muir (1879–1931)

Lost his seat narrowly to a Unionist in the 1924 election though it was regained by John Clarke for the ILP in 1929 who had also been involved in the CWC. Muir led the Workers' Education Association until 1930.

Arthur MacManus (1889–1927)

Served as first chairman of CPGB until 1922 when he took another leading position and was also appointed to the executive committee of the Comintern. He was imprisoned in 1925 along with Gallacher and other Communist leaders. Dying in 1927, his ashes are interred in the walls of the Kremlin in Moscow.

Tom Johnston (1881–1965)

Lost his seat in 1924 but re-elected that year in a by-election and won his old West Stirlingshire seat back in 1929. Initially a junior minister under MacDonald, he joined Maxton and Wheatley in being a stern critic of the government. He lost his seat again in 1931 and joined Labour after the disaffiliation of the ILP, being re-elected for West Stirlingshire in 1935 and becoming wartime Secretary of State for Scotland. After retiral he subsequently chaired various boards and statutory authorities such as tourism, forestry and hydro.

John Maclean (1879–1923)

Continued with his educational work and campaigning before establishing the Scottish Workers' Republican Party, convinced that an independent Scotland was needed. He died of pneumonia on St Andrew's Day 1923 with 20,000 following his funeral procession from his home in Glasgow.

Manny Shinwell (1884–1986)

Lost his Linlithgowshire seat in 1924 but was re-elected in a by-election there in 1928. Served as a minister in MacDonald's government but subsequently became a critic. Lost his seat again in 1931 but was re-elected in County Durham in 1935, ironically defeating MacDonald. Served in post-war Labour government until being elevated to the House of Lords in 1970 as Baron Shinwell of Easington.

Patrick Dollan (1885–1963)

Served as chairman of the Scottish ILP until 1932 when, following disaffiliation, he joined Labour. Lord Provost of Glasgow 1938–41, he was pivotal in many improvements made to the city under the Labour council and was knighted in 1941.

Mary Barbour (1875–1958)

Served on Glasgow Council, becoming one of the city's first female baillies. Also appointed one of the city's first female magistrates, she also chaired the Women's Welfare and Advisory Clinic. Was active in health and welfare issues throughout her active life. A statue of her was unveiled in Govan Cross in 2018.

Helen Crawfurd (1877–1954)

Served on the central committee of the CPGB and became secretary of the Workers' International Relief. Unsuccessfully contested elections for the CPGB in 1929 and 1931. Prominent in Friends of the Soviet Union.

Agnes Dollan (1887–1966)

Stood as the first female candidate for the ILP in council elections in January 1919. Elected to the council in a by-election in 1922 and served until 1928. Sat on the Labour Party NEC and opposed the disaffiliation of the ILP.

BIBLIOGRAPHY

Armstrong, Murray, *The Liberty Tree: The Stirring Story of Thomas Muir and Scotland's First Fight for Democracy* (Word Power, 2014)

Berresford Ellis, P. and a'Ghobhainn, Seumas Mac, *The Scottish Insurrection of 1820* (Victor Gollancz, 1970)

Brown, Gordon, *Maxton: A Biography* (Mainstream, 2002)

Craig, Maggie, *When the Clyde Ran Red* (Mainstream, 2011)

Duncan, Robert and McIvor, Arthur (eds), *Militant Workers: Labour and Class Conflict on the Clyde, 1900–1950* (John Donald, 1992)

Galbraith, Russell, *Without Quarter: A Biography of Tom Johnston* (Birlinn, 2018)

Gallacher, William, *Revolt on the Clyde*, 4th edition (Lawrence & Wishart, 1978)

Harris, Bob, *The Scottish People and the French Revolution* (Routledge, 2016)

Holman, Bob, *Keir Hardie: Labour's Greatest Hero?* (Lion, 2010)

Johnston, Tom, *The History of the Working Classes in Scotland* (Forward, 1930)

Kenefick, William and McIvor, Arthur (eds), *Roots of Red Clydeside 1910–1914? Labour Unrest and Industrial Relations in West Scotland* (John Donald, 1997)

Kirkwood, David, *My Life of Revolt* (George G. Harrap, 1935)

Logue, Kenneth J., *Popular Disturbances in Scotland, 1780–1815* (John Donald, 2003)

Marriott, J. A. R., *Modern England: A History of My Own Times 1885–1945*, 4th edition (Methuen, 1948)

McFarland E. W., *Ireland and Scotland in the Age of Revolution: Planting the Green Bough* (Edinburgh University Press, 1994)

McKinlay, Alan and R. J. Morris (eds), *The ILP on Clydeside, 1893–1932: From Foundation to Disintegration* (Manchester University Press, 1992)

McLean, Iain, *The Legend of Red Clydeside* (John Donald, 2000)

McShane, Harry and Smith, Joan, *Harry McShane: No Mean Fighter* (Pluto Press, 1978)

Meikle, Henry W., *Scotland and the French Revolution* (James MacLehose, 1912)

Melling Joseph, *Rent Strikes: People's Struggle for Housing in West Scotland, 1890–1916* (Polygon, 1983)

Milton, Nan, *John Maclean* (John Maclean Society, 2002)

Morgan, Kenneth O., *Labour People: Leaders and Lieutenants, Hardie to Kinnock* (Faber and Faber, 2011)

Roe, Michael, 'George Mealmaker, the Forgotten Martyr', *Journal of the Royal Australian Historical Society* (1957), vol. 43, pp. 284–98

Smout, T. C., *A Century of the Scottish People 1830–1950* (Fontana, 1987)

Thompson, Willie, *The Good Old Cause: British Communism 1920–1991* (Pluto Press, 1992)

ACKNOWLEDGEMENTS

As ever there are many people and institutions to thank. Firstly, though, I should perhaps acknowledge the debt I owe to the late Nan Milton, daughter and biographer of John Maclean, who both inspired me and encouraged my political activism.

Staff at the National Library of Scotland have again been helpful and accommodating. Family and friends have encouraged and supported. My son Roddy researched early aspects of the book and provided wise comments. My wife, Susan, has been ever helpful in sourcing information and giving assistance throughout; indulging my writing habits yet always supporting me in them.

Stephanie Carey, my editor, has been tireless in her efforts and yet sparing in her criticism of my errors and mistakes. I'm grateful for her wise counsel as well as her skills and support, and would like to thank all the team at Biteback. Ian Johnston at *The Scotsman* was helpful in providing a photograph more reflective of my age.

But, most of all, my thanks go to those I've campaigned with over the years in elections and on other issues – from the poll tax to factory occupations. It's been a privilege, as with knowing Nan, to have worked with them. Times are hard at the moment, but, to paraphrase Thomas Muir, it is a just cause, it will ultimately prevail.

INDEX